AN INTRODUCTION TO

LEISURE STUDIES

AN INTRODUCTION TO

LEISURE STUDIES

PRINCIPLES AND PRACTICE

PETER BRAMHAM AND STEPHEN WAGG

Los Angeles | London | New Delhi
Singapore | Washington DC

Los Angeles | London | New Delhi
Singapore | Washington DC

SAGE Publications Ltd
1 Oliver's Yard
55 City Road
London EC1Y 1SP

SAGE Publications Inc.
2455 Teller Road
Thousand Oaks, California 91320

SAGE Publications India Pvt Ltd
B 1/I 1 Mohan Cooperative Industrial Area
Mathura Road
New Delhi 110 044

SAGE Publications Asia-Pacific Pte Ltd
3 Church Street
#10-04 Samsung Hub
Singapore 049483

Editor: Chris Rojek
Editorial assistant: Gemma Shields
Production editor: Katherine Haw
Copyeditor: Rosemary Campbell
Proofreader: Lynda Watson
Marketing manager: Michael Ainsley
Cover design: Lisa Harper-Wells
Typeset by: C&M Digitals (P) Ltd, Chennai, India
Printed in India at Replika Press Pvt Ltd

Library of Congress Control Number: 2014932676

British Library Cataloguing in Publication data

A catalogue record for this book is available from
the British Library

MIX
Paper from
responsible sources
FSC® C016779

ISBN 978-1-4129-1874-9
ISBN 978-1-4129-1875-6 (pbk)

At SAGE we take sustainability seriously. Most of our products are printed in the UK using FSC papers and boards.
When we print overseas we ensure sustainable papers are used as measured by the Egmont grading system.
We undertake an annual audit to monitor our sustainability.

TABLE OF CONTENTS

LIST OF BOXES

LIST OF FIGURES

LIST OF TABLES

ABOUT THE AUTHORS

Peter Bramham is a Research Fellow, and former Reader, in the Carnegie Faculty at Leeds Metropolitan University, in the UK. His more recent publications in sports studies are *Sport Development* (co-edited with Kevin Hylton, 2008), and two books on leisure (co-edited with Stephen Wagg) *Sport, Leisure and Culture in the Postmodern City* (2009) and *The Politics of Leisure and Pleasure* (2011).

Stephen Wagg is a Professor in the Carnegie Faculty of Leeds Metropolitan University in the UK. He has written widely on the politics of sport, of childhood, of comedy and of leisure. His most recent books are: *The New Politics of Leisure and Pleasure* (edited with Peter Bramham, 2011), *The Palgrave Handbook of Olympic Studies* (edited with Helen Lenskyj, 2012) and *Thatcher's Grandchildren? Politics and Childhood in the Twenty-First Century* (edited with Jane Pilcher, forthcoming in 2014).

ACKNOWLEDGEMENTS

The authors and the publishers acknowledge the permission of the following to reproduce materials in this student textbook:

Les Haywood et al. (1995) *Understanding Leisure* (Second edition). Cheltenham: Nelson Thornes.

Figure 1.1 *Callois' Classification of Games (adapted)* p.17.
Table 2.1 *A Typology of Leisure Activities* p.37.

Jock Young (1974, p.250) *Mass Media, drugs and deviance* in Mary McIntosh and Paul Rock (eds) *Deviance and Control*, London: Tavistock, pp.229–260.

INTRODUCTION

The structure of the book maps out different key stages in the life course; these stages are the ones that primarily interest leisure policy makers, leisure planners and managers. Traditional ideas have suggested and stressed the importance of the human life cycle and the ageing process – that irreversible biological clock that ticks away throughout the social status of living as a child, youth, adult, middle-aged parent and finally old age pensioner. At each developmental stage in the life cycle, individuals face pressing biological and psychological needs and these have changed historically as individuals charted their ways through the institutions of family, education, work and leisure. As we shall argue in Chapter 3, this linear view of the life cycle appropriately described collective experiences of earlier industrial society or modernity. People shared common backgrounds of class, of gender roles and of ethnicity as they grew up and grew old in locally based neighbourhoods. Much sociological research in the middle of the last century was all about the changing nature of social networks, the cohesion and solidarity of urban and rural communities.

The concept of the life course better construes what some writers term late modernity or postmodernity, as, nowadays, people's lives are more episodic, replete with disjuncture and contradiction. Within leisure studies and the social sciences generally there are fierce debates about the nature of these changes and whether we now live inside fragile and globalized postmodern cultures which are seen as qualitatively different and divergent from the solid culture of modernity or industrial society.

The life course metaphor can still be used to divide existence into discrete life stages but one's *Dasein* – that is, one's lived experience of the world – is more accurately captured by a geological metaphor; childhood, youth, adulthood, parenthood and old age are much more like tectonic plates that grind together providing diverse outcomes, challenges and experiences for different people. Some glide effortlessly on through the decades, others become frozen in or addicted to particular stages, whereas others may miss some out altogether. Biological body clocks do not necessarily measure time unequivocally; psychological, social and political processes may have different time scales and projects. Existential time, embodiment and biography must be contextualized with institutional/generational time and glacial time of *époques* and structural change.

This book provides a foundation for students studying within the broad field of leisure studies. It seeks to provide an appropriate and accessible introduction to key principles of leisure studies and leisure research and also to develop an understanding of contemporary leisure and changing leisure practices. The first chapter of the book defines the field of leisure studies. Chapter 2 examines the main traditions, principles and practices of leisure research and the third chapter provides an historical dimension to leisure. The material covered aims to encourage the student to engage in reflexive analysis of his/her common-sense understandings of everyday life. It therefore takes a biographical approach in rendering current debates within the social sciences and amongst leisure researchers. It provides case studies and grounded exemplars to encourage students to engage with social scientific accounts and develop a historical perspective on leisure.

Chapter 4 reflects this biographical approach as it focuses on childhood and play; likewise Chapter 5, which looks at youth and adolescence. Chapter 6 covers the literature around family and leisure, and Chapter 7 explores the traditional adult divisions of modernity around class, race and gender. Chapter 8 outlines the key arguments surrounding the growing individualization of people's leisure (and other) experience and details recent theoretical developments in leisure studies. Chapter 9 examines the position of old age and the retired in terms of leisure. The final chapter returns to policy and planning responses to these age cohorts of childhood, youth and adulthood. At the conclusion of each chapter, there are a series of student exercises and worked examples with key concepts and directed readings. Such exercises are derived from leisure-relevant questions and leisure debates raised in different disciplines.

1

DEFINING LEISURE AND LEISURE STUDIES

THIS CHAPTER

- Introduces students to the concept of leisure and the field of leisure studies and leisure research
- Identifies five main academic disciplines and the research questions they generate about the nature of leisure.

The overall aim of the book is to introduce students to what social scientists have to say about leisure. This is no simple task. First, there is no collective agreement amongst social scientists about how to define leisure. Secondly, there are many disciplines that make up the social sciences and within each discipline there are different complexes of theories or research traditions and diverse methodologies. So, for a variety of reasons, not all disciplines or all social scientists take an interest in leisure research. There are simply more important things to research in the world of say medicine, law and religion. But over the past thirty years, a generation of scholars has emerged who have mapped out a field of study and named it leisure studies.

This book is only concerned with social sciences, so there is no need to worry about what natural scientists get up to in maths, physics, chemistry or biological sciences. But, as we shall see later, changes in understanding science, technology and mass communications, all have real impacts on leisure lives and leisure spaces and thus raise important questions for both leisure theory and research. For example, new technologies of mass communications can transform people's leisure choices in viewing, listening and game playing.

1.1 Why call a social networking company Facebook?

What do you know about Facebook?

- from what people talk about?
- from having your own Facebook account?
- from the film, *The Social Network*?

What social significance do you attach to the following everyday phrases heard in conversation?

- 'I'll try and save face'
- 'God, He has a face on him!'
- 'I must put my face on' (Usually women applying make-up.)
- 'Let's face the music'
- 'I can't lose face over this'
- 'I really couldn't say it to her face'
- 'I suppose I shall have to face up to it!'
- 'Let's face it …'

The very concept of 'social media' such as Facebook and Twitter has dissolved (for some?) the previously more solid division between private and public lives. People can now become 'celebrities' through, for example, posting YouTube clips. The advent of home computers has meant that more and more people want to choose their own holiday via the Internet rather than buying holiday packages from travel agents. As a result, multinational travel companies such as Thomson's have decided to diversify from traditional mass tourist holidays and to develop new markets, new packages of holiday breaks and, importantly, to open up new global destinations. If commercial companies fail to recognize how the Internet or mobile phones transform people's leisure decision-making, they will lose business and market share. But what should public policy do for those sections of the population without access to mobile phones and the Internet – something or nothing?

WHAT MAJOR DISCIPLINES TAKE AN INTEREST IN STUDYING LEISURE?

Before reading Table 1.1 you need to think about what you expect leisure theory and research to look like. Here are some ideas or questions to start with:

- If you turned to a newspaper, what sorts of stories would be about leisure?

- Where would the articles be placed in the paper – front page, page 3, editorial pages, weekly columns, back page?

- Who do you think are the key leisure celebrities in the UK, in Australia, in the USA, in Africa?

- Who are global leisure stars and which are the main global leisure companies?

- What research projects interest you and what do you expect to be studying in the field of leisure studies?

1.2 Academic disciplines and research questions

- Write down the major disciplines you would expect to meet in the new field of leisure.

- What would you expect your key discipline (perhaps you have chosen psychology or perhaps sociology) to say about leisure?

- Construct one research question or project each discipline would undertake if they were engaged in a research project into student lifestyles in a city-based university.

Table 1.1 offers a broad-brush overview of the main disciplines that have shown an interest in leisure, and all have contributed to the field of leisure studies. The disciplinary contribution of history has not been included here as the third chapter is allocated to the history of leisure. The table only generalizes key disciplinary characteristics and approaches, in order to help us think about the different kinds of research questions asked by psychologists, economists, geographers, sociologists and political scientists. But, as becomes clear in Chapter 2, researchers working inside each discipline do not solely ask people questions but deploy a variety of methodologies and techniques of data collection. So, as traditional academic disciplines have single-mindedly focused on psyche, economy, environment, polity, or society, they provide distinctive insights into the psychology of leisure, the economics of leisure, the sociology of leisure, and so on. Indeed, one would hardly expect the same theoretical debates, issues and concepts to shape such different academic disciplines as psychology, economics, geography, political science and sociology. Each has developed its own theories, research methodologies and distinctive techniques of collecting data and writing up. Psychologists set up human experiments and measure sports competencies, economists analyse company performance and market share, geographers pore over maps and study catchment areas of leisure centres, sociologists investigate communities and join leisure subcultures, while political scientists scrutinize the comings and goings of government and judge how key politicians cope with leisure challenges for policy.

Table 1.1 Five major disciplines and leisure research questions

Discipline	Disciplinary focus	Leisure research questions
Psychology	• individuals and individualism • human development resilience • satisfaction and pleasure • personality • self	How does leisure meet human needs? What motivates individuals to engage in sport, arts and physical activity? What is the relationship between self-identity and leisure lifestyles?
Economics	• markets • material scarcity and abundance • leisure spending • leisure-centred business and commerce	What is the market structure and profitability of key leisure markets? How and why is leisure spending changing? What are mass and niche markets in arts, sports, tourism and leisure?
Geography	• demography • population growth and migration • mobility • rural and urban land use and planning	How are city leisure spaces changing? What impact does leisure and tourism have on landscape and local places and environments?
Politics	• democratic power • pressure groups • governance • public policy and public provision	What role does government play in leisure – should it have a role in leisure and/or different leisure sectors? What impact do leisure-relevant policies (e.g. education, transport, health etc.) have on access to and participation in leisure?
Sociology	• divisions of class, race and gender • generations, age and disability • social networks, community and local institutions • social inclusion and exclusion	What are the functions of leisure in different communities? How does leisure differ between different social groupings? How do inequalities shape leisure participation?

The next section suggests what thematic questions each academic discipline can offer to help us understand leisure. All social science disciplines have much to say about people, places and power. Leisure is made up of people, places and power. Each discipline has its own internally diverse traditions and discrete ways of study, so disciplinary perspectives provide diverse and distinctive understandings of leisure practices. These disciplines offer one unique picture or perspective on leisure practices in any society at any one historical moment. What makes leisure studies interesting is its ability to draw on a variety of disciplinary perspectives to provide a comprehensive or holistic view of the field of leisure. As a field of studies it has to be, in its weakest version, multi-disciplinary, and in its strongest form, inter-disciplinary. As the different terms imply, a multi-disciplinary approach features separate disciplines offering unique explanations of any subject matter, whereas an inter-disciplinary approach relies on well-established integrated sub-disciplines to provide a particular focus. For example, key writers may draw on psychology and sociology to provide a social psychology of leisure, as is the case with the work of Michael Argyle (1993, 2001). We shall return to these philosophical debates about the status of knowledge later, but first we must start with the foundation blocks of the single social science disciplines, such as psychology, economics, geography, politics and sociology.

PSYCHOLOGY

Psychology has concentrated on studying individuals and, from a leisure perspective, most importantly on the framing and quality of human experience. One central concept linked to definitions of leisure has been the concept of freedom. Individuals exercise freedoms in leisure. The starting point for early work mapping out leisure studies was a philosophical emphasis on individual choice. Greek philosophers such as Socrates emphasize the importance of leisure to individual self-development. It is in leisure when pursuing the arts, literature and scholarship that individuals exercise human freedom and develop skills and competencies. In the world of ancient Greece, people who were constrained by having to work (essentially slaves and women) were not free to experience leisure. Slaves and women did have free time but, according to Plato (see Sylvester, 1999), they could not experience leisure because they did not possess sufficient intellect and the necessary scholarship. That was the job of philosophers whose sole purpose was to leave the material world of work behind so that they could single-handedly pursue the truth (at their leisure).

In an article of 2000 the English philosopher A.C. Grayling (Grayling, 2000) raises a number of interesting points about the nature of leisure. He suggests that in early autumn many people are 'planning their holidays, leafing through the Sunday supplements to ponder advertisements offering everything from Andes pony trekking to Zimbabwe big-game viewing'. This, we can safely say, is a very partial view of the world, since most people don't read the sort of Sunday newspapers that carry supplements and are unlikely, in any event, to be able to afford the sort of holidays advertised there. Indeed, many people can't afford a holiday at all. That said, we're on safer ground when we suggest that most people *aspire* to a holiday: they'll take one if they can and regard doing so as a priority. Indeed Grayling later acknowledges that 'leisure has typically been the privilege of a few carried on the sweated backs of many' (Grayling, 2000).

Grayling goes on to suggest that a lot of people 'think of holidays as paradigmatic times of leisure, by which they mean opportunity for relaxation, not just of body and mind, but – even if only in the form of a little self-indulgence – of morals too: for holidays and moral holidays go together like cakes and ale'. They are, he adds, 'an opportunity for sin' (Grayling, 2000).

1.3 Holidays and the idea of leisure

The word 'holiday' is a corruption of 'holy day' – usually a saint's day, which in medieval times was marked by revelry of various kinds: dancing round the maypole, engaging in hectic traditional games and general carousing for the duration of the day. There were times thereafter, however, when such pleasure-seeking interludes became frowned upon and suppressed. The Puritans, for example, recognized no holy day but the Sabbath and, in New England, the settlement founded by the Pilgrim Fathers, even Christmas Day was an ordinary working day in the 1620s (Innes, 1995: 146). When the notion of a holiday was re-embraced, it was not necessarily for the enjoyment of everyone. As the historian James Walvin once observed, in the 1830s and 40s, 'the English middle and upper classes were as notable for their pursuit of pleasure as their inferiors were generally devoid of it' (Walvin, 1978: 2).

Grayling (2000) argues that in modern society leisure had to be measured against work and that merely doing nothing was seldom satisfying. He cites two writers in support of this: the eighteenth-century English Christian poet William Cowper and Sam Clemens, better known as Mark Twain, the celebrated American writer of the nineteenth century. In his poem on 'Retirement' (1782), Cowper warned against idleness. He wrote: 'Absence of occupation is not rest, A mind quite vacant is a mind distressed ... An idler is a watch that wants both hands; As useless when it goes as when it stands' (Cowper, 1980: 393 and 395).

This remark can be linked to the teaching of Greek philosopher Aristotle, who is widely quoted on the matter of leisure. For Aristotle, 'the aim of education is to equip us to make noble use of our leisure: ... If work is concerned with securing life's necessities, leisure is concerned with cultivating its amenities' and Grayling concludes that 'leisure is not the opposite of work, it is – as Mark Twain and Aristotle both suggest – something better: the opportunity to work for higher ends' (Grayling, 2000).

We are left, then, with two intriguingly different notions of the holiday and, thus, of leisure: it is, alternatively, an opportunity for sin and moral relaxation, or a time of self-education and improvement.

What do you understand by Grayling's phrase 'most ... think holidays as holidays are paradigmatic times of leisure'?

Consult some dictionaries and find out the origin and early meanings of the word leisure. What do these origins tell you about the meaning of leisure today?

What is the nature of the relationship between leisure and work?

Why do you think the Puritans sought to ban holidays?

What does William Cowper mean by the lines 'An idler is a watch that wants both hands; As useless when it goes as when it stands'? Do you agree with him?

> The saucy seaside postcard could be said to signify the holiday as a period of moral relaxation. In your view, are these cards still popular among holidaymakers? If so, why? If not, why not?
>
> Drawing on your own experiences, as well as the experiences of your family and friends, to what extent is leisure 'an opportunity to work for higher ends'?

This debate about the human potential to be free is also a touchstone of psychology, as theories and research take sides as to whether individuals are determined or can exercise free will. Recent research by the genome project and studies looking into DNA profiles have reasserted the position that humans are genetically determined, that individuals are hard wired by their inherited makeup. Our ancestors are chimps, with whom we share 99% of our DNA, and despite surface appearances we actually share 95% of our genetic makeup with mice. This supports biological determinism. One's potential is pre-programmed by one's biological parents and their ancestors. It is genetic makeup that pre-determines the individual's intellect, body shape, skin colour, morbidity and lifespan. When applied to sport and leisure, some people are naturally talented at tennis and others can't hit a ball; some can sing in tune, others are tone deaf; some can dance, others cannot keep to a rhythm.

This envisages little space for freedom or human agency and choice. It concentrates on neurological processes, chemical reactions fired off in the brain, leaving individuals as complicated biologically programmed machines. If one follows the currently popular arguments of evolutionary psychology, humans are primates, destined to compete in order to survive. Even 'other-orientated' selfless behaviours, often found in the care and intimacy of family life, are just the acting of selfish genes (Dawkins, 1976). Each man and woman has an interest in securing the continuity of his/her own genetic pool, through sexual reproduction, and so they settle down into stable family relations. Over millennia men have been programmed genetically to be aggressive, to hunt and kill for survival. Women are biologically programmed to nurture and care for their children. It is a biological necessity and natural to have this sexual division of labour.

1.4 Sporting violence

How would evolutionary psychologists explain high levels of violence in sports and sports spectators?

What sort of counter arguments could be made against a strong evolutionary psychological approach?

Start from the extreme position that biological determinism is a complete myth and there is no hard evidence whatsoever that chromosome makeup actually connects or determines human behaviour.

Sigmund Freud (1920) took a similar position on determinism with his revolutionary theory of human personality. He suggested that human beings are *sociable* but not fully *socialized*. In *Beyond the Pleasure Principle* (1920) he argued that the death instinct and the sexual instinct were prime motivators of human behaviour. The individual is in constant struggle with these fundamental forces, two basic instincts which he named Thanatos and Eros respectively. Freud's pessimistic view of human beings casts the lives of individuals as caught in complex webs of subconscious instincts. These are ultimately and inevitably in conflict with rational civilized behaviours. Normal society hopes for and expects individuals to be fully formed and well-rounded personalities. From Freud's view, informed by psychoanalysis, individuals will never live lives free from anxieties and neuroses because of their need to repress and control sex and death instincts.

1.5 Freud and leisure activities

Here is a list of different leisure activities. How would you code them in accordance with Freud's view of the sexual instinct (Eros) and the death instinct (Thanatos)? Some of course could be mixed compromises.

Codes: 1 = Eros; 2 = Thanatos; 3 = Mixed

- Speeding in a car on a motorway/a highway
- Racing a friend on a powerful motorbike down narrow lanes in the countryside
- Climbing freestyle in the mountains
- Abseiling down a cliff
- Sailing a dinghy or yacht on a quiet lake/on the sea in windy stormy weather
- Salsa dancing
- Watching pornographic films
- Reading detective stories/murder mysteries
- Reading newspapers magazines about the lives of celebrities
- Watching a live boxing or wrestling contest
- Playing rugby or American football
- Drinking alcohol on a tourist beach

In contrast to Freud's pessimistic view of human nature, many writers take a much more positive view of the human condition. Assumptions about human nature are in part linked to more generic anthropological questions separate from psychological and scientific research. One helpful corrective to a very deterministic view of human nature can be found in the work of Chris Rojek (2000). Writing about the historical development of leisure theory, Chris Rojek maps out three moments in the history of leisure studies – functionalism, critical Marxism and feminism. He suggests that all three major theories lack an anthropological view of culture. He challenges the work-centred view of humanity. This view, so central to Marx's view of history and class, argues that humankind only realizes its true nature in work and material production, dealing with the realm of necessity and reproducing the means of existence, the means to live. For Rojek this approach must be understood in its context. It is historically specific to modern times, to industrialization and later industrial society, to the nineteenth century when Marx was writing and the bulk of the twentieth century when Marxism was particularly influential as a global political ideology. However, by the late twentieth century, with de-industrialization, more flexible employment and with more women working, often in part-time jobs, Rojek suggests that work is no longer central to individuals, communities or classes. Following Johannes Huizinga, Rojek argues that language, communication and play are at the centre of human culture. Nineteenth- and twentieth-century industrial society stresses over-regimentation, calculability and rationality, while leisure is a site for transgression and change, for challenging everyday culture and compulsion. As Table 1.2 illustrates Rojek's work helpfully maps out two ideal types of humanity: *homo faber* and *homo ludens*.

Table 1.2 Comparing *homo faber* and *homo ludens*

Homo faber (Marx)	Homo ludens (Huizinga)
• Realm of necessity • Work and employment • Material production • Scientific knowledge and rationality • Technological control of nature and environment	• Realm of freedom • Play and creativity • Cultural production • Artistic knowledge and emotion • Aesthetic judgement of nature and environment

PSYCHOLOGY AND SELF-ACTUALIZATION

Many American writers in humanistic psychology and social psychology have developed the idea of *homo ludens*, a creative playful self. They stress that everyone has this human capacity for self-development and self-actualization; that within us we have a nature and potential we can articulate and through which we can find meaning. So, unlike the clinician Freud and psycho-analysis that distrusts the individual's own account of his or her behaviour (for good reasons, as we shall explore in Chapter 4), humanistic psychology respects the individual's subjective experiences of reality. It values personal responsibility, goal setting, personal choices and individual freedom.

These humanistic ideas, influential in the development of leisure studies, have come originally from organizational psychology, from the world of paid employment and work, and are derived from the research agenda of the

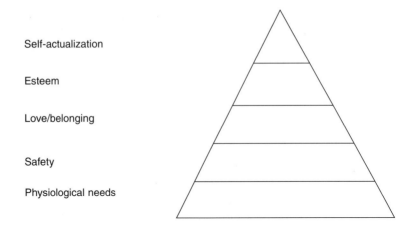

Self-actualization

Esteem

Love/belonging

Safety

Physiological needs

Figure 1.1   Maslow's hierarchy of human needs

American, Abraham Maslow. He argued that all individuals have a hierarchy of needs and once lower level needs (e.g. physical needs for security and material survival) are satisfied, then people strive to achieve higher level needs (friendship, status and creativity) (see Figure 1.1).

So, according to Maslow, people look outwards and strive to achieve status and respect from others in the community. Finally, at the apex of Maslow's hierarchy, he locates the highest need of self-actualization. The assumptions of humanistic psychology are that one can trust human beings to make positive, constructive and conscious choices. In contrast, Freud argued that individuals were often in negative states as they struggled to repress destructive anxieties, driven by unconscious instincts.

Roger Ingham (1986, 1987) made an important contribution by introducing psychology into leisure studies. He challenged the narrow experimental tradition in psychological research, arguing for a social psychology that should study meanings and experience as well as the diverse roles, contexts and opportunities that leisure provided for self-expression.

ECONOMICS

It is worth looking next at what economists tell us about leisure choices because classical economics rests on some very strong assumptions about individuals, human nature and human behaviour. Whereas we may only have passing knowledge about psychological theories, we have practical experience of how capitalist economic systems function. According to eighteenth- and nineteenth-century classical economists, individuals act out of self-interest. In this view, people are rational decision makers and seek to maximize profit and minimize costs in the production and consumption of all goods and services. So, individuals are calculative, with interests focused solidly on meeting their own material needs for short- and long-term personal survival. As we shall see later, in the world of political ideologies, both liberalism and conservatism argue that individuals have a natural right to property; indeed Macpherson (1962, 1977) describes liberalism as 'possessive individualism'. Such rights, linked to economic individualism and personal liberty, were clearly written into the core principles of the US constitution.

Markets are the sites where suppliers of particular commodities and services can meet with consumers who want to buy. Adam Smith (1776) argued the 'invisible hand' of the market price mechanism brought together supply and demand, maximized efficiency, minimized costs and secured common wealth. Open competitive markets mean that firms can freely enter the marketplace and compete with other firms in price, quantity and quality, and this leaves the individual, as sovereign consumer, free to choose. Price is linked to material production. Firms that meet consumer needs and guarantee satisfaction will flourish, whereas firms that produce substandard shoddy goods will lose trade and perish.

Classical economics has stressed that this dynamic balance between supply and demand applied to all goods and services, including markets for labour. Those individuals who have developed scarce highly valued skills will command high salaries and income for their work, whereas unskilled workers in an environment of plentiful labour will receive low wages or even face unemployment. For classical economists any interference with market mechanisms that balance supply and demand is unwelcome. So, government regulation of markets, say by setting a minimum wage for labour or in specifying the number of hours that may be worked on health grounds, will distort the efficient and effective way of allocating resources. Interference by labour in the form of trade union organizations which may control the supply of accredited labour or bargain for higher wages similarly distorts market forces and in the long run will be counterproductive. Unions will price their members out of jobs as other firms employing non-unionized labour generate lower wage bills and, consequently, offer the produced goods at a lower price. Individual consumers can thus buy more and the firm secures a greater market share and potential for economic growth and further investment. Nor should firms organize themselves into monopolistic cartels and engage in price fixing agreements so as to generate surplus or excess profits. Any interference by government, by firms or by trade unions distorts the neutral mechanisms of the allocation of resources by price, according to the classical liberal version of economics. Some economists acknowledge that there are some 'natural monopolies'. Nation states may want to take long-term control over and regulate national resources such as water, energy production, transport and communication networks. In these cases public policy could yield economies of scale, promote the co-ordination of investment and planning strategies, and act to subsidize pricing structures to protect the poor, which would be impossible if left to free-for-all market forces.

In the post-war period Keynes stated that long-term economic growth and full employment should be managed by the nation state's economic policies.

By changing fiscal policies on corporate and income taxation, politicians must manage the economy so as to avoid the 'bust and boom' fluctuations within market forces. Downward pressure on wages leads to deflation and a lack of consumer spending and investment, accompanied by low economic growth, whereas inflation means rising prices, a shortage of labour and an overheating economy. These two approaches, one of classical liberalism, the other of Keynesian economics, have dominated past generations' thinking. There is some irony, within a globalized economic world, that politicians and economists are still working with economic models and theories that have their roots in the eighteenth and nineteenth centuries.

It is, however, the case that liberal economics provides an idealized vision of how capitalism should work and EU Commissions struggle to introduce laws to encourage the free movement of capital and labour, as well as policies to secure fair competition across industries in different EU member states. Nevertheless, wherever one looks at leisure markets one sees monopolies or oligopolies, that is markets are dominated by one (monopoly) or a handful of major companies (oligopolies) which deploy a variety of strategies, including branding and advertising, to legitimate selling their goods and services well above costs and normal profit margins. The global market for trainers provides a good example of oligopolies at work as major companies compete with each other in terms of branding – the cost of producing a trainer is quoted as $5 while a pair sells for much more than $50 worldwide.

In the first chapter of *Leisure and Culture*, 'From ritual to performative culture', Chris Rojek (2000) argues that all societies must organize time and space for economic and social survival, but that there is and has always been a surplus of energy and unused resources. Leisure is how this surplus is consumed. Challenging the assumptions of classical economics and Marxist political economy, Rojek draws on the works of Lewis Mumford (1967, 1970) and George Bataille (1988) to argue that human history is not so much about scarcity, poverty and inequality but rather about abundance, conspicuous consumption and transgression. Again, the realm of material necessity is held in stark contrast to that of freedom and excess. As when purchasing a pair of branded trainers, consumers are not solely looking for value for money, but rather buying a brand or logo that signifies current styles and fashions. Hence, retailers are forced to discount last year's fashions and styles.

It is really only in the past two decades that one can talk about 'leisure shopping' for practically the whole of the population. As we shall see later in this chapter, this has led to emerging, large, out-of-town shopping malls that house not only national retail chains but also multiplex cinemas, restaurants and leisure centres. There has also been substantial urban regeneration and redevelopment. Within pedestrianized city centres, shopping malls, restaurants and bars mushroom along with street animation, for example entertainers, buskers, mobile food outlets and community liaison officers. John Spink (1994) neatly outlines the shift from functional everyday shopping for necessity to 'window' or leisure shopping (see Table 1.3).

Table 1.3 Leisure and shopping

	LEISURE		SHOPPING
Single function trip	Recreation pursuit		Purposive shopping (major item)
			Convenience shopping (time-centred)
Multi-function trip	Leisure	AND	Essentials shopping (bulk purchase)
	Leisure	AS	Pleasure shopping (comparison of goods and services)

1.6 Shopping for trainers

- How many pairs of trainers do you own?

- When did you last buy a new pair?

- Where did you buy your trainers? (City centre, out-of-town retail, local store, Internet?)

- Was the price discounted?

- Did you buy them on your own or were they purchased when out shopping with friends/family?

- Did you take advice about what sort of trainers would suit your feet/ needs?

- Do you know what brands your trainers are – who made them? Where were they made?

- What type of shoes are they?

- Do you use them for competitive sport, recreational sport or simply leisure wear?

- Has anyone commented on your new trainers? What did they say about them?

GEOGRAPHY

Geographers have studied the spatial dimensions of leisure. It is important to think about the location in which leisure takes place, as the context often features as an important ingredient in an individual's leisure experience. People construct their own special and distinctive spaces for leisure purposes and these favourite spaces, gardens and landscapes are often subject to redesign and redevelopment in the search for leisure satisfaction and profit. Indeed, much daytime television is full of design and fashion experts as they buy and refurbish houses, redesign gardens and patios and carry out general decorating. The teams of workers are often constrained by impossible time scales, as the refurbishment has been secretly planned by one partner in collusion with the media company to 'surprise' the other partner, who is cunningly organized to be absent over the weekend when filming occurs. The denouement of the programme focuses on the delighted response of the householder on returning to their newly designed house or garden. This is usually filmed with glasses of celebratory champagne, and the householder is embraced by TV celebrity gardeners, all of which can only serve to ease any lingering disappointment he/she may have felt initially over the inappropriate and distasteful water feature. Writers on postmodern culture (Featherstone, 1988, 1990) celebrate 'fashions' not 'fashion' and there can be a clash between private tastes and a kind of garden design technocracy in which media personalities know best. The individual's taste may be the expert's distaste and vice versa. It is not just gardening either, there are a plethora of media programmes where experts tell novices and members of the public what they should like and what is best.

1.7 TV celebrity programmes

What are the following TV celebrities 'experts' about?

- Alan Titchmarsh
- Gok Wan
- Trinny and Susannah
- Laurence Llewelyn-Bowen
- Sir Alan Sugar
- Kirsty Allsop
- Simon Cowell
- Raymond Blanc
- Mary Berry
- Kevin McCloud

Some geographers have set out to log accurately the amount of leisure time people actually have and to map out precisely where it is spent. One example of this kind of approach in the UK can be found in the research of Sue Glyptis. She devised time-space diaries in which respondents recorded where they spent their time, what they were doing and its precise location, inside or outside the home. The importance of home-based leisure time was a distinctive finding of this research in the 1980s (Glyptis et al., 1987) which compared different patterns in the diaries across age groups as well as marital and family status differences.

1.8 Time-space diary

Keep a time-space diary for four days from 00:00hrs Friday morning to 23:59hrs Monday night.

The X axis (vertical line) denotes time measures in hours/days, whereas the Y axis (horizontal line) denotes the precise location and nature of your time spent during work/study periods and at weekends.

The left half of the Y axis notes the location/rooms where activities take place inside the home, whereas the right half measures the distance and destinations travelled outside the home.

Calculate the amount of time spent in a weekday and weekend inside and outside of the home.

Compare your pattern with the profiles of unemployed people outlined in Glyptis (1989: 112–130).

Glyptis' research discovered that older people spent much more of their leisure time inside the home compared with younger generations, including even couples with young children. Geographers are also keen to point out that present generations will have opportunities to experience much higher levels of geographical mobility than their parents or grandparents did in their lifetime. John Adams refers to this as hypermobility and suggests that pace of life and the distances people are travelling are both accelerating exponentially. Chris Rojek has referred to this growing sense of restlessness, pointing out that individuals nowadays are keen to travel and discover new places. Tourist destinations defined as exotic by grandparents and parents are now simply matters of course for their children to visit and enjoy. Take some examples such as Paris, Barcelona and Florida compared with China, Singapore, Thailand and Vietnam.

1.9 Family destinations

Make a list of the countries your family has visited so far in their lives: who is most travelled and why?

YOURSELF	PARENTS	GRANDPARENTS

But it is not just private households that are eager to design their own domestic leisure spaces; there are professional planners whose job it is to design public leisure spaces. Geographers have long been interested in how both urban and rural spaces have changed over time and particularly how economic forces have determined land use values in terms of their function, whether it be production (e.g. primary, secondary or tertiary), circulation and distribution (transport, retailing) or consumption (residential). Land prices reflect the profitability of land use and functions compete for prime sites so that unprofitable land uses in city centres come under pressure to be transformed and developed into more commercial functions. It is precisely this sort of pressure that has created public anxiety about schools selling off playing fields, most usually to become retailing sites or for residential properties. But all spaces have potential for leisure and each individual quests for greater mobility. Each generation has grown up in a distinctive environment with its own unique historical material infrastructure. For example, the grandparent generation (those over seventy years of age) will have grown up swimming at the seaside or in urban lidos opened in the 1930s, while their children, the parent generation, now middle-aged, learned to swim at primary school in 1960s local authority swimming pools, whereas young people may now only be prepared to swim in new leisure pools, furnished with slides and wave machines.

1.10 Locations and leisure

Think of some rural/suburban/city-centre examples or contexts for leisure activities.

Our initial example (above) concerned water-based resources in different geographical locations but try and think of other forms of land-based resources and sites with their potential for sport, recreational and leisure activities, e.g. walking, running, cycling, climbing and so on. Does the 'leisure' experience change, if the location changes? (See Table 1.4) Compare, for example, riding a bicycle in a multi-purpose leisure centre, in the garage at home on a turbo-trainer, in busy city-centre traffic and in the quiet countryside.

Sharon Zukin (1991) argued that the landscapes we inhabit, or pass through and gaze upon in our leisure, have been moulded by economic, political, social and cultural forces. All landscapes are shaped by human habitation, by continual exploitation of material resources, by consumption processes and by communication networks to enable spatial mobility. To use Zukin's terms, landscapes represent the architecture of class, gender and race relations imposed by powerful institutions. In her book, *Landscapes of Power* (1991), she depicted three different physical landscapes that reflected three different types of society. The first she described as the 'Class Society' of the USA in the 1930s. It was epitomized by

Table 1.4 Locations and leisure

Rural area		Suburban area		City centre	
Natural	Manufactured (artificial)	Natural	Constructed	Natural	Constructed
Mountains Lakes	White-water canoe courses	Urban parks and streams/ becks	Play areas, lidos, swimming/ paddling pools	Rivers	Canals, marinas, waterfronts

local occupational communities of coal mining – the landscape of pit winding gear, slag-heaps, and rows of terrace housing that made up the isolated mining village. It was a world of men's work, of strong class divisions and harsh times of recession, unemployment and poverty. There were distinctive class cultures and strong local identities and a definite sense of place. There were equally strong cultural boundaries between the sexes as men were trade unionists, paid piece rates for hard manual work in close-knit teams and spent their leisure time in working men's clubs. Women were left at home, responsible for keeping a clean household, for cooking appropriate family meals and for child care. A British example of this was Ashton, the mining village in *Coal is Our Life* by Dennis et al. (1969).

Zukin's second landscape from the 1960s was to be found in the gridiron cities like Detroit. She described it as 'Modern Mass Society' and it was the world of large car manufacturing plants, of assembly lines, of new suburban housing estates. It was the world of affluence, featuring new houses with consumer durables such as washing machines, fridges, new cars, TV aerials on rooftops, and telegraph and telephone wires. Male workers were more home-centred and patterns of mass tourism were emerging with the development of high-rise hotel and self-catering apartments at expanding overseas resorts. A British example of similar research can be found in Goldthorpe and Lockwood's (1969) study of affluent workers in Luton and Young and Willmott's later study (1973).

Zukin's third landscape from the 1990s highlighted the architecture of 'postmodernity'. It was the physical landscape of heritage centres, of shopping malls and iconic theme parks. The warehouses, docklands and mines of the class society were refurbished as urban tourist destinations. It was a world of cell phones, laptops and Internet access. Both men and women worked; the boundaries between work, home and leisure became more blurred, with 'fast food' outlets, microwave ovens and burgeoning tastes to 'eat out' in diverse 'authentic' global restaurants. Zukin's particular interest in postmodernity was focused on the theme park as a tourist experience. As we shall see later with George Ritzer's work on McDonald's, Sharon Zukin felt that one company epitomized the complex changes afoot. Disney World exemplified the new simulated and pastiche culture of postmodernity. In Zukin's phrase, Disney was the capital of symbolism and the symbol of capitalism.

Zukin and Ritzer are important writers for leisure studies because their ideas offer a broad and challenging perspective to link changes in the business practices of multinational firms to eating patterns and family networks, and to natural and built environments. Their research challenges us not to take anything for granted in leisure. Urban and rural landscapes are resources produced by people making decisions, some of which are solely leisure based. Taking a long vacation trekking in a National Park or in wilderness territories, 'to get away from it all' and 'to get back to nature', becomes possible because some politicians somewhere have taken a particular view of land-use planning, as in the 'Freedom to Roam' debates in the UK before the passing of the CROW Act 2004 (Ravenscroft and Gilchrist, 2011). This designation may have been fiercely controversial at the time, fought over by international, national and local interests. It may be contested once more by future generations.

POLITICS

Although Zukin as a cultural geographer has written about landscapes of power, the idea of power expression is more usually associated with the business of politicians, pressure groups and decision making. Political processes strive to achieve some sort of balance between individual rights to freedoms and collective rules and obligations to ensure safety and order. Political parties profess different values about the correct balance between national governments, local communities and the individual. At election time, they write manifestos, make TV broadcasts and pay for advertising which set out and promulgate their distinctive policy aims about the economy, health, education and law and order. We have already seen that personal freedom in leisure is central for some psychological perspectives, but leisure choices are inevitably made and played out within a broader political context. Within the boundaries of each nation state, leading politicians hope to develop policies that will be popular and will win media and public support for their re-election to office. The same holds for local politicians as they try to convince usually distrusting and indifferent local communities that local towns and cities have been well governed over the past years and that local interests have been more or less protected.

Whatever they say about 'having no alternatives' all politicians have a wide range of options when they develop and implement public policies. Presumably they have more time and opportunities to refresh or even change direction when newly elected. Over time it seems that politicians simply run out of steam, and faced with many major problems institutional inertia sets in. In the 1970s leisure policies were left under the guidance and providence of the local state. However, by the 1980s the politics of neo-liberalism sought to restrict local government expenditure; certain types of localized leisure spending came under increasing pressure from limited budgets and central state auditing. So when it comes to leisure, that may be some way down their personal policy agendas of 'things to do'. They can simply not regard it as a legitimate arena for government action, but not taking action is a policy decision in itself. If politicians choose to 'take action', they can and do act as direct providers of leisure services, or they may prefer to be facilitators by encouraging partnerships, grants and subsidies or as regulators by creating agencies to set standards and supervision. Haywood et al. (1995) have devised a useful typology for mapping out dimensions of leisure on an active to passive leisure continuum. They argue that governments want to encourage active leisure pursuits like arts, sports and outdoor recreation while they tend to favour licensing and regulating for passive leisure such as mass media consumption, shopping and gambling. As a rule of thumb, Republican and Conservative governments tend to resist government intervention, whereas Labour and Democrats favour a strong collective state presence. But things are not always so straightforward and politics, particularly in the field of leisure, yields some surprising initiatives and outcomes.

In any country leisure policies are potentially both broad and complex. They clearly are of interest to both national and local politicians as well as policy advisors. One major issue with leisure policies and managing leisure is the need to take a broad view of the interdependencies between the main leisure policy areas – such as sports, arts, tourism, mass media, countryside recreation and urban leisure. There is also growing interest in hybrid or mixed policies such as sports tourism or media-led cultural policies to regenerate cities and regions. Most national states are becoming more interested in elite sport development, building sports stadia and hosting global mega-events like World Cups or the Olympics. Many policy makers claim that huge investments in sports facilities will leave behind a viable heritage to secure future sports participation and leisure opportunities for ordinary citizens. City politicians legitimate their decisions by arguing that local citizens have a right to access world-class facilities.

Fred Coalter has produced a useful distinction between 'leisure policies' and 'leisure-relevant policies' to help clarify our thinking. The leisure impact of some policies is obvious as they focus on free-time activities, whereas other policy areas may have an indirect tangential impact on leisure participation, such as access to transport and employment.

1.11 'Leisure policies' and 'leisure-relevant' policies

Which of the following policies would you classify as 'leisure policies' and which as 'leisure-relevant' policies?

- Funding a National Institute for Sport

- Designating a wilderness area as a National Park

- Introducing preventative health care strategies for small children

(Continued)

(Continued)

- Building a sports and leisure centre
- Planning an out-of-town shopping, cinema and restaurant complex with lakeside water features
- Opening a long-distance cycle path
- Introducing more physically active programmes in school education to combat childhood obesity
- Providing subsidies for rural and late-night urban public transport
- Providing tax incentives to encourage charity donations to the arts
- Developing comprehensive child care facilities in deprived areas
- Regulating satellite and digital channels' access to pornography
- Providing free Internet access for all schools
- Developing a sustainable 'green' energy policy
- Subsidizing the purchase of bicycles to encourage people to cycle to work
- Implementing EU health regulations that only permit individuals to work a maximum 48-hour week.
- Introducing a carbon tax on aircraft fuel and airport flights
- Improving the visibility of the police in city centres at weekends
- Providing a minimum wage for all workers in the service sector, e.g. hotels, restaurants, bars, etc.

It is no easy task for politicians to defend individual freedoms while simultaneously seeking to secure collective duties and obligations in wider society. This balancing act is drawn into sharp relief in debates about 'the war against terrorism'. What powers should nation states have to ensure safety and law and order for citizens? American and British governments have been criticized by judges, lawyers and by international media for infringing the rights of suspected terrorists because of undercover surveillance operations, illicit telephone tapping, internment without judicial trial, and so on. To what extent do governments have a mandate to intervene in people's working and leisure lives? To start thinking about the politics of leisure let us look at the political debates contesting any change to the licensing hours for drinking alcohol.

Governments often feel mandated to tackle moral panics – stormy periods during which the mass media amplify concern about a supposed problem, without either explaining it or assessing its extent. As Chas Critcher (2003, 2011) explains, moral panics have often centred on the drinking habits of the public.

An early example was the so-called 'gin craze' of the early eighteenth century. In England in 1721 the Middlesex magistrates called gin 'the principal cause of all the vice and debauchery committed among the inferior sort of people' (Chisholm, 2002) and five acts of parliament, designed to restrict the consumption of gin, were passed between 1729 and 1751. Similar political anxiety informed early-twentieth-century America, where, under the Volstead Act, alcohol was banned between 1920 and 1933 out of the belief that it would improve public morality and health. But Prohibition, as it was called, was difficult to enforce and is widely seen to have played into the hands of organized crime syndicates, who became the main providers of alcohol. It is doubtful that alcohol consumption decreased during 'the Long Thirst' (Coffey, 2013).

1.12 Leisure and the licensing laws: 24-hour drinking?

Moral concerns about drinking have re-emerged in the early twenty-first century with widespread denunciation of 'binge drinking'. In an article entitled 'My name is Britain and I have a drink problem' (Kettle, 2003) the *Guardian* columnist Martin Kettle compares Britain to Italy, noting that the consumption of alcohol per head is more or less the same for each country: 'But', he adds, 'that's where the cultures diverge. Italians spread their drinking out. Notoriously, we concentrate ours. And Italy's alcohol consumption is dropping, in line with the pattern in the majority of countries in Europe. In Britain, we are in the minority of countries where alcohol consumption is rising' (Kettle, 2003). Deregulation failed in Ireland in the 1990s and the country's politicians have had to reverse the liberalizing legislation of that decade because of a rising tide of drunkenness and disorder amongst young people.

In 2011 leading medical experts called for similar restrictions in Britain: combining drink-related diseases with drink-induced accidents and violence, a quarter of a million lives could be lost to alcohol by 2031. As the *Guardian* reported, referring to a recent article in *The Lancet*, 'raising the price of alcohol and restricting its availability are the two proven ways of reducing drink-related harm, the authors argue. Yet ministers, they say, have rejected major changes in both areas' (Campbell, 2011).

Often we see society pulling in different directions on issues such as this. The sociologist Chas Critcher comments on the 'contradiction between moralistic attacks on binge drinking and policies fostering night-time economies in city centres which depended wholly on consumer hedonism' (Critcher, 2011: 41). In these city centres, as two other sociologists have observed, young people are 'encouraged to play with the parameters of excitement and excess' (Hayward and Hobbs, 2007).

Let's also remember the influence of the drinks industry lobby who have their own solutions to the problem.

List the arguments for and against 24-hour drinking.

(Continued)

> *(Continued)*
>
> Who are the key stakeholders in this debate?
>
> Why should the Irish government and the New Labour government become interested in providing new laws and regulations concerning alcohol consumption times?
>
> Why have the two governments taken very different positions on regulating drinking times?
>
> What do you see as the short- and long-term effects of these new policies?
>
> Select three countries with different rates of alcohol-related crimes and illnesses. Suggest reasons for these differences.
>
> In what ways are young drinkers 'encouraged to play with the parameters of excitement and excess'?

So governments do become involved with leisure, if only through their interest in creating and maintaining law and order. They may be more concerned with more serious issues of managing the economy, modernizing health services, supporting families, but all these directly and indirectly affect people's leisure. Politicians produce legislation to regulate and deregulate time and people's life timetables such as hours of work, dates for pensions and possible retirement, as well as holidays, Sunday retail trading and paternity and maternity leave.

As we shall argue later, governments also decide how much risk is permissible in public places and who precisely is legally responsible for safety and negligence in public and private places. Risk and risk taking are essential ingredients across the gamut of sporting experiences and similar issues have been raised about children growing up in urban environments when they become involved in illegal activities, drug and alcohol abuse and unsafe sexual behaviours. Indeed, Rojek (2000) has encouraged leisure studies scholars to think beyond their more traditional concerns around rates of active leisure and rational recreation and start to explore 'dark leisure' and policing free-time desires. This takes academic debate controversially into the expanding world of pornography, drugs, the Internet and media interest in serial killers.

SOCIOLOGY

Of all the social sciences, sociologists have shown the keenest involvement in leisure studies and leisure research. They have drawn on their own interest in the sociology of leisure and have made major contributions in establishing leisure studies internationally. The 'founding fathers' of leisure studies in the UK were Ken Roberts and Stan Parker and both have had an enormous influence in developing and organizing leisure studies at an international level. From its inception in the UK, leisure scholars have long been concerned with the relationship between work and leisure. Drawing on the work of American sociologists such as Dubin (1956) and Wilensky (1960), leisure theory became interested in the idea of people's 'central life interests'. Research was straightforward in that the sociological task was one of asking different social groups whether work was their 'central life interest'. As one would expect, much higher percentages of professional occupations stressed work as centrally important and rates were far lower amongst non-manual and manual workers. The latter two groups were more likely to take a neutral or oppositional approach to work, as satisfactions were to be found elsewhere in the worlds of leisure and family.

1.13 Social research and work

What are the strengths and weaknesses of social research asking people questions about work as a 'central life interest'?

Discussion points:

- How would you set about collecting data from different social groups using interviews, questionnaires, focus groups and participant observation in different work settings?

- Where would you choose to conduct the research? In the individual's workplace? In a leisure setting? At home?

- Which groups are included or excluded by this type of approach?

By definition sociologists have concentrated on the social aspects of leisure. They are interested in the phenomenon of leisure and how it functions inside different societies. So how does leisure relate to other major institutions such as family, work, religion and politics? One classic UK study is summarized below because it highlighted both the democratic functions of leisure and leisure's importance in establishing people's identities in modern society.

1.14 Leisure and the voluntary sector

J. Bishop and P. Hoggett (1986) *Organizing Around Enthusiasms*. London: Comedia.

In this study the two authors completed innovative research into leisure and the UK voluntary sector. The research was funded in the 1980s by the Economic and Social Research Council to order to explore the diversity of the voluntary sector in leisure.

(Continued)

(Continued)

The study focused on two different local areas – Kingswood (suburban Bristol) and Leicester (focusing on the north east corner of the city that included inner-city council estates and multi-occupied households (both Asian and 'English')). Their survey discovered 300 groups in Kingswood (assuming a membership of about 90) – this meant that 28,500 people were leisure active in a neighbourhood with a population of 85,000. The research sampled 71 organizations in Bristol and 63 in Leicester. The explicitly stated purposes of the clubs were coded: a third were multi-functional (e.g. youth clubs, Women's Institutes, OAP clubs), another third were sports clubs and the remainder were for arts, crafts and hobbies clubs. Over half of all clubs were for adults or youths of at least 15 years old. Women were well represented in arts, crafts and hobbies, with higher involvement rates in adult education classes. Ethnicity was an important fact and class less so.

They defined these leisure groups as 'collectivities which are self-organised, productive and which by and large consume their own products' (1986: 40). Leisure goods and services are organised 'by *us* for *us*' and consumed and enjoyed locally by family, friends and other enthusiasts. It was best described as communal leisure – mutual-aid organizations with the focus on reciprocity, self-help and self-organization.

Enthusiasms are defined as 'activities freely given yet [they] typically assume the form of highly skilled and imaginative work, whilst remaining leisure not employment'. Enthusiasts form groups or 'communities of interest' and constitute an essential ingredient in national, regional and local culture.

Such activities are non-commercial. Such groups are not just settings in which leisure activity takes place, instrumental means to ends; they are fragile and open to the commercialization of leisure. Communal groups offer aid and mutual help, while producing goods and services for their own enjoyment. So leisure clubs are self-run and self-organized mainly into arts, sports, crafts and hobbies and multi-functional community groups.

Bishop and Hoggett offer four main reasons as to why people join leisure groups:

- Activities are collective and members are essential to producing the leisure experience.
- Facilities are collectively shared and maintained.
- Clubs provide competition, clubs and leagues.
- Clubs provide a wide range of opportunities for sociability.

Discussion topic:

Cookery and DIY are the only two activities around which enthusiasms are not organized.

Given Bishop and Hoggett's research, how would you set about explaining this finding from their original survey? Do you think this is still true?

As we shall see in later research into volunteering in sport (Nichols, 2003), people are drawn to help out in clubs, primarily because of their stage in the family life cycle, for example they want to help sports clubs so that their own and other children can participate locally in their favourite sport. But there are also time pressures from work, from other domestic responsibilities, from the desire to pursue their own leisure interests, so that sports clubs are finding it increasingly difficult to replenish and replace their older and long-serving volunteers.

One key concept within the history of sociology has been the influence of class on people's lives, social networks and opportunities. Like any other institution, there is no reason to suspect that leisure relations would be exempt from class direction and influence. Indeed, there is a well-established school of sociologists who locate class as their starting point for understanding society generally and leisure in particular.

1.15 Leisure and social class

Which leisure activities do you associate with each class in society?

Code each activity from the list below: Aristocracy/elite; Professional middle class; White-collar non-manual middle class; Manual working class; 'Class-free', i.e. all social classes participate.

Leisure activities:

- Attending opera
- Playing a musical instrument
- Watching television
- Listening to the radio/music stations/downloading music from the Internet
- Watching football
- Playing snooker/darts
- Reading a daily newspaper
- Belonging to a book group
- Eating at McDonald's
- Working out in a gym
- Cycling
- Swimming
- Playing sport
- Leisure shopping

(Continued)

(Continued)

- Cinema-going
- Visiting historical buildings/museum
- Going on a seaside holiday
- Gardening
- Playing cards

The above exercise has hopefully started you thinking about some of the ways in which the material and cultural resources of class divisions inform leisure choices. We shall see in Chapter 7 that leisure is defined as an important site for class expression and conspicuous consumption. But sociologists are also interested in other social divisions and inequalities such as gender or race or age or disability. Goffman (1971a) has referred to these as master roles, which are significant in all social encounters. In everyday life, these markers are the first thing we see about a person before we get to know them.

The history of popular culture – television, sport, film, comedy and other things that we enjoy in our leisure time – is full, unfortunately, of examples of racism and racial stereotyping. It also offers plenty of examples of the fight against these things. The American music scene is a good place to start. Until the second half of the twentieth century there was a clear racial divide in popular music in the United States, especially among the nation's working class: many white folks listened to country music and rural African Americans had the blues. When these musical forms began to combine in the 1950s there occurred one of the most famous instances of mistaken racial identity in the history of popular culture: when his first records were released in 1954, many listeners thought Elvis Presley, a poor white from Mississippi, must be black. At that time many musicians in the United States still played to segregated audiences. Presley became known as 'the white boy with the black voice'; his record producer Sam Philips later claimed 'I knocked the shit out of the color line' (Guralnick, 1995: 134). Similarly, the English singer Dusty Springfield has been called the 'white negress' (Cole, 2008: 3). In 1964 she was deported from South Africa, having refused to sing to segregated audiences there.

1.16 Racism and racial stereotypes in popular music

In Britain the BBC broadcast *The Black and White Minstrel Show*, which ran from 1958 to 1978 and, at the height of its popularity, had viewing figures of 18 million. The show featured white artists singing in blackface. Critics suggested that it perpetuated stereotypes of black people and in 1967 a petition was presented to the BBC, calling for it to be taken off the air.

Since the late 1950s and early 60s there has been much mingling of different kinds of music, but racial division and exclusion have not gone away. In 1969 the white American rock band Lynyrd Skynyrd released 'Sweet Home Alabama' a tribute to their home state which was seen as a defiant riposte to liberals and anti-racists. At their concerts the band displayed the Confederate flag, the symbol of the breakaway union of southern, slave-owning states in the 1860s (Hoskyns, 2012). Similarly, in August 1976 the English guitarist Eric Clapton told an audience that they should vote for the right-wing politician Enoch Powell to prevent Britain becoming 'a black colony'. This was ironic, given the influence of the blues on Clapton's music, and it led to the founding of Rock Against Racism (Huddle, 2004).

Indeed music and musicians have long been an important source of opposition to perceived racism. In 1939 the black singer Billie Holiday began performing the song 'Strange Fruit' which condemned the lynching of African Americans in the American South (see Margolick, 2000).

In 1964, the African American soul singer Sam Cooke released 'A Change is Gonna Come', a song which was adopted by the civil rights movement in the United States. In 1968, the white English singer Petula Clark recorded a TV show for NBC in the United States during which she took the arm of Jamaican American artist Harry Belafonte while they sang a duet. Doyle Lott, vice-president of the Chrysler car company, who were sponsoring the broadcast, objected to this 'inter-racial touching' and called for the duet to be re-shot with the performers standing apart. Clark refused, Lott lost his job and the show commanded a huge audience (Doyle, 2009).

More recently, in 2005, the hip hop artist Kanye West told the audience of a telethon to raise money for the (mainly black) people of New Orleans following Hurricane Katrina that the President (George W. Bush) 'didn't care about black people'. This led to the release of the protest song 'George Bush Doesn't Care About Black People' by the hip hop duo The Legendary K.O.

Questions to consider:

- How is it possible to describe plainly white artists such as Presley and Springfield as 'black'?

- Find a clip of *The Black and White Minstrel Show*. Assess the claim that it stereotypes black people.

- Some commentators now suggest that the emergence of predominantly black musical forms such as rap and hip hop is part of a re-segregation of popular music. What do you think?

- What role has popular music played in (i) promoting racism and (ii) fighting racism?

Social divisions of class, race, gender, age and disability work through individuals, families, friendship networks and leisure institutions to include some and exclude others. Some have insider status, feel comfortable and belong in a leisure setting. Conversely, these very processes may serve to exclude others who feel strange, uncomfortable, out of place. It is interesting that most nation state politicians and policy makers often look towards leisure institutions as a way of integrating people into local communities. But, as we shall see, many sociologists feel that societies have changed and are disintegrating. The common blocks of culture that used to bind people together – belonging to a nation state, working in a social class, sharing a common ethnic background, living in a traditional community – all are more or less changing. New fissures are appearing around lifestyles, consumption patterns and sexual orientations. Social movements have broken up traditional divisions, and the functions of leisure may have become more diverse than in earlier times.

1.17 Racism and racial stereotypes in sport

The Sri Lankan writer Ambalavaner Sivanandan observed in 2004: 'In football, by and large, it's the fans that are racist but in cricket it's the establishment. It's institutionalized racism. The smell of imperialism is in your nostrils all the time' (*The Observer*, Sport Section, 25 July, p. 5). Cricket culture has also, however, thrown up one of the most eloquent rebuttals of racism in sport history. When John Arlott visited South Africa as a cricket commentator for the Test series of 1948 he was handed an immigration form containing a box marked 'Race'; in it he wrote the word 'Human'.

In America, between the mid-1870s and the 1960s, the country was racially segregated under the purportedly 'separate, but equal' Jim Crow laws. This gave a special edge to boxing contests between black fighters and whites. In 1908 Jack Johnson became the first African American heavyweight champion of the world and between then and 1915 promoters worked hard to find a 'Great White Hope' to take him on. Equally, American boxing produced probably the most articulate and influential of all sportspeople – Muhammad Ali – who in 1964 renounced his original name as a 'slave name' and three years later refused induction into the US army to fight in Vietnam because 'no Vietcong ever called me nigger' (Marqusee, 2005).

Moreover, racial inclusion in sport did not necessarily mean that sportspeople were not racially excluded in the wider society: the famous clenched-fist salute by African American athletes Tommie Smith and John Carlos at the Mexico Olympics of 1968 was performed to remind the public that athletes like Smith and Carlos would still be second-class citizens when they got back to the US.

Since the decline of racial exclusion in sports participation, other issues of a racial nature have emerged in sport. Stereotyping is one. This most often takes the form of imputing fixed racial characteristics to sportspeople in terms of their performance. African footballers making a defensive error, for example, have invariably been called 'naïve' by commentators and black footballers in England were for a long time held to lack 'bottle' – that is, to recoil from the more physical aspects of the game. Some research has been directed to investigate 'stacking' in various sports – a process by which players of a certain ethnicity are placed in particular positions because of stereotyped assumptions about their abilities.

Questions to consider:

- What are the dominant stereotypes of black men and women? Try and think of examples in relation to:

  o specific sports roles, e.g. players, trainers, coaches and managers
  o specific sports, e.g. athletics, boxing, cricket, cycling, golf and football.

- On balance, do you think sport has helped or hindered the struggle against racism?

- Consider your favourite sports. Can you think of examples of stacking in those sports?

During the past thirty years a generation of scholars has sought to map out a field of study called leisure studies with more or less success. Several major social science disciplines have been plundered and in some cases synthesized to ask interesting research questions about changing leisure patterns in industrial societies. The next chapter starts to examine some of these theoretical debates and describe the research tools that writers have deployed to tackle leisure research.

2

STUDYING AND MEASURING LEISURE

THIS CHAPTER

- Introduces students to the key social science disciplines interested in leisure
- Outlines the emergence of leisure studies from a sociological perspective and the diverse methods used to study leisure.

The previous chapter very much represents a starting point in an intellectual journey. Its aim was to introduce students to key social science disciplines, the research questions they generate and to think about the interests that psychologists, economists, geographers, political scientists and sociologists have in studying leisure. This chapter takes one step further as it looks at the ways in which leisure scholars have developed a distinctive field of study from these various disciplines and appropriately named that field leisure studies. This may not appeal to students who want to know how key ideas can practically inform and guide leisure policies and leisure management. Indeed, some students will already be wanting to bypass general arguments about leisure and focus more on dimensions of leisure that specifically interest them in sport, arts, countryside recreation, outdoor pursuits, tourism and leisure consumption. But to concentrate on just one particular leisure form is to miss the bigger picture of leisure and what we shall later term the leisure project. It is the big picture that provides a distinctive context, a holistic perspective, within which to make sense of more intricate detail. For once, size is everything. It is the bigger picture that generates important comparative questions about people's lives and leisure. However, what shapes the big picture and puts it in focus is leisure research, which often starts from different standpoints and deploys different research methods. The choice of sociology as a disciplinary vantage point reflects the authors' backgrounds but also the dominance or hegemony of sociological ideas in the development of leisure studies, particularly within the UK.

Whenever one starts to ask questions about academic disciplines and how they generate knowledge, one enters the world of philosophy. This is in one sense a parasitic discipline: it feeds off other disciplines that make up the natural sciences, social sciences and humanities. It raises questions about what counts as knowledge and what this can tell us about ourselves and the world we live in. Philosophy asks second-order questions about the scope and nature of each discipline, whereas those academics working inside the disciplines get on with the primary research questions they have set themselves (see Ryan, 1970).

2.1 Asking philosophical questions

Which questions are questions of philosophy?
Remember the distinguishing criterion: philosophy asks second-order questions about disciplines whereas 'non-philosophers' ask more factual questions inside their own disciplines!

1 What percentage contribution does international tourism make to the Gross Domestic Product of the UK compared with USA, Australia and India?

2 How do we know that the argument presented in this case study is logical?

3 How much time do 'white' American women have to spend on leisure in an average week compared with 'black' American women?

4 Is freedom and rationality in decision making possible?

5 How do different teaching styles in school physical education classes affect measures of pupils' enjoyment of sport?

6 What proportion of older people are regular members of gyms or regularly attend keep-fit classes?

7 To what extent did gender equity policies in Australia and Canada increase sports participation amongst younger women during the 1990s?

8 How does scientific method produce reliable and valid knowledge?

9 Have attendances at out-of-town multiplex cinemas in the UK increased annually since 1985?

10 Is it possible to refute Einstein's theory of relativity?

Another cutting edge to philosophical inquiry rests on the distinction drawn between facts and values. Philosophers argue that scientific knowledge is accurate because of its rigorous cyclical method. Scientific method studies the real material world, develops theories, provides hypotheses and collects objective data to test new theories against predicted facts. It then continues to correct theories that cannot explain or fit with material facts. One can only then press on with further research. In contrast, values belong to another ('other') ethereal world, a more aesthetic world of beliefs, of political ideologies and spiritualism, of religion and moral codes, of ethics and plain common sense. For Max Weber (see Giddens 1979a: 89–95) this is a world of warring gods, where values clash irreconcilably. One can only believe and hold one's position, even if challenged by others. On the one hand, scientific knowledge is *factual*, that is, it is objective and empirical, satisfied only with hard facts, whereas non-sciences can be *fictitious*, unconstrained by the necessity of generating accurate facts, and so they can offer intuition, along with creativity, by using personal stories or narratives. Philosophical inquiry is therefore interested in the precise truth of claims made by different disciplines. It scrutinizes the theories and the methodology thinkers deploy when routinely doing research. (see Table 2.1)

Table 2.1   Science and common sense

SCIENCE	COMMON SENSE
Scientific Knowledge means Theories.................. Explanations Hypotheses..............Predictions Empirical data...........Facts	Common sense means a 'natural' attitude or practical way of 'going on' or 'getting on with' everyday life.
Scientific knowledge is corrigible, it can be tested and interrogated. It is public, valid and reliable. It is always conditional on further research.	Common sense is based in custom, unquestioned routines and rhythms which shape private life plans and personal projects.
Scientists learn from mistakes.	People are usually certain about 'what is going on here' and ask, 'What is this about?'
Scientists are objective and detached observers.	People are subjective, emotionally involved in their personal life plans and projects.

2.2 Sociology as a science

Sociology as a social science

Sociology is defined as the scientific study of society or the social order. Social sciences collect empirical data by quantitative and qualitative methods.

Quantitative methodology means collecting 'hard' data; this involves setting up experiments and collecting and measuring data taken from representative population samples. The subjects (participants) all know that they are involved in a research study and there are clear ethical protocols to guide data collection, data storage and publication. There are hard (usually statistical) techniques of data collection and reactive ones (where the researcher interacts with his/her subject matter). Social facts can be gathered through large-scale representative surveys and subjecting findings to statistical analysis between measured variables.

Social science is different from common sense as it views taken-for-granted things, popular culture, values, attitudes, etc., as strange and worthy of further investigation. Just as anthropologists study pre-literate cultures, the workings of institutions such as work, family, class, community and leisure in modern societies are examined and compared.

Qualitative data collection means understanding social meanings via participant observation, interviews etc. Qualitative strategies are 'soft' and non-reactive in that the researcher and the researched must share the same language and engage in social interaction so as to make sure social scientific accounts are valid and relate back to the respondent's account of what is going on. Some traditions in qualitative strategies see people as co-researchers. There is a demand that sociologists reflect on their own personal values, prejudices and interests and, not least, the impact their research findings may have on the lives of those who are part of the study, as well as the wider community.

Within the social sciences there has been a long-standing debate about whether it is possible to study social facts objectively. Writers such as Max Weber have been keen to stress that social sciences must be 'value free', as he was concerned that nineteenth-century academics working within German universities used their professorial status to present their own personal and political prejudices as objective scientific truths. Weber allowed that professors, as citizens, could engage in politics and demand policies in line with their personal values; however, when engaged in academic research, they should detach themselves from their own values and describe objectively and without bias, the value positions that people hold in society. It is crucial from the start to recognize the difference between facts and values, if any kind of scientific commentary can be made about society or about leisure.

2.3 Research questions and value judgements

Which of the statements listed below offer hypotheses for social scientific research and which are personal value judgements?

Divide the statements into three categories: FACT, VALUE and UNDECIDED.

(Continued)

(Continued)

Why do you think you have problems with the statements you have allocated to the undecided column?

1 Extreme sports such as mountaineering, paragliding, base jumping, etc. are very dangerous and too risky for young people to participate in.

2 Young people involved in extreme sports ought to take out special personal insurance to provide cover in case of accidents.

3 Young people involved in extreme sports are more likely to have extrovert personalities than non-participants.

4 Young men involved in extreme sports belong to distinctive subcultures which value risk taking and 'macho' behaviour.

5 Women should not participate in extreme sports because they are not strong or brave enough to do so.

6 18–24-year-olds are more likely to suffer injury from driving a car in the city than from doing extreme sports.

7 If people get into difficulties while participating in extreme sports they should pay the full cost for rescue services if accidents occur and the rescue services are called out to help.

8 Extreme sports and outdoor challenges can reduce deviant and criminal behaviour amongst 'at risk' teenage boys.

FACT	VALUE	UNDECIDED

If we are aware of the important philosophical distinction between facts and values, between 'is' and 'ought' statements, we are better able to detect when and how writers smuggle in their own personal values and prejudices when studying leisure. Indeed, the history of leisure studies has been disfigured by writers who valued certain leisure forms above others. They have traditionally advocated the development of certain 'serious' leisure activities such as sport or physical exercise while fearing the growing popularity of 'casual' leisure such as watching television, playing computer games, surfing the Internet or texting/chatting on mobile phones. As we shall see in Chapter 5 there is a general anxiety that young people, as the next generation, are choosing unsuitable and in some cases harmful leisure activities – the dark side of leisure as manifested in alcohol, drugs and youthful sexual activity.

So, when one starts to examine how leisure studies has developed, what standpoints and methodologies have been adopted by researchers to study institutions of leisure, we are travelling down, or at the very least alongside some philosophical path of inquiry.

Scholarship in the realm of leisure is often quite different in each nation state. For a variety of reasons, leisure research has developed under different nomenclatures; for example, it is predominantly called 'leisure sciences' in Northern America, whereas in the UK and Australia, it is labelled as 'leisure studies'. Different nation states in Europe carry different leisure research traditions, often linking leisure with adult education and community development. At this point, there is obviously little need to worry about those nation states and languages that do not even have a word or direct translation for leisure and who research under another sobriquet such as 'free-time studies' (see Mommaas et al., 1996)! This is simply a further twist in the complicated narratives about leisure and the different national struggles to develop leisure studies. In each nation state, different cultural, economic, political and social processes have shaped the trajectory and institutional positioning of academic endeavour in the field of leisure.

The following section outlines the main features of modern industrial society or modernity and spells out the distinctive standpoint of leisure studies. We also shall be looking at other interdisciplinary approaches to social science research, designated broadly as cultural studies, because cultural studies academics argue that, as the foundations of modern industrial societies have changed, so has leisure. So, according to some writing and working within cultural studies, modern industrial society or modernity is over. It is history, and therefore we all live, without exception, in its aftermath – postmodernity. Clearly this new standpoint needs some investigation as it carries some quite radical implications for how we should approach the study of leisure.

CULTURAL STUDIES AND MODERNITY

Modernity is a term developed by writers in cultural studies to explain the nature and direction of modern industrial societies (see Hall and Gieben, 1992). Modern societies should be understood and captured historically by researching distinctive economic, political, social and cultural formations. Modernity is made up of four distinctive facets – the economic, the political, the social and the cultural. Such formations have their own history, institutional trajectory and momentum. Each has a separate domain: the economic entails material distribution, price mechanisms, supply and demand in markets; the political concerns the nature of authority and distribution of power in governance; the social is to do with face-to-face relations in families, neighbourhoods and local communities; finally, the cultural is no longer the exclusive domain of humanities but must broaden out to include material and intellectual signification in mass communications. Cultural Studies has focused on communication and semiotics; the importance of style and symbolic content of leisure; and the communication, transmission and penetration of mass media, mobile phones and the Internet.

2.4 Semiotics and leisure studies

(On semiotics, read David Harris, *Key Concepts in Leisure Studies*. London, Thousand Oaks, New Delhi: Sage Publications (2004), pp. 229–237.)

Semiotics is the study of the meaning of signs, how they interrelate and what they mean.

What does the Swoosh logo on Nike products mean?

How might you interpret the three stripes on Adidas goods?

Similarly, what do you think the two golden arches of McDonald's might symbolize?

Each has a distinct cultural message or slogan. What are they? What kinds of people are targeted or are expected to listen to or read the advertising message?

Rather than treat the social as the only standpoint from which to study modern societies, writers in cultural studies have demanded more interdisciplinary approaches to break down the artificial and (now perhaps obsolete) boundaries which have served to divide academics as they worked away, isolated in their separate disciplines. As we shall show later in this chapter, sociology effectively recast itself as social theory and became interested in individuals and self-identity – two concepts that had long been sequestered in the exclusive and fiercely protected domain of psychology. There has also been a surge of interest in anthropology as researchers started to theorize about human nature, culture and signification in post-colonial societies. Anthropology was used to explain the lifestyles of various ethnic minorities or diasporas (enforced migrations) who found themselves living inside modern industrial societies. Nation states were now more culturally diverse, with global flows of refugees and migrant workers, and anthropologists felt that they were best placed to explain the relationships between indigenous and migrant cultures.

At its historical birth in mid-nineteenth-century Europe, sociology crowned itself as 'queen of the social sciences'. The founding fathers of sociology immediately staked a claim to be the only academic discipline that could explain the changing structure of emerging modern industrial societies. Sociologists felt that it was uniquely their own discipline that could contextualize the more narrow approaches of economics and politics, while simultaneously updating pre-modern, pre-literate anthropological studies. Sociologists have self-consciously placed modern industrial society at the heart of their investigations. This generic brief gathered momentum when faced with the crucial question

Table 2.2 Modernity: its four major formations

	Economic Formations	Political Formations	Social Formations	Cultural Formations
Major Discipline	Economics	Political Sciences	Sociology	Humanities/ Cultural Studies
Major Institution	MARKET	STATE	SOCIETY	ARTS/ MASS MEDIA CULTURE
Key Focus	Material production and price mechanisms	Power and public policies	Neighbourhood and community relationships	Literature and Mass communications
Approach to Leisure	Leisure as private goods and services	Leisure as public policy	Leisure as social networks	Leisure as creative arts / Leisure as popular culture

famously framed by C. Wright Mills (1970) in his bestseller, *The Sociological Imagination* – what kind of society do we live in? That was and remains the important question.

Philosophers claim that questions are always more important than the answers. One response to Mills' question that emerged in the 1970s was that we live in a leisure society. Leisure was seen as the product of modernity (although some were eager to dismiss it as an inconsequential by-product) and leisure studies scholars set out to explore the institution of leisure and its central function for modern industrial societies. Whereas economics had concentrated on the world of production and work, and political scientists were exclusively concerned with power, with allocating resources or managing legitimacy inside the nation state, leisure studies scholars turned their academic attention to the neglected world of free time, to non-work as a site for reproduction and consumption. Leisure researchers focused on important questions about the quality of people's lives. They were the harbingers of emerging economic, political and personal issues that would dominate social movements and politics in advanced industrial societies for the next thirty years.

LEISURE STUDIES AND THE LEISURE SOCIETY

During the late 1960s most Western industrial societies were experiencing strong economic growth and development. What was new about this particular period following the Second World War in Europe was that economic growth was both rapid and sustained, year after year. At that time, social commentators heralded with confidence the arrival of a new social order. The world was now made up of affluent societies that had access to innovative and powerful machines, advanced information technologies, which would transform by automation the harsh world of work and employment. All would live inside a leisure society, as most people would only need to work at most a 20-hour week. Because of gains in productivity at work the remainder of their time would be leisure. Where their grandparents and parents had lived through the 1920s and 1930s, a workless world of poverty, unemployment and economic recession, working- and many middle-class people in the 1960s were not only growing up in affluent Western welfare states but also having to face up to 'leisure shock'. The fears amongst political commentators were that people had been brought up with certain ideas about work, with expectations of lifelong careers and full-time jobs, whereas the future would be about leisure, changes in careers and part-time, flexible employment. Cultural formations were locked into a nineteenth-century view of hard work, whereas what was needed was a twenty-first-century leisure culture which would accommodate seismic change in traditional economic formations. Policy makers started to talk about 'education for leisure', about how to prepare people for living within a future leisure society.

This leisure scenario applied to both liberal capitalist societies in the West and also to communist nation states that at that time made up the Soviet bloc in Eastern Europe. It was then argued that new technologies, new patterns of social mobility and new occupational hierarchies would override any political differences between the capitalist West and the socialist East and all would soon live in advanced industrial societies. There would be an 'end to ideology' and the Cold War. The Eastern European socialist states would eventually catch up with the living standards and leisure lifestyles of people in the West. In the 1960s this argument was labelled the 'convergence' thesis. It implied that differences between capitalist and socialist societies would slowly weaken and that these societies would become similar and so ultimately converge. However, the thesis, unsurprisingly, failed to predict the dramatic collapse of communism and state socialism by the late 1980s, which meant similarity and convergence was achieved overnight, affirming the dominance of Western liberal capitalism. State socialist societies could not offer freedom of expression, leisure and individual choice as enjoyed in the West. Many journalists and media commentators had argued that it was consumer goods, satellite mass media and communications and the prospect of freedom of movement and travel that fatally undermined the control that socialist states had over their citizens.

Table 2.3 West versus East

	West	East
Economy	Capitalism: Market price mechanism and profit motive; commercially focused investment	State socialism: Command economy and centralized economic plans; focus on heavy industrial investment
Ownership	Individual private property, home ownership, capital and profits	State ownership and collective state investment, social housing

	West	East
Wealth distribution	Unequal income, wealth, inheritance and property ownership	Equalizing of income, state regulation of wealth, inheritance and scope of property ownership
Politics	Democratic elections; pluralistic parties and interest groups	Single party government of Communist Party elite; party leadership has control of key organizations
Society	Civil society – free trade unions, separate voluntary sector and community organizations	Civil society organizations led by communist party – e.g. youth clubs, communist trade unions, 'social' planned tourism and managed destinations
Travel	Freedom of mobility: reliance on private cars/transport	Urban mass public transport; collective infrastructure and limited private car ownership
Leisure	Private hedonism	Sport and rational recreation to serve community and the nation state
Popular culture	Commercially led consumption	State sponsored leisure forms
Mass media	'Free' press, market driven media/ advertising	Censored media, state control, propaganda
Shopping	Cornucopia of shopping – 'leisure' shopping, luxury goods and services	Modest living standards, functional shopping, queuing and rationing, shortages of necessities and absence of luxuries

DEFINING LEISURE

The liberal capitalist values of Western democracies have been one key to understanding leisure and leisure studies in modern societies. There are few people who have done more to explore this relationship in the field of leisure studies than Professor Ken Roberts at Liverpool University in the UK. He has written several books since the beginning of the 1970s, when he embarked on an academic career which has remained focused on leisure (Roberts, 1970, 1978, 1999, 2004). The left-hand column in Table 2.3 expresses the conventional view of Western industrial society and it captures the three key values that 'together offer a philosophy for the society with leisure' (Roberts, 1978). The first value that should be emphasized, argued Roberts, is hedonism, that is the desirability and the pursuit of pleasure. The second core value is humanism which celebrates the diversity of human experience – sensual, sexual, artistic, physical and intellectual. 'The third cardinal value is liberalism, acknowledging that each individual is the best judge of what is pleasurable for himself [sic] and that choosing for oneself is an intrinsic quality of leisure' (Roberts, 1978: 167).

In the 1970s, the starting point for leisure studies was the assumption that individuals were free to choose the leisure activities from which they derived satisfaction and pleasure and that changes in the world of work in modern societies would release more leisure time for more people. Researchers in America and Europe set about defining leisure and its key characteristics. To take Max Kaplan's (1975) lengthy definition:

> Leisure consists of relatively self-determined activity/experience that falls in to one's economically free time roles, that is seen as leisure by participants, that is psychologically pleasant in anticipation and recollection, that potentially covers the whole range of commitment and intensity, that contains characteristic norms and constraints and that provides opportunities for recreation, personal growth and service to others. (1975: 26).

2.5 Defining leisure activities

How would you define the following activities: are they work or leisure?

- Gardening in an allotment
- Playing a musical instrument
- Performing on a stage
- Metal detecting
- Reading a book
- Going to an aerobics/Pilates class
- Visiting a historical building or monument
- Singing in a choir
- Cycling to work
- Swimming in a charity event

Would you classify activities differently if you were given additional information? See below:

- A semi-professional footballer playing soccer
- A TV critic watching a soap opera
- A fitness instructor/personal coach working out in a multi-gym
- A hospital patient taking walks as part of a recovery programme after a major operation
- Taking the family dog for a walk in poor winter weather
- Cooking a meal while entertaining friends

What is important about leisure? What role does payment play? How important are the social relationships which provide the context for activities? What if one is 'obliged' to do the activity?

However, the Cambridge philosopher, Ludwig Wittgenstein posited that such a task was actually fruitless. He held that it was impossible to define a concept, say leisure, so accurately as to distil its essence, to exclude all forms of non-leisure. To do so was to be caught in the 'fallacy of essentialism'. For Wittgenstein philosophy involved different sorts of 'language games'; that favoured by natural sciences posited a one-to-one relationship between a concept and its material existence in the real world. However, for the social sciences, it was regarded as more appropriate to deploy language in terms of 'family resemblances'. Just as one can identify children in a family by their similar, but not identical features, the same perspective applies to the similarities and differences in social life. Social institutions share similar characteristics, allowing them to be grouped together, but there are also important differences.

Early leisure studies sidestepped some of these difficult philosophical issues by defining leisure as free time, time left over from work and paid employment. It was therefore taken for granted that people understood what leisure was and consequently the challenge facing researchers was to collect leisure facts. So, some research during the 1970s and 80s developed time-budget studies to measure how much time people had and to ask people to keep time diaries about how that time was spent. This created large-scale research into demographics of age, gender, ethnicity and location in order that researchers could compare and contrast leisure time within and between nation states (Gershunny, 2000).

If researchers were interested in leisure activities, one obvious way forward was to collect survey data on patterns of leisure participation and non-participation. One corollary of defining leisure as residual time was to collect data on the activities that people were involved in, as well as mapping the leisure spaces they inhabited and the social networks they belonged to. All that was needed was some measures of the frequency and intensity of people's participation in different leisure forms. Haywood et al. (1995) have provided the most useful framework for understanding the diversity or dimensions of leisure activities (Table 2.4, see oppostie).

Populations were surveyed over a range of leisure activities – art, indoor sports, outdoor recreation, museum visits and short- and long-haul holidays. Policy makers and planners were keen to assess the recreational demands of local and regional populations so that they could supply appropriate facilities and thus plan for growing future demand. National and local governments became more interested in developing parks and transport and leisure services as part of public health policies. In the 1970s there were emerging policy debates and experiments about 'quality of life' issues and leisure was felt to play an important role in improving individual happiness and community vitality. So, leisure studies researchers felt well placed to offer useful knowledge for interested policy makers and so contribute to building the future leisure society. While acknowledging that leisure is a problematic and contested concept, leisure scholars started to map out a field of study which worked within three

Table 2.4 Dimensions of leisure

Leisure activity	Formal dimension			Contextual dimension			Examples
	Process	Location	Provision/ Management	Provider	State control	
Recreations (Arts, sports, countryside)	Active production of experience; control over outcome	Outside home	Self-programmed or external provision	Mainly public or voluntary	Encouraged	Sports, drama outdoor activities
Hobbies/craft/education	Active production of skills or knowledge or objects	Home or outside	Self-programmed or external	Mainly public or voluntary	Encouraged	Gardening, collecting pottery, reading
Tourism/holidays	Consumption of experiences (some active production)	Outside home	Mainly external	Commercial	Neutral	Day trips, tourism, packaged holidays
Consuming entertainments	Active production and consumption of experiences	Home or outside	Mainly external	Public or commercial	Encouraged but Licensed/ consigned	Dancing, speaking, TV, cinema, cheerer
Consuming commodities and shopping	Consumption of goods	Home or outside	Self-provided or external	Commercial	Licensed	Drinking, eating out, shopping
Gambling and gaming	'Passive production'; no control over outcome	Home or outside home	Mainly external	Commercial	Licensed	Pools, horseracing, bingo, routines

broad overlapping traditions of research. One important tradition was, as we have seen, to define leisure as *residual time* and secondly, to explore participation in *leisure activities*. The third and dominant theme in leisure studies focuses on the nature of *leisure experience*. For Ken Roberts in the UK, DeGracia in Spain, Dumazadier in France and Kaplan (1975) in the USA, leisure offers a qualitatively different experience from the more serious concerns of work, politics, family and religion. Leisure is the distinctive product of industrial society and is valued as a sphere, a space for individual freedom and self-expression. So leisure is pleasure and yet philosophers and leisure theorists argue about what counts as leisure. Many writers are keen to stress that leisure must involve active play or some form of rational recreation for it to count as leisure rather than simply as indulging in relaxation, recuperation or suffering boredom in one's free time. In the current jargon of the mass media, it must be 'quality time' rather than just 'free time'. The Venn diagram shown in Figure 2.1 should help to unravel the different ingredients to leisure.

Think of moments, minutes, hours, episodes or holidays when all three circles at the centre of the Venn diagram overlap. This is at the site, occasion or condition which some philosophers (as we have noted earlier) define as pure leisure. Here pure leisure/pleasure appears in a confluence of free time, freely chosen activity and a positive psychological experience. It is often referred in everyday life and the chat-show media as 'quality time' or 'me-time'.

Think about the other circle sectors when two circles do not fully overlap or stand alone.

Where would you locate these daily routines (*la vie quotidienne*)?

- work and other work commitments such as commuting or homework
- domestic work such as cleaning or cooking, washing the car/motorbike
- sport or physical exercise such as playing for a Saturday team, working out in a gym, swimming
- non-work family commitments such as baby sitting, looking after children, caring for an elderly dependent relative
- helping neighbours, attending community meetings or religious observance, etc.
- passive leisure such as listening to music, background TV, free-time boredom/*ennuie* of waiting in transport queues, texting, surfing the Internet.

Figure 2.1   Understanding the concept of leisure

CHANGE, LEISURE AND POSTMODERN CULTURE

Another different recent answer to C. Wright Mills' important question, 'What kind of society do we live in?' is that we now live in a postmodern society. As many theorists now see it we have left behind industrial society, broadly described as modernity, and we now live in postmodernity – that is, under different or 'postmodern' conditions (Harvey, 1989). The postmodern or cultural turn in theory has challenged many assumptions of social scientific endeavour and has struck at the very roots of conventional wisdom about epistemology – our knowing about the world around us. Indeed, since the 1980s there has been a long-running debate between leisure studies and cultural studies scholars as witnessed in the title of Alan Tomlinson's article, 'What side are they on? Leisure studies and cultural studies in Britain.' (Tomlinson, 1989).

2.6 Leisure studies and cultural studies

Read A. Tomlinson (1989) 'What side are they on? Leisure studies and cultural studies in Britain'. *Leisure Studies*, 8: 97–106.
Answer the following questions:

- What is meant by 'postmodernity'?

- What are the key differences between 'modernity' and 'postmodernity'?

- Assuming that we live either in a 'modern' or 'postmodern' society, which group of scholars do you think is right and why?

But if the debate is about anything, it is about change, as we shall explore in the final chapter of this book. Both leisure and postmodern theorists struggle to develop better models, problem-solving devices or theoretical perspectives to analyse the nature of changes and predict their general direction. Many writers, including those in leisure studies, have been reluctant to accept the idea of postmodernity and have been more comfortable with less apocalyptic labels, such as 'high modernity', 'late modernity' and 'Modernity II'. These terms are invariably set against earlier forms deployed as yardsticks or templates, such as 'simple modernity', 'early modernity' and 'Modernity I'. What all these models have in common is the argument that culture and leisure have become more important in people's lives. But there remains a sceptical ambivalence about the postmodern and the significance of postmodern changes. However, it is clearly beyond the scope of an introductory leisure textbook to provide a comprehensive review of all the different positions taken. The best overview of such debates and their significance for leisure can be found in the extensive works of Chris Rojek (see e.g. Rojek, 1993, 1995, 2000, 2005).

If we start from Stuart Hall and Bram Gieben's (1992) conceptualization of modernity we are forced to think beyond disciplinary boundaries. We need to grasp both the character of the four separate, distinct formations – economic, political, social and cultural – and also their interrelationships and tensions. In the past social scientists have usually thought about these four dimensions as structures that fit together to form a whole, like large pieces of a child's jigsaw puzzle or steel girders that are bolted together to form the shell of a building, which is then fitted out with walls, windows and a roof. So the traditional focus of attention has been on the completed picture or the shape of the building. What Hall and Gieben suggest is that social science would be better served if it were to pay more attention to edges, to joints and cracks, to tensions or (to use Marx's phrase) to contradictions. It just might be that all the jigsaw pieces had not been put away into the right box or that the building materials used were incompatible, perhaps leaving a legacy of concrete deterioration or damp.

To adapt this analogy, if social science conceives of the economic, political, social and cultural as four overlapping processes rather than rigid static structures, it compels us to think about change and contradictions. Social science can no longer assume that all four formations move or change at the same pace or travel in the same direction. There may be untidy overlays. Consequently, there is an urgent need to adopt some kind of historical perspective for understanding different institutional domains and the tensions and dislocations that may occur between them. Briefly to take the UK as an example, its economy in the nineteenth century was at the forefront of world production and it had developed a skilled workforce with an individualized culture of labour power, yet its political system remained fiercely anti-democratic, locked into a seventeenth-century style monarchic regime, without any constitutional Bill of Rights for individual citizens or universal suffrage, but still capable of developing an empire and a colonial mission overseas. So, one reading of nineteenth-century UK history would map the way in which economic changes in the sexual division of labour and growth in trade union organization either connected with or were insulated from partisan politics. This would entail studying efforts at widening suffrage: looking at, for example, the Chartist and suffragette movements, changes in class consciousness and the growth of nationalist and xenophobic culture, sometimes called 'jingoism' in the late nineteenth century.

ERODING SINGLE DISCIPLINES: COLLAPSING SOCIOLOGY

One major failing of early sociological theory related to the question of scope – the failure to appreciate the dynamics of the four formations in modernity and/or a failure to theorize the particular relationships between those four separate elements of market, state, civil society and mass communications. Throughout the 1970s, sociology was confronted by growing Marxist critique, which emphasized economic and material foundations to

society, politics and culture. During the 1980s feminist analysis also challenged the failure of 'malestream' approaches in both sociology and Marxism
to acknowledge and engage with foundational divisions of gender and their
consequences for economy, society, politics and culture. What has further
complicated theoretical debates has been a general reluctance to acknowledge that modernity as a concept has been rooted in a myopically bi-polar
view of the world, divided between the 'West and the Rest' (Hall, 1992).
Post-colonial theories demand that there can be no single story or meta-
narrative about modernity, no one definitive universal account, especially
one that ignores or marginalizes dependency and power relations of colonialism and the implications imperialist histories have regarding development
in non-Western nation states, national identities and the history of the
'Other'. The task remains to understand modernity, leisure and change. As we
shall see in Chapter 7, Marxist, feminist and post-colonial thinkers demand
an awareness of the processes of class, gender and race. For their part post-
modernist thinkers are keen to highlight weaknesses in these radical
approaches, suggesting that both leisure and culture have moved on.

It is worth taking a little time to look at the recent history of sociology as a
single discipline and its response to the challenge of Cultural Studies because
leisure studies has experienced similar waves of theoretical debates and controversial challenges. In its early history sociology had always focused on the *social*:
networks of face-to-face relationships within families, in local communities, at
work, and so on. Social relationships had been contained within the boundaries
of nation states. In the post-war period, there were unchallenged assumptions
about a uniform consensus in society, shared values and beliefs sustained within
nation states by definite institutional structures (made up of tradition, normative
rules, roles and obligations) and constituent social systems. Sociologists took it
for granted that society was commensurate with the territorial and cultural
parameters of politics, within the nation state. One was superimposed on the
other and both were self-contained, self-regulating systems. During the 1960s
and 70s conflict theorists (principally Marxists) subscribed to a holistic territorial view of a class-divided society, with economically dominant groups seeking
to impose a capitalist ideology onto a national populace. There was then an
assumed objective concreteness, a solidity to social structure, just as Durkheim
(1982) suggested, and a sense that social facts *did* constrain and shape people's
lives. According to the then influential Althusserian perspective, individuals were
swimming in a tideless sea of ideology.

Friese and Wagner (1999) opened up a postmodern debate between structuralist and culturalist accounts of the nature of social life. Structuralist
accounts emphasize the determined nature of social life, whereas culturalist
accounts focus on the meaning and interpretations that individuals give to
their social experience. This was not simply a return to internal debates
between functionalist structuralists and interactionists demanding that sociology 'bring people back in' to break away from perspectives that treat humans
as 'cultural dupes', passive recipients of structural relations and processes.

That debate merely reproduced the historic dualism in sociology of the micro and the macro, the individual and society, agency and structure. The claim from Cultural Studies, as a harbinger of the more postmodern turn, is that social order itself has changed and is now stretched over time and space. Writers such as Giddens (1994) emphasize the importance of the *spatialization* of social theory. This is tantamount to arguing, alongside Gregory and Urry (1985), that sociology should become like geography and vice versa. Space and locality have in the past been taken for granted and consequently they are neglected dimensions in sociological analysis. Such processes of *time-space distanciation*, particularly stimulated by innovation in computing and fibre optics, have had radical implications for our key institutions – work, families, communities and, importantly, leisure – which are no longer recognizable as they once were. Societies have been changed by technology, not least by new information technologies and telecommunications.

Thus, perhaps one might expect postmodern theorists to argue that culture and leisure have become more important in people's everyday lives. Postmodern theorists also feel that the politics of modernity have changed to the point where the relevance of the nation state and its governance has been called into question. Transnational or global culture has invaded society and has simultaneously weakened the resistance of the host nation state to 'alien' forces. Social systems are now penetrable by other societies or nation states and by transnational processes – for example multinational global corporations such as Nike, News International and Microsoft. The nation state no longer has a boundary impenetrable by 'outsiders' nor is it a secure and safe container for society and the social system. Does theory now need to concentrate on culture at the boundaries, the crossovers and the margins rather than focusing on the centre or heart of the nation state? One important metaphor of postmodern theory and change was one of implosion; inside the bourgeois nation state lay difference and diversity. The centre will no longer hold. For example, post-colonial theories developed because the occidental grip on modernity and its single meta-narrative has been challenged. Writers such as Paul Gilroy have argued that many people living in the age of modernity were characterized by a 'double consciousness' (see Gilroy, 2000). That is to say, industrial society grew out of the slave trade. Colonialism and imperialism were crucial developments of the Enlightenment rather than merely being contingent or sites where other causal structural processes were playing out or unfolding. Migrants to Britain in the period after the Second World War (and their children) were defined both by their slave and colonial origins and by their Britishness: their identities were therefore constituted by a 'double consciousness' or 'hybridity'.

Traditional societies and nation states were no longer containers of everyday worlds as people could see beyond local horizons. Society was now global. There were global flows (Appadurai, 1990) of diverse people, ideas, technology, finance, information, and so on. In modernity, people's lives were shaped by collectivities – families, local communities, social classes and nation states, but these are now uprooted from locality and from tradition. Expert systems of knowledge, communication and other processes of time-space distanciation

disembed them. Other major consequences of this process are growing individualization, changing gender roles, hypermobility and further dissolution of
nation states that progressively dislodge and disembed individuals from traditional collective morality, rules, roles and obligations. The challenge for leisure
studies is how to think about and research these seismic changes in culture and
draw out their implications for leisure.

BRITISH CULTURAL STUDIES

Inspired by writers such as Raymond Williams and E.P. Thompson, British
Cultural Studies sought to distance itself from more structuralist accounts found
in the work of the French Marxist philosopher Louis Althusser. In the 1970s
French structuralism was influential in a variety of disciplines, particularly
anthropology, linguistics and psycho-analysis. It was Althusser's reading of the
later writing of Marx, his demand for scientific Marxist praxis and his analysis
of ideology that proved most corrosive, not only for sociology but also for more
humanist and empiricist versions of Marxist analysis. Althusser and others influenced by his approach (see for example Poulantzas (1973) on the state and
politics) launched a theoretical assault on social science. Although maintaining
the Marxist shibboleth of the economic base determining the superstructure 'in
the last instance', Althusser suggested that the ideological superstructures of
society could be 'relatively autonomous' from the economic base. The concept
of over-determination permitted class contradictions of capitalism to find their
expression in the ideological superstructure: for example, in the Ideological State
Apparatuses (ISAs) such as the family, education or politics. Althusser therefore
challenged ideas of history and human agency. English Marxism and Italian
Marxism, indebted to Antonio Gramsci, were deemed equally guilty of histori-
cism and of theoretical naïveté by engaging with a false problematic. By focusing
on the agency of human subjects, such analyses were ideological. Both British
and Italian theoretical traditions failed to develop scientific categories of
Marxism which could locate and explain structural contradictions of capitalism.

   In contrast to Althusser, British Cultural Studies were keen to embrace Italian
Marxism and, in particular, Gramsci's newly translated work on hegemony and
its purchase on struggles over and cultural consent in modernity. Indeed, as
Stuart Hall's (1980) introduction to the theoretical problematic of cultural
studies acknowledges, Gramsci was one crucial strand of thinking that gave
shape to subsequent diverse epistemological, theoretical, methodological and
practical interventions in the social sciences. Researchers working in the Centre
for Contemporary Cultural Studies (CCCS) at Birmingham University were
keen to map out a new field of study, a new territory or space for engagement
so as to flesh out sociology, with its narrow skeletal focus on the social, and to
challenge its more traditional, elitist sub-discipline, the sociology of literature.
In a variety of ways, the CCCS sought to raise new problematics and new questions. It sought to refocus attention on class, on the mass media and on popular

culture as sites for both resistance and identity. By drawing on Gramsci's concept of hegemony, the CCCS defined capitalism holistically, as a totality structured in dominance, with social, political and cultural ramifications. This shift
in perspective away from early sociology and the emergence of new problematics appeared in a plethora of multi-authored publications, but was most
graphically illustrated by Hall et al. (1978) in *Policing the Crisis*, a critical study
of the media panic about black street crime in the UK, orchestrated by the
authoritarian state response to crime through the police and the courts.

DISORGANIZED CAPITALISM AND DISORGANIZED STUDIES

Lash and Urry (1994) argued that Western societies had now entered the
period of disorganized capitalism and that new regimes of accumulation were
constructed particularly around the economy of signs as commodities were
no longer priced in terms of their exchange value, so that their symbolic value
and significance became crucial. We have already seen in Chapter 1 that this
feature may well be a crucial ingredient of certain emergent forms of leisure.
Disciplinary boundaries surrounding economics became more permeable as
research and scholarship embarked on making sense of the business of culture. The more applied perspectives of business management, media studies,
marketing, public relations and consumer psychology became of increasing
interest, not least to commercial consultants, journalists and think tanks, as
well as universities. Theorists working within Cultural Studies accepted, perhaps unsurprisingly, that culture had assumed central significance in this
phase of modernity. There was now an autonomy of cultural forms – the
growth of individualization (what Featherstone then called the 'autonomiza-
tion of culture') empowers cultural intermediaries to assume growing significance as experts on consumer culture (see Featherstone, 1995). So cultural
formations had become more central, or conversely less peripheral, if scholarship wished to understand and explain changes in modernity. For example,
the Polish émigré social theorist Zymunt Bauman (1992) argued in *Intimations
of Postmodernity* that politicians as legislators were no longer committed to
a cultural mission of transforming people into citizens who belonged to nation
states but rather were content to allow markets to bind people into consuming
lifestyles. Instead of encouraging and subsidizing appropriate leisure forms for
all citizens, nation states became less prescriptive and less interventionist,
thereby permitting more autonomy to markets to recast citizens as consumers.
One challenge for nation states remains how to manage those individuals
excluded by markets, what economists refer to euphemistically as market
imperfections, and what role leisure may play in the development of inclusive
public policies.

What is so striking about this phase of human history is its global scope (see
Bauman, 1999) and, as we shall see in subsequent chapters, processes of globalization have made a profound and noticeable impact, penetrating local

institutions of leisure. For example, one major attraction of traditional local working men's clubs in the UK (often, perhaps to avoid sexist terminology, renamed as social clubs) is the opportunity to watch live global sports on satellite broadcasting. In any major city around the world, there are 'authentic' Irish pubs, South African and Australian sports bars where large plasma screens enable drinkers to watch for instance World Cup Rugby and consume adverts for Fosters, Heineken, Budweiser, Carling, John Smith and Guinness.

DEAD DISCIPLINES, NEW EXPERTS AND DISORGANIZED PEOPLE

Following the cultural turn in sociology and the rise of cultural studies, writers became increasingly interested in posing more psychological questions such as 'who am I?' and then providing sociological answers. It was felt that traditional sociology and traditional psychology offered 'zombie' categories. These established disciplines were increasingly seen as dealing in dead or old tired concepts (such as class, community, family and state) and they made little sense of how people were currently living their lives. The cultural turn in sociology encouraged writers to think less about work and politics and more about people's free time and leisure choices. New writers argued that we had to move on from past thinking and the constraints of traditional disciplines and come up with new ideas to explain people's experience of change. One influential concept introduced in an attempt to capture the shifting processes of psychic and social change was reflexive modernization. For leisure scholars this was an important paradigmatic shift as this concept focused on key leisure issues, namely individual choice, human agency and self-expression.

Reflexive modernization means that each individual can critically construct and reflect on his or her own life narrative (see Giddens' *Modernity and Self-Identity* (1991)) as well as on structures and processes within contemporary institutions. In this new approach, individuals take centre stage and social research must focus closely on the life course of individuals and how they make sense of different stages in their changing lives. In what Giddens terms post-traditional societies, individuals are free to choose how they spend their free time, how hard they work, whether to marry, have children, and so on. In traditional society, this is hardly the case as moral codes prescribe social roles closely, mapping out the lives of men and women. In traditional society, the coercive, compulsive nature of obligation is natural and taken for granted, whereas in post-traditional societies, such compulsions are recast as addictions, as unjustifiable no-choice commitments to lifestyles.

CONCLUSION

This chapter has outlined the major issues confronting scholars hoping to make sense of modern leisure. From its inception, leisure research was confined within the carapaces of nation states and their distinctive funding regimes and policy priorities. In the US the field of study was labelled 'leisure sciences' whereas in Europe it was named 'leisure studies'. However, leisure researchers have been buffeted by wider theoretical debates about the nature of social theory, social science research and the globalization of culture.

3

TIME, HISTORY AND LEISURE

THIS CHAPTER

- Introduces students to key debates in history about free time and leisure
- Describes three different measures of time – the *lifetime* of the individual's lifespan, the *epoch* of generation cohorts and the *era* of structural time
- Argues that leisure is a product of historical 'clock time' and the work discipline that characterizes industrial capitalism
- Contrasts pre-industrial time with industrial and post-industrial time
- Offers three case studies of leisure forms in different times – the carnival, the football match and the theme park.

There is a strong tradition within leisure studies of defining leisure as residual time, as time left over from work. Such an approach is not without difficulties but it remains an important starting point for understanding leisure. Before tackling debates about the changing nature of leisure, free time and work time, let us attempt a brief history of time. It is hardly necessary to start with Stephen Hawking's analysis of black holes or creation of the universe, or even Bill Bryson's more accessible account of the history of 'nearly everything' (Bryson, 2004). We only need go back to pre-industrial society, some 300 years ago, to find a jumping-off point for history to start. Any historical approach serves to illustrate the importance of context to an understanding of leisure. As Jeffrey Hill (2002) has suggested, it is important for historians to understand the meaning and significance of sport and leisure as culture that changes over decades. Leisure time is best understood as a distinctive product of industrial capitalism. It is only during the nineteenth century that specialized and differentiated leisure institutions were created. They have remained in place and shape leisure still.

Taking an historical approach helps develop one's grasp of leisure theory and explanations of social and cultural change. There have been many worthwhile attempts to construct models of social change and to locate different societies at different historical periods on some kind of continuum or cyclical time scale. Many writers, including Burke (1980), Tilly (1981) and Callinicos (1989) have argued that historians and sociologists have much to learn from each other. Indeed, society can be seen as fixed and stable, a persistent structure, but at the same time viewed as a process of breakdown, renewal and development. Some historians look on the past as process, a perpetual movement of destruction and reconstruction. Consequently, different societies can be viewed as travellers in both time and space. Historians such as Braudel (1949) have stressed the uneven nature of time with changes taking place at different speeds: the fast moving time of events (*histoire événementielle*), the time of economic systems, nation states, and so on, with their slow rhythms (*histoire conjoncturelle*) and finally, the history of mankind and the environment – with its constant repetition and ever-recurring cycles (*histoire structurale*) (see Burke, 1980: 94).

Since its inception as an academic discipline, sociology has sought to explain the emergence of new types of societies. It has done so usually by taking an evolutionary theory of social change in which it has been assumed that human societies followed a path of 'progress' from comparatively simple to more complex forms as time marches on. There is here a powerful idea of inevitable Darwinian progress and sustained development, captured most clearly in what some writers term the 'Whig' view of history – a term coined by the Cambridge historian Sir Herbert Butterfield. Such historical writing describes humankind and nation states as gradually exerting control over the forces of nature through scientific advances in technology, communications and medicine. This way of writing history is both optimistic and teleological. This means that there is an implied logic to history, so that political institutions, for example, work towards a predestined goal or end, such as the emergence of democracy, or a communist nation state or the defeat of fascism. A similar evolutionary perspective shaped the work of Harvard sociologist Talcott Parsons and of US sociology in the 1960s in general. Parsons argued that institutions over time gradually become more functionally specific as social structures become both differentiated and complex and so more adaptable to the demands of advanced industrial societies. As work moves into urban-based industrial factories and out of the home, farms and rural production, people earn their living through paid employment and time left over in the evenings and at weekends becomes time for leisure. In industrial societies each institution serves a specific function and so contributes to the maintenance of shared values, social order and stability. So the emergence of industrial societies from rural ones brings new institutions of work, politics, education and leisure, now sitting alongside more traditional institutions of family, monarchy and religion. This greatly important transition had important implications for the perception and recording of time.

DIFFERENT TIME SCALES: INDIVIDUALS, INSTITUTIONS AND SOCIETIES

A sensible starting point for any analysis concerned with the social construction of time is an understanding of three distinctive time scales with very different chronologies. In advanced industrial society, we take it for granted that units of measurement are standardized – although they are set quite arbitrarily against Greenwich Mean Time in the UK. Although there are slight variations or conventions with British Summer Time and Winter Time, time is measured accurately in seconds, hours, days, months and years. There are global time zones and we adjust our watches when travelling continental-scale distances by air. Even within this received industrialized view of time, there are still fierce debates amongst physicists about rounding up rogue milliseconds so as to adjust time on a global scale in order that Internet computers agree and work to some conventional international standard of measurement.

But for most individuals the only important currency in time is one's own lifespan. Time can only be experienced within one's personal biography and everyone faces the core existential anxiety of having little idea of how long one will live. Even when faced on a daily basis with terminal illness, doctors and carers are usually reluctant to be specific and predict the time of the patient's death and, of course, there is always the possible hope of remission. So individuals must live their lives in the present, in the Here and Now (or what some German philosophers term the *Dasein* of the individual). So each individual not only has his or her own subjective experience but also has a personal history or biography with important moments or milestones in the individual's life course – birth, childhood, adolescence, adulthood, and so on. Major life events such as marriage or remarriage or a birth or a death in the family may lead individuals to claim that they are starting again, turning over a new leaf or starting a new chapter in their book of life. So we can measure time in the Here and Now, the immediacy of the individual's personal experience, grading where they are in the ageing process and within the life course. As we shall see later, the concept of career is very significant in social sciences: we can use it to chart the way individuals plan the length of their education and work experiences as well as commitments to family, leisure and wider community.

In contrast to the immediacy of the single individual's lived experience (how else can one be in the world?) are the collective experiences of generations, cohorts of individuals who are born in a particular decade, go to school together, work together and grow old together. Karl Mannheim (1952) argued that each generation shares a common location in the socio-historical process. Each generation grows up in, experiences and makes sense of its historical setting or context, shaped by distinctive economic, political, social and cultural formations. Yet each generation has periodically voiced identical fears about its young people. Time here is best measured in blocks of thirty years or so, the chronological difference or the 'generation gap' between parents and children.

So one can write about the pre-Second World War generation facing unemployment, war and poverty, as the post-war 'baby boomers' who became affluent teenagers during the 1960s and 70s, and their children, Generation X, as young people growing into adults in the 1980s and 90s with computers, mobile phones and credit cards. These become the characterized cohorts of 'hippies', 'teddy boys', 'mods and rockers' and 'punk rockers' of popular media depiction.

It is useful therefore to adopt some kind of historical perspective, as prescribed, for example, by the late Philip Abrams (1982). To understand present leisure lifestyles one needs to explore the changing collective experiences of generational cohorts and how these are expressed over a lifetime. This requires some Durkheimian analysis which focuses on the 'conscience collective', that social solidarity which crystallizes at distinctive historical episodes. Durkheim's work on deviance stresses the functions of social rules and rituals, the effervescence and celebration of shared experience and memories. Peer pressure and shared historical experience are crucial contexts and resources for individuals growing up and growing old together, producing a distinctive 'spirit' for every age. Each generation inherits both material and cultural resources from the previous generation and in modernity each generation endeavours to win some cultural space from its parents and from the past. So the second level or measure of time can best be described by the word, *epoch*, which refers to a distinctive historical period or perhaps decade, when a generational cohort set about shaping their own institutions and history.

The third and final measure of time is not measured lightly in individual lives or in generational decades but in a much weightier and lengthier currency, which spans one or more centuries. This measure represents major phases of human history such as medieval times or modern industrial society. Giddens argues that we should think in terms of these times as *eras*, periods of long-term seismic structural change. It can be compared to glacial time when change, hardly noticed by individuals or generations, may be quite radical in character. Environmentalists have this time scale in mind when they express concern about population growth, pollution and global warming. Riding around town in 'gas guzzling' 4x4 'all terrain sports' vehicles and enjoying cheap air flights suits our generation in the first decades of the new millennium but our grandchildren and their children may face a bleak, environmentally depleted future. A recent report for the UK government has argued that if we do not deal with global warming now, at a cost of just 1% of global GDP, the world economy could lose 20% in economic growth and so plunge into economic recession by 2050.

It is precisely this long-term structural change from one sort of society to another which created leisure. It is the shift from pre-industrial society to industrial society that created leisure time. The following exercise is to encourage you to think about what life was like in pre-industrial and industrial times. You can draw on any sources you wish to fire your historical imagination – your own knowledge of history, for example, cinema films, TV documentaries and any novels you may have read that cover the period.

3.1 Comparing pre-industrial and industrial times

What image do you have in mind when you think about Britain in the mid seventeenth century (the time of Oliver Cromwell) and then 200 years on in the late nineteenth century after industrialization (during the reign of Queen Victoria)?

	PRE-INDUSTRIAL BRITAIN	INDUSTRIAL BRITAIN
Landscape		
Buildings and dwellings		
Work		
Family		
Child care		
Food/diet		
Community networks		
Politics		
Religion		
Leisure		
Medical care		
Role of local government		
Policing and military		
Crime and deviance		

'LEISURE' IN PRE-INDUSTRIAL TIMES

Most historians stress the importance of local custom and tradition within agrarian pre-industrial society. The traditional landscape is one of smallhold-ings, farms and village communities, usually situated in the shadow of huge landed estates, punctuated by imposing mansions and parkland, owned by the county aristocracy. Geographers write of open and closed communities depend-ing upon the degree of religious, economic and political power and control exerted by rural elites over local territory and populations. The aristocracy can have leisure but it soon becomes seen as idleness amongst the lower orders; the aristocracies have the duty to spend their wealth ostentatiously, as it 'trickles down' to benefit the lower classes, whereas labourers and servants need poverty as an incentive to work hard. During the seventeenth and eighteen centuries, many landowners used their legislative and judicial powers to enclose common land for hunting, riding, shooting and fishing (the theme, for example, of E.P. Thompson's famous book *Whigs and Hunters* (1977)) and, in so doing, often to tie independent labourers and their families to work on or for their country houses and estates. There is inevitably some rural nostalgia in descriptions of pre-industrial societies which ignore the dependency, famines, poverty and class differences that divided wider society. Part of such nostalgia related to the seasonality of the agrarian way of life. People were locked into 'natural' rhythms of agricultural production: there were 'task-based' cycles of sowing crops in the spring, cultivation in the summer and harvesting in autumn with the dark nights of winter, leading to quieter, less busy times and more sociability.

Not everyone was tied into the rural economy or lived under aristocratic influence. Professional middle classes and artisan manual workers, as well as semi- and unskilled labourers, lived and worked within the parishes of market towns and within the city walls of regional centres. Patterns of work were not so much driven by natural rhythms or traditional sexual divisions of labour as by work skills and craft practices which were carefully controlled by town guilds. These were professional and trade associations that organized apprenticeships which taught work skills, provided qualifications and set down the parameters for both work, regarding conditions of employment, and holidays.

Much has been made by historians of the religious outlook and values among the medieval populace, the enormous influence in the society of the early modern and Middle Ages of various religious institutions. The Anglican and Catholic churches and parsonage, as well as Methodist chapel wielded much influence within local communities. Sabbatarianism which forbade recreations on Sunday was strong – leaving it dull or drunken for many. However, the monthly calendar was permeated with holy days to celebrate saints, religious festivals and local feasts. In 1761, the Bank of England was closed for 47 weekdays in the year. By 1834 this had been reduced to four (see Walvin, 1978). Artisans were frequently reluctant to return to work on the Monday after a weekend of drinking, resting and entertainments. If labourers and their families could manage to live the week on four days' pay, they would not turn up for work on the Monday – hence the term, 'St Monday'. So the medieval calendar witnessed a plethora of religious 'holy days', festivals, fairs, feasts and carnivals. The timing or duration of these events was determined by local tradition: see for example, the Nottingham Goose Fair. Such events were closely linked to excess and disorder. To quote Jeremy Paxman's book *The English* 'Tis no revel unless there be some fightings' (1998: 248). Drink and drinking were the cornerstones of pre-industrial leisure. Those in authority, such as judges, magistrates and the clergy, all feared the worst, especially during times of political unrest, exacerbated by conditions of poverty and unemployment in the local economy.

3.2 Pre-industrial leisure – the medieval carnival

Pre-industrial leisure occurred on 'holy' days or holidays which, given local custom and community practice, often meant ironic inversions of traditional hierarchies of status and privilege. For example, on the 5th of November Bonfire Boys, in disguise, burned effigies of local manufacturers and dignitaries in market towns in Southern England (Storch, 1982).

The distinguishing features of wakes, the dedication of local parish churches, in early nineteenth-century Lancashire were rush carts and their parades or processions, Morris dancing, heavy drinking, blood sports, stalls, exhibitions, children's rides, new clothes and whitewashed housing (Walton and Poole, 1982). The rush cart symbolized the local identity of the village and often pitched battles raged around them. There were fairs, sports, amusements and extraordinary common feasts, 'madness' and drinking (Reid, 1982).

Before the industrial revolution, popular culture during festivals and fairs (Cunningham, 1980) focused on subversive disorder, and what Bernice Martin (1981) refers to as 'liminality' the reversal and suspension of traditional hierarchies and obligations. It was a time of excess and role reversals, with the aristocracy often as joint participants, as the forces of law and order turned a blind eye to general drunkenness, debauchery and sexual licence among the lower orders. This popular culture was well supported by the Tories of the landed gentry, for whom, 'beef, ale, field sports meant Englishness' (see Cunningham, 1980), whereas the middle classes and the radical edge of working-class culture tried to ban festivals and fairs. They saw them as an unnecessary diversion from honest toil. The Tories often cast the liberals and labour politicians as 'kill joys' and out of touch with the instincts of British people.

In what sense are 'stag nights', 'hen party' weekends and 'binge' drinking simply residues of the 'carnivalesque' traditions of the past?

INDUSTRIAL TIMES

If pre-industrial times was symbolized by the tolling of village church bells, industrial time is sounded by the factory hooter or, on a more personal level, the loud tapping on bedroom window panes of the town's 'knocker up'. His job in the morning was to get workers out of their beds ready for the next shift in the mills, mines and factories. In the evening he would light the gas standard lamps which provided artificial 'daylight' or more appropriately 'worklight', enabling factories to run machinery through the night. The natural rhythm of sunrise and sunset, of changing seasons, became less and less important for the majority of the urban population, as industrial capitalism imposed a standardized 'clock time' on everyone, management and workers alike. Following the strictures of the Protestant work ethic and Evangelicalism, leisure or 'spare time became something to be earned by hard work, remission for good conduct, a reward for responsibility' (Lowerson and Myerscough, 1977). In the Christian teaching of the period, time must not be wasted. Religion demanded that leisure must be disciplined – entailing a search for self-education, self-improvement and respectability.

Protestantism was at the heart of English culture and its experience of industrialization. It marked the cornerstone of Max Weber's analysis of the emergence of capitalism and the rational organization of work. Weber was struck by the apparent historical patterns wherein industrialization in Europe grew stronger and faster in Protestant cities, regions and nation states than in Catholic areas. Weber argued that it was the ideas of Protestantism which most strongly informed 'the spirit of capitalism'. Its motivating force was 'vocation', the faithful were literally 'called to serve God' by working hard, pursuing a methodical, frugal and abstemious life in this world in order to be rewarded in the next world with a place in heaven. To become one of God's chosen few each individual must practise devotion and self-denial. There could be no space for Catholic confessions, absolutions and indulgences with the individual's soul and welfare ministered to by priests, bishops and the Vatican. It was as if the Catholic Church could offer 'vacations' for the soul when material and corporal pleasures had beckoned the individual towards sin and sinning.

For Puritans and many others in the Protestant Reformation movement (Calvinists, for example) one could not allow these 'mini-breaks' from the serious business of securing eternal life. In economic terms this meant that any wealth accumulated from hard work could not be spent on pleasures and amusements as that would be self-indulgent. The only acceptable solution was further investment and reinvestment, to provide work opportunities for others and riches and wealth to confirm one's own status as one of God's chosen few. The title of a powerful Marxist analysis of contemporary leisure in Britain tells the whole story, *The Devil Makes Work* (for idle hands to make mischief, see Clarke and Critcher, 1985). The idea of work as a 'vocation' was not only central to Protestantism but also to the more radical anti-capitalist doctrines of Marx in the 1860s, William Morris' 'Art and Crafts' movement in the 1880s, the labour movement in the 1910s and G.D.H. Cole's Guild Socialism in the 1920s and 30s.

E.P. Thompson (1967) has written in great detail about the making of the English working class, and, for him, industrialism is symbolized not by satanic mills in the North nor fiery smoking chimneys nor engineering works in the 'Black Country' of the Midlands, nor dockside cranes in the Port of London, but rather by the clock. For Thompson the factory clock, and the work discipline it imposed, transformed people's lives. Under capitalism workers were transformed into commodities that could be bought and sold depending on business and market forces. They were no longer people as such; they were literally, in the new vocabulary of industry, reduced to 'hands' to work the mechanized mill machinery. Traditional hierarchies of skill, based on class and gender, were changed as even children were capable of minding the fast-working, more productive machines. So people became employees of factory

owners, selling their labour power in return for wages. Some resisted new technologies and destroyed machinery, such as the Luddites or Captain Swing, but
not for long. Time was no longer 'passed' while working at agricultural tasks
until completion but it was rather 'spent' at work, often 12 hours each day, six
days a week. Sunday, the Sabbath, remained the one day of rest; for religion,
recreation and recuperation for the next week's toil.

3.3 Time and industrial work

What do the following phrases tell you about the world
of work?

"Here's your card for 'clocking on' and 'clocking off'."

"You are going to have to work nights all next week."

"You can do that in your own time."

"I'm not working those hours it is against EU regulations." "I am sorry but
you are going to have to work late to meet this project deadline. The report
has to be sent off by nine o'clock tomorrow morning."

"You're not here to waste time!"

"It is 'time and half' for working Saturday afternoons and Sundays."

"Piecework is much better than being paid by the hour or the day rate on
this assembly line."

When a person retired from work, they were traditionally presented by their
employer/manager with a pocket watch or a carriage clock as a leaving
present. Why?

One view of nineteenth-century Britain stresses class and industrial conflict,
as the new industrial manufacturing middle classes struggled to impose work
discipline on a workforce accustomed to a more relaxed set of traditional
working practices. Labour power had to be regulated and controlled so that
employers could maximize labour efficiency and their own profits on their
capital investments. Part of the onslaught on pre-industrial culture was to
make people work harder and longer. The pre-industrial religious holidays
were felt to be too numerous and local practices of 'St Mondays' had to be
stopped (see Reid, 1976). In the 1830s the Temperance Movement sought to
control excessive drinking patterns and thereby encourage thrift through
local Friendly Societies, Building Societies and the Co-operative Movement.
There was a substantial reduction in the numbers of local feasts, fairs and
statutory bank holidays, with the UK experiencing the greatest reduction in
holiday time in European countries during this period. Legislation centred on
controlling the alehouse, banning popular animal sports such as bull running,

bear-baiting, dog-fights, ratting and duck hunting so as to minimize the gambling associated with these activities. Such activities ran contrary to the now-entrenched Puritan ethic: 'The puritan', wrote Thomas Babington Macaulay, 'hated *bear baiting*, not because it gave pain to the bear, but because it gave pleasure to the spectators' (cited in Richard Holt, 1992: 29). Horse racing and prize fighting still enjoyed patronage from the leisured rich and cricket and pedestrianism were popular recreations.

It took a long-term project by powerful middle-class interests to wean pre-industrial labour off their relaxed uneven version of local time and onto a national standardized version of clock time. Capitalist development required national time to co-ordinate emergent communication networks – for example, the railways – in order to open up local markets and populations. One way of thinking about this change is to see the nineteenth century as bringing both mechanization and standardization. Watches and clocks measured out time in regular hours and minutes and thus divided people's days and nights up into work time and time left over for recuperation and leisure.

3.4 No time to lose?

Jay Griffiths (1999a, 1999b) relates conceptions of time to notions of progress and questions industrialism and its use of contemporary technology.

Many writers have studied both the difference and distance between rural and industrial time. In tribal and agricultural societies, time was measured either in relation to routine tasks – a half hour, for example, might be described as the time it takes to boil rice – or the seasons: many tribal societies, therefore, have seen time as cyclical, rather than linear. Their days would be regulated by nature and need, rather than strict routine and the clock.

When industrialism came, bringing with it new technologies and new conceptions of time, there was political resistance. One obvious example are the machine-breaking 'Luddites' in the 1840s. The word survives into contemporary usage and is taken to mean 'wreckers' and 'destructive opponents of progress'. Today, writes Griffiths, 'urban modernity lives under an assault of clocks' (Griffiths, 1999a: 3). Many of us prefer 'fast food' or to cook quickly in microwave ovens, rather than wait for the more traditional food preparation methods of 'slow food' to run their course. Agriculture, once governed simply by nature is now often organized around the imperatives set and regimented by big corporations.

Another example of contemporary time 'saving' can be seen in the proposal by the British government at the time of writing to build a new high-speed rail link (HS2) between London and the north of England. The current estimated cost is around £43 billion and one of the chief arguments put forward in favour of the project is that it will shorten journey times between the capital and towns and cities in the north of England by around thirty to

(Continued)

(Continued)

forty-five minutes (see the British government website: http://www.hs2.org.uk/phase-two/facts-figures (accessed 11 November 2013)).

But we must remember that time constrictions are not confined to the worlds of industry and business; we see them equally – and ironically – in the field of leisure. Think of how we conceive and consume sport today. In previous years, the county game of cricket was played over three or four days but now the most popular form of cricket is probably Twenty20, in which matches are completed in around six hours.

Questions to consider:

- What is the difference between cyclical and linear conceptions of time?
- What is the colloquial meaning of the word 'Luddite'? What were the aims of the Luddites? Which groups, if any, might be called the modern equivalents of the Luddites, and why?
- Griffiths argues that time is being 'split from nature'. Can you think of examples of this, other than the ones given here?
- Why do you think that Twenty20 cricket has largely superseded longer forms of the game?
- Drawing on contemporary life, think of ways in which you might measure time if you weren't able to use watches, clocks and the other apparatuses of industrial time.

Historians have fiercely debated the nature of social change in the nineteenth century, especially in relation to changing work patterns and whether there was much class consciousness and resistance to the new work discipline introduced by managers and supervisors in factories, mines, steel works and the docks. Marxist writers have sought to document how collective organizations, such as trade unions, Guilds, Friendly Societies and the Co-operative movement, all sought to challenge the power of industrial and commercial employers and their detailed plans for work discipline. By organizing collectively, trade unions sought to control pay rates, hours and conditions of employment, holiday times and half-day working on Saturdays. This resulted in industrial disputes, demonstrations, 'working to rule', strikes and lock-outs, as well as secondary picketing of recalcitrant employers who refused to honour agreed wage rates and conditions. Very occasionally, county lieutenants and magistrates mobilized volunteers, yeomanry and the military when local fears of social disorder arose. Such actions often had disastrous results, as at Peterloo in 1818. A little later, in 1823, a Master and Servants Act was passed by parliament, making 'breaches of contract' by workers punishable by prison and/or hard labour. As the century progressed, with London's Metropolitan Police Force held up as an exemplar of good policing, it was felt that unarmed constabulary should act as 'domestic missionaries' to police urban crime and industrial disputes. (For example, see the extensive writings about policing northern towns by Robert Storch (1975, 1976, 1977).)

One strong and recurring theme in historical narratives has been to explore ways in which the middle classes hoped to exert social control over subordinate groups by encouraging law and order, religious observance, self-help through education and rational recreation. Many middle-class industrialists were themselves moral reformers. They joined voluntary societies and sought 'improvement', to reshape 'rough' working-class culture, turning the 'ungovernable people' (Brewer and Styles, 1980) of the proletariat into respectable citizens. This 'cult of respectability' was actively pursued by enlightened employers who, as religious philanthropists, were prepared to build model communities offering good houses, schools, Mechanic Institutes and leisure facilities to compliant workers. There are examples throughout the nineteenth century – Owen's New Lanark, Salt's Saltaire, Cadbury's Bournville and Lever's Port Sunlight – of such model communities. Some working groups, often designated as the 'aristocracy of labour', were keen to develop radical or religious opposition to the dominant forces of capitalism. In so doing they developed a collectivist culture in the hope of gaining independence from the individualistic middle classes, as well as securing political suffrage and some influence in national political debates (Cunningham, 1980; Gray, 1974).

The work of Malcolmson (1973), Morris (1979) and others has suggested that the nineteenth century witnessed a wholesale decline in popular culture, customs and amusements because of the relentless onslaught of the 'tyranny of the clock' and the imposition of stricter work practices. The emphasis on history, on lived experience and human agency were central tenets of the socialist historian E.P. Thompson's life and work, particularly in his seminal study of emergent working-class consciousness, *The Making of the English Working Class* (1968). In short, by the 1840s the English working class had made itself. It was different from the middle classes. For example, in support of Thompson's thesis, Foster (1974) even suggested that working-class consciousness in Oldham had a radical and even revolutionary edge and was challenging bourgeois control of the town. There is clear evidence that working-class leisure had forged its own distinctive character – in music such as brass bands, operatic and choral singing, church and chapel choirs as well as the theatre, music halls and most importantly of all, the public house (see Bailey, 1978; Gammon, 1981).

Any radicalism that remained in the Chartist movement had collapsed by the mid-nineteenth century. This left the victorious middle classes to consolidate their political and cultural dominance – what Antonio Gramsci would later term as 'hegemony'. By this he meant that the ruling class established a kind of moral leadership, dominating the nation state's ideas, values and culture, with subordinate groups actively consenting to their own subjugation inside hierarchies of class, race and gender. During the late nineteenth century, as part of the Enlightenment project, most European nation states sought political solutions by encouraging shared inclusive national consensus around '*invented traditions*' (see Hobsbawm and Ranger, 1983); the wrinkles of local, ethnic and class differences were ironed out by the missionaries of domestic metropolitan culture. Rather than becoming radical and challenging bourgeois ideas of work discipline, market forces and industrial capitalism, the working classes were prepared to work within capitalism, albeit at a price. Many writers feel that leisure time was a crucial feature of that settlement.

There have been fierce historical debates about the relative autonomy of working-class culture and its independent forms of organization. In his book *Languages of Class* (1983) English historian Gareth Stedman Jones explores the incorporation of the working classes into commercialized leisure. Politically, he suggests, working-class people settled for what he calls a capitalist 'culture of consolation', rather than seek all-out confrontation with the employing class. His work challenges any simple functionalist view of social control (that social order breaks down, control is reasserted from above and social equilibrium prevails). He argues that social order is negotiated and contested. His primary worry concerns historians who deploy sociological concepts carelessly. His meticulous historical research emphasizes that the working classes were controlled in capitalist society through the wage relationship at work rather than through leisure institutions. Hugh Cunningham (1980) too sees the late nineteenth century in terms of a wholesale expansion of commercial leisure industries and opportunities – seaside holidays, excursions, music halls, spectator sports and the ubiquitous public houses (see Bailey, 1978). Rather than embarking on economic and political change for a radical and socialist future, the English working class settled down within British culture. There was no radical working-class consciousness to make connections between economics and politics. In Britain at least, these two formations were separated and were to remain separate. Although there were frequent outbreaks of economic struggle and dispute between capitalist employers and workers, there was also sustained political consensus in support of the British state and, not least, of its imperial role. There may have been dissensus about relative rates of pay and economic rewards for labour power, but such conflicts did not extend to politics or to the reshaping of liberal democracy. Immiseration and alienation at work, the cornerstone predictions and motors of Marxist revolutionary analysis and revolutionary class struggle, did not lead to radical political change in the UK.

3.5 Industrial leisure: The game of football

Leicester University has conducted a substantial amount of research into the history of football as well as providing a social and contemporary history of football hooliganism. Drawing inspiration from Norbert Elias' work on figurational sociology and the 'civilizing process', Eric Dunning et al. (1986) have suggested that violence between supporters and crowd disorders were not only a feature of the 1960s and 1980s but existed in the late nineteenth and right through the early decades of the twentieth century.

Anthony Delves (1991) has provided an interesting case study of medieval street football or 'hugball' in Derby, a game played by the whole community on a local two-day holiday with money collected for the victor. Pre-industrial football was a violent, drunken and riotous affair with the aim of the game to get the football from one side of town to the other. There were few rules, uneven sides, no playing area and no goal posts. In 1845, the Mayor pronounced the game illegal and special constables and troops were drafted in to police the game, with players bound over to keep the peace. If working-class people employed in the hosiery, silk and lace work trades took possession of the streets to play riotous games of football, the *Derby Mercury* argued, no one was safe, as ruffians threw bags of soot at respectable people and engaged in 'the usual acts of insubordination'. The middle classes attempted to organize alternative sports – athletics with prizes.

Historical research has documented how the round ball game was transformed and codified into a sport, with 11 players on each side, a referee and a playing area delineated in time and space. Many writers have suggested that the ending of the spontaneous pre-industrial game mirrored changes in work discipline. Football was gradually transformed into a rational sport with specialized playing roles, the development of players' skill and competencies and its creeping commercialization, with players playing for money.

What do you see as the defining characteristics in pre-industrial, industrial and current Premiership football?

What has changed and what remains the same?

Think about the following dimensions of the game:

local.................global
informal...............formal
amateur...............professional
male ....female
white ....black

Taking each of these five binary distinctions in turn, which word (left or right) best describes the following, and why?

- Players

- Officials

- Coaches/Managers

- Fans

- Casual spectators

- Media interests

POST-INDUSTRIAL TIMES

In the 1990s sociology as an academic discipline took 'a cultural turn' which meant that social theorists and research projects were less interested in the industrial world of production and more interested in the world of consumption, popular culture and leisure. In this account, the growing individualism of the 1980s in the UK challenged previously definitive contours of industrial society such as class, race and gender. Personal identities were no longer seen as determined by class culture but rather as articulated in diverse lifestyle choices around flexible employment, 'hybrid' or a mixture of ethnicities and contested sexualities. To paraphrase Karl Marx and Marshall Berman, 'All that was solid seemed to melt into air'. The taken-for-granted certainties of the industrial society of class, hard work, careers, heterosexuality, traditional sexual division of labour, child care, self-contained nation states, imperialism with Western military and cultural dominance of world affairs, no longer held.

The argument was first articulated by Daniel Bell (1973) in his book portentously entitled *The Coming of Post-Industrial Society*. His arguments and other versions explaining the shift into this third type of society have been neatly summarized by Krishan Kumar (1978). The story is a familiar one of long-term structural change; people were living in a new kind of social order. The main institutions of industrial society – family, education, work, politics and religion were facing seismic change which led some Marxists, such as Stuart Hall and Martin Jacques, writing in the magazine *Marxism Today*, to speak of 'New Times'. However, for Marxists the 'new times' still related to the old economic system of capitalist exploitation, but what had changed capitalism significantly was a new regimen of capital accumulation – a more flexible regime of 'just in time' production for niche markets rather than standardized mass consumer products. Capitalism was no longer contained within nation states but operated a global economic system. Countries in the West experienced unemployment in primary and secondary sectors of their national economies with multinational companies relocating production to 'Asian Tiger' economies of the Far East such as Japan, Malaysia, Korea and China. A radical change had taken place in information processes, with new computer technologies and then later digitalization producing global communications networks. Global financial markets were created and financial transactions in Tokyo could now impact on London and New York. New times meant more flexible work practices and a 24/7 society. Gone were the work patterns of Mondays to Fridays and 'nine-til-five'; shops opened on Sundays, restaurants and bars could serve late at night and there was always the Internet. The rigid time and space boundaries between work and leisure became increasingly blurred or 'de-differentiated'. The mobile phone and e-mail meant that individuals were expected to be contactable at any time, including evenings and weekends, and to respond immediately.

3.6 Timetables and peak times

Map out a week's calendar for the following organizations ... all more or less dealing with people's leisure choices and their outcomes. Then insert three categories of work-flow timetables (*Very Busy, Busy, Quiet*).

Think too about the impact of seasons (*Spring/Summer/Autumn/Winter*) on such leisure organizations.

- Inner-city public houses
- Tennis clubs
- Restaurants
- Cinemas
- Hospital Accident and Emergency Departments
- Gym and leisure centres
- A café in an out-of-town shopping complex
- Taxis
- Newsagents/off licences
- Art galleries and arts centres
- Public libraries
- National Trust properties
- A seaside B&B hotel
- IKEA
- Tourism and travel agencies

In leisure studies literature, there are few things that capture the shift to post-modern leisure better than the emergence of the theme park. It has an iconic status as it signifies new leisure as fantasy time. It offers families an opportunity to spend quality time as holiday tourists immersed in a world of what Rojek (1995), echoing the French philosopher Jean Baudrillard, has called simulacra, in an artificially built environment. It is an opportunity to step into a 'magic kingdom' to be met by friendly staff, or 'cast members' who make sure that tourists 'have a nice day' as well as spend time and money in cafés, restaurants and shops.

3.7 Postmodern leisure: Developing theme parks – Disney World

Walt Disney's first theme park was built in 1955. Disney presents the vernacular of small-town nineteenth-century America as an image of social harmony, entitled Main Street, USA. Disneyland is located in Orange County, California and boasts a castle, railroad stations and five themed areas or destinations: Adventure Land; Lilliputian Land; Fantasy Land; Frontier Land and Holiday Land. One can consume or experience very different places in the same afternoon.

Disney World Orlando was the futuristic EPCOT (Experimental Prototype Community of Tomorrow) – planned in 1966, finished in 1982, and developed in partnership with other mega-corporations and franchises. The four main elements of the archetypal theme park are present – amusement rides, stage-set replicas of vernacular architecture, state of the art technology and an ideal community. It has fantasy theme parks (Captain Nemo, Pirates of the Caribbean, Space Mountain) plus facades of tourist architecture (Eiffel Tower, St Mark's Square, Italy) and solar powered cars which function to manage and control blocks (60) of visitor flows.

Magic Kingdom has 10 resort hotels (5,700 rooms), 1,190 camp sites, 580 vacation villas/time shares, three Convention centres, Lake Buena Vista, Walt Disney World Village (+7 hotels; 3,700 rooms). The hotels are branded theme parks in themselves – such as space adventure, wild west, ancient Rome.

Disney itself symbolizes global capitalism. Walt Disney himself was a racist and fiercely anti-union. The film corporation has diversified into international markets (Europe, Japan, China as well as USA) and earns money from theme parks franchises and video markets.

The corporation has been subject to various take-over speculations, with tensions reported between the parent company and Euro Disney. In the late 1980s, before the publication of Sharon Zukin's book (1991), the US Disney workers or 'cast members' faced pay cuts of 16% over a three-year period and there have been strikes and changed work practices because of automation.

For Sharon Zukin (1991) Disney is not only the capital of symbolism but also the symbol of capitalism. The powerless immerse themselves in 'hyper-reality'. Disney symbols, cartoon characters and Disney stories determine the limit of the imagination. Merchandising branded cartoon characters in toys, games, clothes, stationery, and so on, provides children and adults with a myriad of opportunities to consolidate a global brand identity. Marketeers look for synergy in products so that the original film must generate sales of videos, DVDs, games and, most importantly, sequels, in order to 'grow' the business. There are now over fifty theme parks in the UK; one of the most recent – Peppa Pig World, dedicated to the children's cartoon character, opened in Hampshire in 2011.

Another of Zukin's couplets, power of fantasy and fantasy of power, suggests that the capitalist market economy suffers from, or at least conceals, a deep-seated cultural problem – how to resolve the tension between weakness and power; image and reality. Individuals may immerse themselves in science fictions such as Star Wars, Star Trek, Harry Potter and Matrix movies, but what power do people have in the face of uncertainties in the real world of business, religion and politics?

As we shall see later, there have been intense debates about the precise value of escapist media and such processes of Disneyfication, wherein multinational corporations seek to re-enchant the world of leisure and tourism with precious, 'authentic' experiences. Hotels and restaurants are recast as spaces for 'quality time' where paying visitors or 'guests' are pampered, their physical and emotional batteries recharged, and there are ample opportunities to reconnect with partners, families and friends. In the case of Disney, it is a fantasy world where happiness is guaranteed in the magic kingdom, one can meet and be photographed with cartoon characters and visit places seen only on television, film and DVDs. Postmodern times offer immediacy too in that one does not even have to wait for photos to be taken to the chemists to be developed. They are ready to view immediately, digitally, and at the same split second one texts them to friends with video phones to prove that one is here, having a good time on holiday.

3.8 'Living life like in the movies?'

What are the arguments FOR and AGAINST people wanting to 'live life like in the movies'?

Make a list of the possible costs and benefits of building theme parks.

What would be the arguments for and against visiting a theme park?

Environmental	Economic	Social	Political	Cultural

CONCLUSION

This chapter has argued that the concepts of time and residual time provide an important dimension and context to our understanding of leisure. Historical and social analyses have stressed the significance of historical sequences of events as they have impinged (and, of course, continue to impinge) upon individuals, generations and society. Giddens has argued that one must differentiate between individual time (*lifetime*), generational or institutional time (*epoch*), and structural time (*era*). So, moments in time can have biographical, generational and societal relevance and impacts. However, this chapter has concentrated on what historians have written about societal and structural changes, the shift from popular culture and custom into rational recreation and leisure. We have mapped out the debates about time in what writers define as preindustrial, industrial and post-industrial societies. Leisure institutions and leisure experiences are seen as the product of industrial society and the standardization of the clock time of capitalism. In the UK, leisure institutions expanded in the late nineteenth century to free time in the evenings and Saturday afternoons and Sundays when most people were not at work. In the postmodern era, de-differentiation has meant the blurring of the boundaries between work and leisure time. Part-time employment, flexi-time working hours, overtime and weekend working have all resulted in more individualized and less routine timetables shaping people's lives.

4

CAUTION – CHILDREN AT PLAY

This chapter explores the usefulness of major perspectives in psychology and social psychology for understanding leisure experiences. This chapter will:

- Distinguish between the life cycle and the life course
- Identify the traditional perspectives of psycho-analytic, behaviourist and humanistic approaches to play and childhood
- Apply the concept of 'flow' to diverse leisure experiences
- Explain the contribution that social psychology can make to understanding leisure.

LIFE CYCLE AND THE LIFE COURSE

The previous chapter has outlined three distinctive timeframes – the *life time* of the individual, the *epoch* of generations and the *era* of societies. Individuals take for granted the immediacy of the 'Here and Now', as they constantly make sense of their lives, of what other people are saying and doing, how organizations work and how power is exercised. The social psychologist Erving Goffman (1974) has suggested that individuals, when entering social situations, and novel contexts in particular, always carry the question, '*What is going on here?*' in the back of their minds. We shall return to his 'new' approach to social psychology towards the end of this chapter but it is worth remembering that the first of Chris Rojek's four basic rules for leisure research suggests that adult leisure should be juxtaposed with conventional notions of children and children's play:

(1) Leisure activity is an adult phenomenon which is defined in opposition to the play world of children.

(2) Leisure practice is an accomplishment of skilled and knowledgeable actors.

(3) The structure and development of leisure relations is an effect of the legitimating rules of pleasure and unpleasure.

(4) Leisure relations must be sociologically examined as dynamic, relatively open-ended processes. (Rojek, 1985: 180–181)

One place to start trying to make sense of children's lives and childhoods is with the established 'old' approach of developmental psychology. This academic tradition is held to be objective: to replicate the scientific methodology of the natural sciences by collecting 'hard' empirical data under experimental conditions in order to be able to isolate cause from effect in human behaviour. Individuals are seen as biologically programmed to move through distinctive life stages which constitute the life cycle. Stated in simple terms, every individual is born with a hard-wired genetic makeup, develops language, learns cognitive and body skills and competencies, passes through puberty, has the sexual capacity to produce children, and gradually experiences a myriad of ageing processes which together diminish physical strength, mental abilities and result often in illness and eventually, of course, death. These traditional perspectives stress sex differences between males and females. Males are seen as biologically and instinctively programmed to be hunter gatherers so are aggressive, competitive and combative risk takers, whereas women are by nature fit for nurturing, 'home/nest building' and child care. The same biological cage is built around traditional ideas of race and disability; biological differences in genetic endowment must explain the difference between 'us' and 'them', 'black' and 'white', 'special needs' and 'normal' children.

In stark contrast, later perspectives take a 'softer' approach to the human condition by suggesting that nurture, the cultural environment children grow up in, is just as, or even more, important than nature in shaping human lives and destinies. Consequently, sex becomes gender: divisions and differences between male and female have been, and continue to be, translated into the unequal social, political and economic forms of 'masculinity' and 'femininity'. As we shall see in later chapters on postmodern culture, these two traditional dominant forms of 'hyper-masculinity' and 'hyper-femininity' have been further deconstructed into diverse 'masculinities' and 'femininities' to acknowledge different and/or ambivalent sexual identities.

4.1 Gender stereotypes

Think about gender stereotyping of 'boys' and 'girls' at different stages of childhood: as babies, toddlers, at nursery, primary and in secondary schools. Can you think of good examples in terms of the following?

- clothes
- shoes
- toys
- nursery rhymes
- dressing up
- pets
- games
- bicycles
- 'out of school' clubs
- mobile phones

From your experience, are there gender differences in the language and behaviour of parents, relatives, neighbours, teachers, and others in the following situations?

- when talking to children
- when sorting out bumps and bruises
- when settling arguments between children
- when 'messing about'/playing with children
- when coaching skills in sports
- when children start taking risks

How about stories in books, children's television, DVDs, play stations, Internet games, and so on? Are any of the following more gender-free than others?

- *The Gruffalo*
- *Teletubbies*
- Characters in *In The Night Garden*
- *Peppa Pig*
- *Thomas the Tank Engine*
- *The Octonauts*

However, sex role stereotyping is crucial to the biological processes of growing up. Each individual carries within him or herself a biological clock which is ticking away at its own predestined pace. The great existential fear for most people is if their body and mind clocks are not synchronized later on in life, so old age may be experienced as dementia (healthy body, diseased mind) or as disability (diseased body, healthy mind). Doctors and health promotion experts constantly remind us of safe lifestyle choices, such as eating a balanced diet, not smoking, engaging in safe sex, drinking moderately, avoiding drug abuse, and routinely taking on appropriate physical and mental exercises in order to prolong the quality and quantity of the life cycle. It is important to remember that all the above activities are leisure choices of the individual, although there are fierce medical and political debates about the causes of dependency and addiction in modern lifestyles.

Mention of lifestyle choices raises the question that a rigidly determined view of the human life cycle is only part of the story. Indeed, the biological sciences acknowledge that there are substantial variations in individual genes, more than first suspected, which may lead some individuals to experience stages of the life cycle at different points than others: children can be intellectually advanced and study university degrees, teenagers can remain childish in interpersonal relations whereas some others are sexually experienced and mature at the age of 16. This scope for individual choice, ability and performance has led some writers to concentrate on the idea of life course rather than that of life cycle. The life course suggests that each individual's development and stage in the life cycle is negotiated and planned differently. There are no biological or psychological imperatives to follow as each individual negotiates his or her own way through local social, economic and cultural circumstances. The person reading a university textbook may be an 18-year-old undergraduate fresh from school, a 25-year-old mature student looking to change careers, a 40-year-old mother on a 'return-to-study' access course or a retired 65-year-old man studying with the Open University or on a University of the Third Age course. In part, the difference between life cycle and life course is a reflection of the paradox about nature and nurture. Is the life cycle pre-determined by nature or is human development shaped by circumstances within the life course? In common sense, the answer to this question is either one or the other. It is an either/or question: *nature versus nurture* but what if it is a both/and question: *both nature and nurture*?

4.2 Nature or nurture?

Here is a list of sport and leisure activities.

Do you think an individual's participation and enjoyment of the activity is determined either by nature or nurture?

- Aerobics
- Amateur dramatics

- Athletics – sprinting
- Basketball
- Ballroom dancing
- Choral singing
- Cricket
- Crown-green bowling
- Cycling
- Darts
- Football
- Gymnastics
- Horse riding
- Marathon running
- Modern dance
- Motor cycling
- Rambling in the countryside
- Rock climbing
- Skate boarding
- Snooker
- Swimming
- Tennis

Do you link any of the above activities with a particular age group?

Does it make a difference if we talk about elite sport performance rather than casual participation? So, does natural body shape, size and motor skills become more important as one moves through the Sports Council's pyramid from foundation, participation, performance to excellence?

FREUD, PERSONALITY AND PLEASURE

It is hard to overestimate the contribution that Sigmund Freud and his psycho-analytic ideas have made to twentieth-century thinking, with the essence of his argument being that our personalities are formed in childhood.

The term *Zeitgeist* was coined by the German philosopher Georg Wilhelm Friedrich Hegel to describe the spirit of a particular historical period or age: 'no man', he once wrote, 'can surpass his own time, for the spirit of his time is also his own spirit' (Magee, 2011: 262). Hegel felt that history witnessed the human spirit progressing towards the absolute spirit or truth itself. Freud set himself a similar lifetime project to use scientific knowledge to uncover the truth about neurology and the brain. More recently *Zeitgeist* has been used loosely to describe cultural qualities of any period such as the 1960s or the 1980s or 2000s. It is in the context of nineteenth-century Vienna that Freud's extraordinary ideas were shaped as he explored the nineteenth-century taboo of sex. Thinkers in the second half of the twentieth century have struggled to digest the full and all-pervasive impact of Freudianism. His theories and methodologies have generated much controversy and debate among both supporters and enemies alike. The intricacies of these visions and revisions of Freud's work, not least by Freud himself during his own life time (see Appignanesi and Zarate, 1992), need not detain us, but we must gain some grasp of Freud's approach to childhood and personality development, in particular his approach to pleasure and happiness. The latter feelings are often defined, by Freudians and non-Freudians alike, as an indispensable part of leisure, a defining common characteristic of all leisure experiences. Indeed, Freud's position suggests that everyone has deep biological drives to seek physical and mental pleasures, not all of which are socially, culturally or politically acceptable.

Initially a researcher at the University of Vienna, Freud was drawn into clinical practice and started to work with patients suffering from hysteria and neurosis. Although still working within a scientific rationalist paradigm, he began to deploy non-experimental strategies such as hypnosis, free association and interpretation of dreams to collect data. 'All dreams represent the fulfilment of wishes and the functioning of dreams provides systematic evidence of the unconscious' (Appignanesi and Zarate, 1992: 60). But the clinical role of the therapist is crucial here because 'dream work' means that the individual's wishes are well hidden, disguised and distorted, so the therapist must be relied upon to interpret the dream.

It is the role of the therapist, with the patient lying on the couch working through the 'talking cure' to relieve tensions, that has caught the popular imagination of Freud's important legacy of psycho-analysis. Such therapies were developed because of Freud's belief that hysteria and neuroses were caused by unpleasant memories, traumatic experiences that were buried, or rather actively repressed, in the unconscious mind. Consequently, psycho-analysis was often quoted as 'the royal road to the unconscious' to help the therapist explore hidden sources of the patient's unhappiness. Freud studied the 'extraordinary' – hysteria, neuroses, dreams, obsessions, language slips, anxieties and pathologies in order to understand the 'ordinary'. For Freudians, the difference between the normal and the abnormal is that 'healthy' people have socially acceptable neuroses, developing culturally acceptable practices to repress the unconscious.

If developing psycho-analysis and establishing the Vienna Psychoanalytical Society was not enough, Freud also published *Three Essays on the Theory of*

Sexuality in 1905 which highlighted the crucial importance of the early years of childhood. For Freud, all babies are born with a basic sex drive, an instinctual force which he termed *libido*, which is unstructured. Sexuality is pleasure for the human body. The source and power of the libido lie deep within the unconscious and with experience it develops a specific aim focusing on particular erotogenic zones (areas prone to arousal) and objects. During the first five years of childhood, Freud argues that there are three stages of psycho-sexual development: the oral, the anal and the phallic stages, whereupon the sexes divide with Freud's Oedipus complex phase – during which a child is thought to develop a sexual desire for the parent of the opposite sex. From five or six years old to the onset of puberty, individuals experience a latency phase when the earlier stages as well as aggressive and sexual feelings towards mothers and fathers are repressed. Problems occur when one becomes fixated or stuck at one stage of development in childhood or when the transitions are associated with traumatic memories that somehow must be repressed. Freud initially thought that psychic disorder stemmed from sexual trauma and repression during childhood, but later believed these were oral, anal and phallic signs or symbols, fixations mixed up with the individual's fantasies and desires of the erotic (Elliott, 2002). Contemporary critics teased Freud that his habit of smoking was because he remained trapped either at the oral or phallic stage, but his enigmatic reply was, 'Sometimes a cigar is just a cigar'. As we shall see later, individuals do develop strategies or defence mechanisms for dealing with problems. One must trace the contradictory patterning of social desire with opportunities for autonomy and leisure in the face of repressive forces. Freud felt that psycho-analytic method was a science which would help patients face the world and the inner demons of the unconscious that were controlling individual lives and behaviours.

Freud's psychology raises some challenging questions – indeed, Norman Brown (1968) has remarked upon his 'excremental vision' of human nature; for the child human faeces exist as a gift, as property and as a weapon. Brown argues that money is faeces, as anal eroticism is repressed, and misers save money just as they resisted potty training as a toddler. Most writers stress Freud's ubiquitously erotic view of human nature as basic sexual instincts permeate the whole body. For civilized society sexuality is distilled and fixated on particular body parts: the mouth, anus and male/female genitalia. Herein reside adolescent and adult fantasies as our own and other human orifices are forbidden sights and sites and therein lie sensual and sexual pleasures. But few people can talk about 'it', few are confident about their own sexual prowess, and to be fearful of the potency of others is common, while many are content to be spectators rather than participants. Therein lies the potency of online pornography and the immense success of 'pornographic' literature such as *Fifty Shades of Grey* and, not least, the columns and columns of sexual advice offered by 'agony aunts' in newspapers and magazines.

4.3 Freud and leisure experiences

Taking an unashamedly Freudian approach, how would you explain the following leisure experiences?

- Buying 'boys only' magazines such as *Loaded, Zoo* or *Nuts*
- Dance moves in the Salsa or Tango
- Downloading pornographic images from the Internet
- Drinking 'to get drunk'
- Drinking water from sports bottles
- Gossiping about parents/partners/friends/work mates in a restaurant
- 'Locker room' talk or 'banter' of sportsmen and women after a game
- Listening to racist or 'dirty' jokes by stand-up comedians
- Masturbation
- Reading erotic literature
- Riding a motorbike
- Subscribing to gay or straight chat-lines
- Taking recreational drugs such as cannabis, ecstasy or speed
- Watching romantic films

How convincing do you find Freud's analysis?

NB: Freudians would probably say you are 'in denial' if you disagree.

What do you think that phrase means? If you don't know find out!

A Freudian perspective on human nature means that individuals grow up to develop complex personality structures of which there are three major constituents – the id, the ego and superego. The id is the unconscious, wherein lie the instinctual drives of sexuality that Freud termed the biological *libido*. But having witnessed the barbaric killing of the First World War, Freud concluded that humankind could lay no claim to being civilized and so added another instinctual drive to the unconscious, the death instinct or Thanatos. The death instinct seeks to return life to stillness, rest and the peace of death. For Freud, the goal of life is death. This primary instinctual force is adaptable: when confronted by obstacles from others it results in aggression but when directed at the self, self-destructive behaviour ensues such as self-harming and suicide. In addition, superimposed on the individual is the superego; this consists of moral pressures and the civilizing constraints of parents, peer groups, teachers and wider society. These are the moral police who lay down conventions, ethical codes and religious teachings to secure social and moral order. The ego is trapped in the middle following 'the reality principle' mechanism, trying to manage tensions between the dark subversive worlds of the id, driven by the immediacy of 'the pleasure principle', and the white pristine glare of the superego. Individualized guilt and the social stigma of shame lie just around the corner.

So children are constrained to control basic biological functions and to negotiate bodily sexuality through what Freud had mapped out as three major stages of childhood – the oral, anal and genital stages. Therefore neither parenting nor growing up are easy matters, as we shall explore in Chapter 5. Freud offers very different views on male and female sexuality. He developed his idea of the Oedipus complex from interpreting his own wish to slay his father and possess his mother; the relations between sons and daughters with both their parents are seldom comfortable or pleasant. Single parenting may now seem a very attractive option to some. Consequently, it is probably not a coincidence that there is currently a surfeit of media programmes and chat-lines around the world that focus solely on the aggressive, disruptive behaviour of small children. Accredited and self-styled media experts (e.g. educational psychologists, cognitive behavioural therapists, super nannies, and so on) are drafted in to give advice to parents and thus improve family relationships and school matters.

4.4 Freud, psycho-analysis and smoking

How would Sigmund Freud explain the attractions of smoking to individuals, for example to teenagers aged 14–16?

Sigmund Freud's cousin, Edward Bernays was a PR consultant in America. His brief from a tobacco company in the 1920s was to encourage women to smoke and to break the taboo against women smoking in public.

- How might he have gone about it?

- How would you develop this niche market?

It is worthwhile noting that young women represent the fastest growing market for cigarette consumption in the UK, as well as in developing countries. Why do you think that leisure trend is developing?

So Freud's view of human development stresses the importance of childhood experiences and the constant struggle that adults face throughout everyday life to manage tensions between the primeval urges of the id and the demands of the superego, transmitted through the morality of civilized society. Freud would not be surprised at the levels of violence in modern societies, nor by the centrality of sex in all its forms in people's lives: in the language they use, the jokes they make, the clothes they wear, and the relationships they develop. Individuals can lose themselves and their inhibitions within crowds and discover excitement in an unexciting society.

Much of psycho-analysis encourages people to examine the taken-for-granted, often unacknowledged defence mechanisms they routinely display.

4.5 Defence mechanisms

Drawing on Freudian psycho-dynamic perspectives, the following list summarizes seven possible strategies to protect the self of the individual from pain and anxiety in everyday life.

- *Denial.* The source of distress is not acknowledged or perceived because it is too threatening. The person refuses to admit being frightened by an event or action of another individual.

- *Repression.* Unacceptable or anxiety-provoking thoughts or feelings are blotted out of consciousness. People forget threatening occurrences.

- *Displacement.* Emotions are transferred from the original person or object to a less formidable or safer target.

- *Sublimation.* Directing a socially unacceptable desire or activity into a socially or culturally acceptable one; for example, releasing sexual urges through dance. One translates or transposes instinctual desires into legitimate social relationships and cultural practices.

- *Projection.* Rejecting an unacceptable thought or feeling by blaming it on another person. By attributing it to someone else, the unacceptable thought or feeling is removed from the person. Clients in therapy often project or transfer their feelings, anxieties and fears onto the psycho-analyst. '*You're* the one who is aggressive.'

- *Intellectualization.* Painful emotions or feelings associated with an event are explained away by use of a rational explanation.

- *Rationalization.* A socially acceptable reason is given to avoid having to face a non-acceptable belief about oneself.

See Kerry Thomas (1997)'The defensive self: a psychodynamic approach'.

Exercise:

Think of athletes, coaches, managers interviewed immediately after a poor performance or poor result, what sorts of explanations or defence mechanisms do they articulate for the interviewer?

Do you think they would provide the same explanation in a changing room immediately after the loss?

What is your usual excuse?

MAKING LEISURE CHOICES: EXISTENTIAL PSYCHOLOGY AND 'FLOW'

Freud's view of the individual is very much one of an embodied self driven on by sexual energy. Indeed, for Freud and the Vienna School, learning, thinking and the pursuit of science should be uninhibited and emancipatory as they are essential for psychological health and well-being. For Freud it is impossible to separate the mind from the body, the *psyche* from *soma*. By way of contrast, existentialist philosophy is more concerned with cognition, what individuals know and how they feel about the world they inhabit. Like Freud, European existentialists such as the Danish philosopher Søren Kierkegaard, writing in the first half of the nineteenth century, and Czech philosopher and mathematician Edmund Husserl a century later, simply do not make happy reading. Both are philosophers inquiring into human nature and the human 'predicament'. Everything else in the world simply exists but humans are conscious of their existence and therefore have the potential to understand it. Unlike everything else in the universe, individuals have a capacity for self-awareness. Stated simply, individuals can choose

> The moment of choice, the leap into existence, comes between two fixed points: the nothingness from which we come and the nothingness to which we return after we die (McLeish, 1993: 267).

Kierkegaard stressed the importance of the personal, the irreducibility of each individual's subjective existence, of being in the world (*Existenz*). No individual can avoid the challenge of developing his or her human potential by an act of will, of 'becoming an individual', by making choices and commitments. So individuals are confronted by a constant state of transition, by a relentless search for meaning, purpose and values. The world itself is indifferent to us. It is no wonder people worry about what is going on and what will happen in the future. For existential philosophy, the key to understanding the human condition or human predicament is fear or *Angst*, an awareness of the fragility of one's own life and the certainty of death and non-being. If anxiety is a defining characteristic or condition of living in the world (what we have termed as *lifetime* in Chapter 3's discussion of time scales), it also paradoxically signifies individual freedom of choice. Individuals are free to choose in their actions how to make their way in life. This positive side of freedom, the human freedom to choose, reminds us of the starting point of leisure studies and leisure research. It is in leisure and the choices that people make in leisure time where people are free to be themselves.

But existentialism has raised some dark questions about individual freedom. Each individual is faced with the anxiety of choosing, of creating a never-secure identity in a world that lacks intrinsic meaning. Perhaps the solutions one wants or seeks will change as the life cycle or life course unfolds – the existential problems facing children, young adults, parents and older people may differ. These may be mediated by wider differences imposed by divisions of class, race, gender and disability. But there are psychologists who can help the individual in the elusive pursuit of happiness. For some it is not a question of chance or 'going with the flow', as only dead fish swim with the current, but rather of exploring how people's everyday lives can be enhanced.

One person who has done more to develop an optimistic psychology and to apply it to leisure is Mihaly Csikszentmihalyi, working alongside a variety of colleagues in the USA. Csikszentmihalyi's roots are deeply buried within humanistic research and he is most closely associated with work on 'flow' and its importance for the human mind and human happiness. Happiness is not a property that exists outside events but rather a matter of how individuals interpret them. This deep sense of participation in life is an optimal experience; it is a question of making something happen, mastering or accomplishing something difficult and worthwhile. This short word flow captures the essence of Csikszentmihalyi's work – or, as he himself put it in a much longer academic phrase: 'the phenomenological model of consciousness based on informational theory' (Csikszentmihalyi, 1992). So, he is interested in events as we perceive them and also those sensations, thoughts, feelings and intentions that they generate in our lives. All are combined in consciousness and are directed by the experiencing person. Psychic energy therefore involves synthesis of both mind and the body where there is congruence between incoming information and the intentional goals of intellectual and bodily engagement. Flow is what gives us zest for life-enjoyment not pleasure, fulfilment not frustration, activity not relaxation. For Csikszentmihalyi flow involves autotelic behaviour – the individual's complete absorption in doing something for its own sake, with a loss of self-consciousness and any sense of time. It is an optimal experience: 'people become so in involved in what they are doing that the activity becomes spontaneous, almost automatic; they stop being aware of themselves as separate from the actions they are performing' (1992: 53).

For the past three decades Professor Csikszentmihalyi has been engaged in studying flow in the Department of Psychology at the University of Chicago, but his main contribution has been to popularize his ideas by arguing that happiness in life can be achieved by people who choose to do activities which generate flow within the individual's consciousness (see Csikszentmihalyi, 1990). He sees no single path leading to learning the practice of self-discipline and the ability to think for oneself and to realize that one's boundaries encompass others and other forms of life. His original model is both simple and compelling and is captured in the title of his first important book, *Beyond Boredom and Anxiety* (Csikszentmihalyi, 1975). As the diagram shown in Figure 4.1 implies, to experience flow, individuals must develop skills and competencies that prove to be a match for the action challenges.

Csikzentmihalyi's research has found that not all individuals experience flow in their work, family and leisure lives, but those people who do are happier than the rest of the population. Affluence and material comfort all too often bring listlessness, boredom, reduced attention spans and, for many, a deep sense of frustration, which they may try to offset by the relentless drive for visible success or hedonistic consumption. Yet there are individuals who lead vigorous lives, open to a variety of experiences, keep on learning until the day they die and have strong ties and commitments to other people and to the

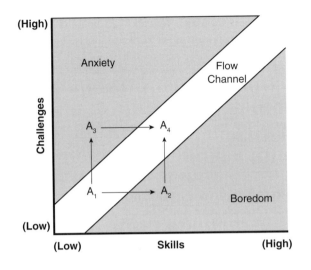

Figure 4.1 Flow

Source: Csikszentmihalyi (1992: 74).

environment. Csikszentmihalyi's work has involved cross-cultural studies as well as comparative research on surgeons, artists, musicians, basketball players and chess masters. This research has involved innovative techniques of data collection – i.e. the Experience Sampling Method – asking people to stop and note their experiences when they have them – 'right then, right there', rather than trying to recall them later. This has entailed such strategies as attaching electronic tags or pagers to participants and buzzing them to write down their feelings whenever the pager signals, which means eight times each day at random intervals. At the end of the week respondents write up experience diaries as running records of their experiences and thoughts.

Flow focuses on the intentionality of consciousness as a form of self-consciousness which usually results in a loss of self and any sense of a passage of time. Flow may be possible in work, family relationships and tourism, but particularly within sport and forms of leisure. These involve challenging activities, skill, merging of action and awareness, clear goals and feedback, the possibility of control, lack of self-consciousness and the transformation of time. Csikszentmihalyi's diagram helps us to understand the psychological make-up and pressure on players when playing sports. Some individuals are capable of staying in the 'zone' and 'delivering', to use terms favoured by coaches and personal trainers, whereas others become too anxious and 'choke or bottle it' by failing to live up to performance expectations. One's potential for achieving flow may also be dependent upon or constrained by others. Take, for example, the different experiences available when comparing participation in individual rather than team sports. Many leisure writers have stressed the importance of playing and experiencing sport and leisure in relationships with others. Some individuals may prefer solo climbing or competitive climbing forms, whereas others value shared routes and team expeditions. But in both cases, sporting or leisure experiences may be shared with others, in planning and shared travel as well as in recall after individual or collective sporting experiences are over. Much pleasure can be gained from sharing stories and experiences pre- and post-sporting, leisure and tourist experiences. Anticipation and recall of leisure experiences are as valuable to mental health as the immediate sporting and leisure experiences themselves. Many of these characteristics of flow are present in the American leisure studies academic Robert Stebbins' view of serious leisure, which will be explored in Chapter 8.

Csikszentmihalyi argues that certain conditions are conducive to flow experiences and these include:

4.6 Conditions for flow experiences

Goals	Individual has a clear sense of purpose, usually immediate feedback both for short- and long-term goals
Concentration on the task in hand	'Focused' consciousness or 'in the zone', ability to banish irrelevant thoughts, dismiss anxieties
Paradox of control	Person experiences a sense of control, of minimizing risk in extreme activities and sports
Loss of self consciousness	This 'does not mean a loss of the self, and certainly not a loss of consciousness, but rather only a loss of consciousness of the self (1992: 64) i.e. the individual 'loses' him- or herself in some activity.
Transformation of individual's experience	Time passes more quickly that in ordinary life; time 'flies' by when having fun; time 'drags' when involved in toil.

4.7 Generating flow: What sorts of activities are likely to produce flow?

Rank the following activities and contexts in terms of their potential for generating flow consciousness in the individual (i.e. LOW/MEDIUM/HIGH):

- Playing the piano in a music competition

- Running a PB (personal best) time in a half marathon race

- Having a relaxing drink with friends in a pub

- Entering an Orienteering event

- Working hard as a volunteer at a charity jumble sale

- Playing a round of golf

- Taking the dog for a walk last thing at night
- Reading a favourite novel in bed
- Playing a play-station game
- Playing a game of cards – Snap, for example, or a hand of bridge
- Strolling by the seaside on holiday
- Performing a leading part in a local pantomime or amateur dramatics production
- Playing a game of chess

What kinds of leisure activities generate 'flow' in your experience?

Csikszentmihalyi (1992: 251–252) suggests that individuals often develop individual routines and rituals to keep boredom at bay (e.g. whistling, doodling, humming, twiddling their hair, finger tapping, etc.).These he defines as 'micro-flow' experiences whereas 'macro-flow' activities generate more positive feelings of self-enhancement and engagement in the individual.

PLAY IN CHILDHOOD

As suggested in Chapter 1, Roger Ingham has demanded that traditional psycho-logical work on leisure should move away from behaviourism. Behaviourist approaches have usually focused on natural scientific and experimental method and particularly on the role of conditioning – that is, positive and negative rein-forcements that strengthen behaviours. Stated simply, humans are no more than animals (the usual subjects for learning and conditioning experiments), and they too can be conditioned into learned behaviour, just as rats can be taught to run through complex mazes, pigeons to pick out square nuts from an assembly line producing hexagonal ones and dogs to learn to obey their owners' commands.

Behaviourist perspectives exert their most powerful influence over popular mainstream books or manuals on parenting and child care, but they also dominate the practice of the courts and penal system in dealing with criminal and deviant behaviours. To take one example, the task (or trauma as Freud would have it) of toilet training is usually held to be best achieved with the help of a behaviourist strategy or regime which positively rewards children for appropriate behaviours. Poor parenting of children, it is widely argued, stems from inconsistent, indulgent or punitive responses. All these are deemed inap-propriate. 'Smacking' children and physical and verbal abuse often stem from the individual parent's own experience of childhood. Rather than ordering children to 'go and play outside' or 'just play quietly' or 'watch the DVD for half an hour', parents are encouraged to play with the children and positively praise the children for remaining task based, for finishing the game, jigsaw, painting or for not hitting siblings or sharing spaces and toys.

The 'common sense' of parenting has been reproduced in research into children's play patterns by Edward Deci and Richard Ryan (1985). Research in which the children were rewarded with sweets for appropriate play behaviours demonstrated the importance of rewards in children's play. Interestingly, once rewards were withdrawn the children changed their play patterns. Both Deci and Ryan (Deci and Ryan, 2002; Ryan, 2012) have written extensively about the fragility of relying solely upon tangible rewards such as prizes, money and grading, which may be demotivating for others and inadequate to generate appropriate effort. Much research by Bandura (1971a, 1971b, 1986) into social efficacy has focused upon the importance of internal drivers to behaviour such as the quest for autonomy, competency and mastery of task and social relatedness to secure long-term commitments and enjoyment among children. Other research into sport performance has drawn a clear distinction between ego involvement and task-based involvement in sport and physical education. The task-based child is intrinsically motivated by the task of developing skill and mastery of the sport and believes increased performance is due to hard work, practice and training. By way of contrast, individuals who are ego-involved are more concerned with competition and beating others, and therefore success is mainly due to natural ability. Drop out and 'burn out' amongst athletes are more prevalent amongst ego-involved than task-involved athletes. Task-involved athletes are more motivated, determined and are committed to skill development and self-expression in sport, whereas those focused upon winning are easily de-motivated or a-motivated and apathetic when results do not go their way. They are less likely to be resilient and 'bounce' back in adverse circumstances. Some individuals just may not be interested in competitive sporting forms as they become sites for sexual and racial bullying.

4.8 Lessons in the gym

Think back to when you were at secondary school in Physical Education lessons. How did the teacher encourage involvement and participation in 'games' and sports?

Were your classes streamed in any way – by size, by athletic ability, by gender or by race/ethnicity?

In the teacher's opinion were particular students seen as 'gifted and talented'?

There are one or two literary examples which highlight how people can be put off sport and, as a consequence, drop out of it as soon as possible. *A Kestrel for a Knave*, Barry Hines' novel about a 15-year-old boy, Billy Casper, at a working-class secondary school in South Yorkshire captures the tensions and the processes nicely. Mr Sugden, the games teacher, immaculately and enthusiastically kitted out in purple tracksuit, bedecked with badges and qualifications, discovers Billy in the changing room; he is not ready for the games period. As usual, Billy has turned up at school with no PE kit, and withers under the teacher's furious stare.

Billy Casper is then made to wear a huge pair of spare blue shorts and is the last person to be chosen when Mr Sugden divides the boys into two teams. Mr Sugden proceeds to pick the best players for one side, allows them to play downhill, and himself acts as referee, commentator and player. He actually retakes the penalty when he misses the first time. Unfortunately, Billy, who is forced to play in goal, is caught swinging from the crossbar: he ends up missing his dinner, but not before letting in the deciding goal so that Mr Sugden's team wins. To round off a cold, degrading, miserable experience Billy is duly punished for not taking a shower, is given a cold one and runs off home to feed his pet kestrel (Kes) in his wet clothes, as he forgot to bring a towel.

There have been acrimonious debates about the nature of sport and the specific role of teachers and coaches in shaping all children's experiences of sport. Previous research has often worked within a pro-feminist perspective (Bramham, 2003), acknowledging growing demands to explore 'the crisis in hegemonic masculinity'. Mac an Ghaill (1996) stresses *that schools do not produce masculinities in a direct, overly deterministic way, but that the construction of students' identities is an active process of negotiation, rejection, acceptance and ambivalence* (1996: 394). Researchers must listen to the girls' and boys' accounts of their experiences of physical education and sport. This is just the first step towards an understanding of how masculine and feminine identities, physicality and power find expression in sport, physical education and schooling.

In the late 1980s Roger Ingham's (1986, 1987) overview of leisure studies in the UK demanded that research must draw upon the social psychology of Rom Harré and Erving Goffman to explain leisure behaviour or, more accurately, human actions. Social psychology should focus on concepts that provided insight into *meaning* and *order* for leisure participants. We should start treating individuals as social agents rather than as victims (of genetic codes, personality types or behavioural conditioning). Throughout childhood and adulthood individuals follow social rules, acting out social roles rather than being physically conditioned into behavioural patterns by batteries of rewards and punishments. This creative capacity of individuals is one defining characteristic of the non-serious play world of children. It is not just the case that children and adults take on roles, but they also make them and to a degree construct their own social order.

Children come to learn through play when a situation is serious and when it is not. Play breaks down when other children fail to play properly and 'spoil the game'. The cheat is tolerated, but the spoilsport who refuses to recognize agreed rules lies beyond the pale. Small children gradually learn to accept rules in play although, energized by temper tantrums, many find it very hard when they lose, demanding 'just one more go' or exerting intense pressure on adult players 'not to be mean' and to let them win.

As Haywood et al. (1995: 12–26) have suggested, both Dutch historian Johan Huizinga and French intellectual Roger Caillois have contributed a great deal to our understanding of both play and leisure. Both Huizinga and Caillois see the defining qualities of play as free, self-contained and regulated or rule governed. This may be highly formalized and codified (e.g. sport) or informal (e.g. a child's game). Play is limited in time and space and it often includes an element of 'make believe' or secretiveness, as well as escapism. The outcome of play is uncertain, creating a pleasurable tension – hence a one-sided match is uninteresting. Early psychological accounts saw play as neutral and instinctual but in more recent times, influenced by the work of Jean Piaget, developmental psychologists have claimed that learning of rules and their balance fosters creativity. Ellis (1973) has argued that play represents a human need for stimulation. Psychological health and well-being depend on the individual's need periodically to experience heightened levels of arousal. Echoing Csikszentmihalyi's work, Ellis has suggested that individuals must find psychological states of optimum arousal, striking a balance between boredom and over-stimulation.

Roberts and Sutton-Smith (1971) have argued that playing games helps socialize children into the prevailing values, roles, practices, beliefs and conventions of normal society. Consequently, games serve two main functions. First, they defuse the conflicts that inevitably arise between children and their parents as they are disciplined to conform to the adult world. Secondly, the games children play encourage enculturation as they endorse acceptance of both rule-governed behaviour and also exemplify the traditional values that society holds to be important. So, a family that plays together stays together. According to this mode of explanation, games of chance will predominate in pre-literate societies which believe in superstition and rely on fate. Games of vertigo will predominate in societies wherein overcoming harsh environmental conditions is crucial for physical survival. Games of skill and competition will predominate in societies with developed economies, which are based formally on equality of opportunity.

In part following Freud, Caillois has explored the psycho-social functions of play for the child (and clearly we should also be interested in how adults play as adults). Caillois himself has suggested that play has an important functional role in providing a means of compensation or sublimation for attitudes and activities which cannot find an expression elsewhere in social life; games are a cathartic release from everyday life.

Understanding children's play and games Haywood et al. (1995: 17) have neatly summarized Caillois' main assumptions:

- *All play* manifests itself in the form of games. Games are of four major types, which he calls competitions (agon); chance (alea); make-believe (mimicry); and disequilibrium (vertigo). Ways of playing games may be located on a continuum from simple to complex, which he calls childlike (paidia) to structured (ludus).

- In games, players *express themselves* in ways not readily available to them in other aspects of life.

- Games may be *corrupted* if the qualities they require are taken to excess; this may result in cheating in sports, e.g. ball-tampering in cricket; drug taking in cycling and athletics.

- The nature of games prevalent in a society, or its subcultures, is a powerful indicator of *dominant* values in society.

4.9 Caillois' classification of games

	AGON (competition)	ALEA (chance)	MIMICRY (simulation)	ILNX (vertigo)
PADIA (simple) (tumult agitation)	unregulated contests, wrestling, athletics	counting out rhymes, heads or tails, patience, solitaire	fancy dress, dressing up, games of illusion, masks, disguises, charades	'whirling/ swinging fairground rides, water lumes, dancing (some forms)
LUDUS (complex) (control, skill)	boxing, fencing, snooker, football, chess	lotteries, football pools, roulette	Theatre, opera, drama, spectacles in general	skiing, sky diving, mountain climbing, wind-surfing

Competition is regulated to foster equality which may not be available elsewhere in life. Hence, sports are always designated as 'equal playing fields' where class, ethnicity and 'race', sexuality, religion, and so on, do not matter. Games of chance are equal in the sense of odds reflecting the chances of winning. Mimicry and make believe, can compensate for the disappointment of reality. Vertigo can supply stimulation. Thus activities provide a bulwark for social order. Public spaces can be set aside by policy makers for children and adults alike to play outside.

4.10 A child's right to play

The UN Convention on the Rights of the Child includes a right to leisure, play and participation. Brian Simpson (2005) traces their possible expression

(Continued)

(Continued)

in two recent documents – one by the Children's Play Council (2004) and the other one is the DCMS Review, *Serious about Play* (2004). However, adults often define children's play as anti-social behaviour and, for example, demand that skateboarding in cities should be contained, regulated and subject to adult supervision, with safety as a paramount concern. Inspired by the work of Bach (1993), Simpson argues that children's play generates spontaneous informal sporting-like activities and children should have a legal right to flexible risk-taking spaces and be actively involved in deciding access, design and location. Drawing on Flusty (2000), he argues that city spaces are increasingly commodified, privatized and corporatized, yet those engaged in play in these spaces – buskers, skaters, and street theatre artists, for example – refuse to disappear from the urban scene.

But as Caillois' table (see Box 4.9) suggests, playing games does not solely take place in leisure but also finds expression in adult lives and in institutional forms. This has led exponents of social theories such as figurational sociology to think of games, and sport in particular, as a fertile metaphor to explain nature and processes constitutive of social networks and relations. However, we shall return to figurational sociology and its approach to sport and the 'civilizing process' later. Eric Berne (1967) an American psychologist, has provided the clearest approach to strengthening the view that adults play games. Popularizing Freud, Berne suggested each individual personality is made up of three elements – the child, the adult and the parent. The child is made up of all the feelings, emotions and behaviours one has as a child, the parent is the voice of parents and authority while by way of contrast the adult represents a rational grown up making one's way in the world. Berne introduced transactional analysis which studied the conversations, encounters and interactions between any two individuals, A and B. If A and B are adults one should expect Adult–Adult interactions and take the ensuing conversations at face value. However, Berne introduced the possibility of different kinds of exchanges or 'games' so that A may routinely emphasize the parent side of his personality when talking to his wife or partner B, treating her not as an adult but as a child. So it becomes more like a Parent–Child exchange. Partner B may be happy with or at least go along with this imposed child-like subordinate status (i.e. Child–Parent exchange) so that husband A always drives the car, takes financial decisions, decides where to go on holiday or what to watch on television, while B acquiesces as a supportive wife. But rather than acting as a subservient child-like adult and playing the traditional husband–wife game, B may subversively fight back, as witnessed in the following exchange:

Husband A, getting dressed up ready to go out to attend a formal dinner, asks wife, B, 'Darling, where's my blue tie?'

Wife B replies, 'Where you last left it.'

This first round or transaction can turn into the 'complaining husband' game.

> A continues, 'You just never help me, do you? Why not try for once? I have been out working all day! You are just like your mother – no bloody use to anyone.'

The second round could easily develop into the 'mother-in-law' game,

> B replies angrily, 'Why don't you leave my mother out of this. You've never liked her! If you can't say anything nice, just don't say anything at all!'

So Berne would not be surprised when people admit that it's all 'only a joke', 'I was only teasing', 'I just wanted to see how you would react', 'I was just winding you up' indicating that some people are well aware of the nature of playing games with others.

In her cartoons, the feminist Jackie Fleming suggests that women should not have to be taken for granted as traditional wives who are meant to be at their husband's beck and call or routinely treated like children:

> Husband, arriving home from work, 'Where's my dinner?'

> Wife, sitting down, reading a book at the table, 'It must be around somewhere, dear. Where did you last see it?'

THE 'NEW' SOCIAL PSYCHOLOGY OF LEISURE

When explaining the 'new' social psychology, Roger Ingham (1990) has mapped out what he terms the *'role-rule model'* or *'ethogenic'* approach, both of which most sociologists would feel more comfortable depicting as symbolic interactionism. For Ingham's part he cites Nigel Armistead's (1974) *Reconstructing Social Psychology* and Rom Harré and Paul Secord's (1976) *Explanation in Social Behaviour* as two key critical and influential texts. The implications of this psychology are, once again, that individuals do not have determined personalities and behaviours, but rather construct their own personal and social identities. For Roger Ingham (1989) the move away from behaviourist psychological approaches can best be achieved by synthesizing the playing games metaphor for social life with Erving Goffman's dramaturgical approach (using theatrical metaphors to interpret social life) to making sense of social interactions. During the 1970s and 80s Goffman's micro-sociology was a popular way of studying social interaction. His influential book, *The Presentation of Self in Everyday Life* (1971a) introduced a variety of interlinked and distinctive concepts which suggested that individuals did not have integrated personalities but rather presented different 'selves' when in the presence of others. Just as actors in the theatre must learn the script, immerse themselves in the character they are playing and move about the stage as directed, so people in their ordinary everyday lives develop, and routinely deploy, similar dramaturgical skills. Social life becomes reframed as a performance in front of others – the audience that monitors and respond to the individual's presentation of self – for example, in the role of a student, girlfriend, employee or cricketing enthusiast. Roger Ingham has offered a long list of key concepts for leisure researchers and they include: roles and choices, style, biography, monitoring, rehearsal, role distance, episodes, props, scripts, front and back regions, intelligibility, accountability and justifiability, rule structures and breakdowns in social order. There is insufficient space to map them all out here but it will be useful to work through one leisure example.

4.11 Notes on becoming a cricketer

Here is a glossary of the key concepts from Roger Ingham's 'new' social psychology; your challenge is to use any or all of them to make sense of the cricketing issues and incidents suggested below.

- **Roles and choices:** social roles are reciprocated interactions; to be a cricket player one needs other supporting roles, e.g. teammates, opponents, umpires, and so on.

- **Style:** whatever role the cricket enthusiast adopts, one can bring to it one's own distinctive style – there are different styles of play, bodily demeanour and 'attitude'.

- **Biography:** associated with roles are biographies – those bits of past life (real or invented) that support and reinforce one's identity.

- **Monitoring:** all performances are constantly monitored both by one's self and by colleagues; performances when playing cricket provide clear indicators of success and failure within roles.

- **Rehearsal:** sometimes referred to as 'mirror work' where performances are practised and coached.

- **Role distance:** one mustn't become so involved in one role so that it takes over the individual's whole identity (especially in leisure); it is, after all, 'only a game of cricket'.

- **Episodes:** social interactions have discrete time demarcations – 'there is a time and place for everything'.

- **Props:** role performances in sport are usually heavily dependent on props and locations; brand names and sponsorship abound in all sports.

- **Scripts:** all episodes are characterized by suitable and unsuitable topics of conversation and behaviour.

- **Front and back regions:** this refers to on or off stage behaviour, between actual performance of a role and actions used to prepare, rehearse or recover a performance.
- **Intelligibility:** we need to be able to explain our actions to others.
- **Accountability and justifiability:** one needs to be able to justify one's actions with reference to moral codes.
- **Rule structures:** most social interactions are governed by legal, moral and taken-for-granted rule structures; sport is uniquely codified and one can rely on umpires to interpret and enforce the rule book.
- **Breakdowns in social order:** social worlds are regulated by systems of roles and rules; actions taking place within these social contexts acquire meaning and individual identities are created and maintained.

Examples: What's going on here?

- 'Sledging', i.e. the verbal abuse of batsmen by the fielding side, is now deemed a normal sporting strategy and umpires usually fail to intervene. West Indian bowlers stereotypically bowl fast and aggressively, so choosing not to wear a cricket helmet when batting can be seen as an indicator of one's masculinity in the face of intimidating bowling (see Carrington, 2011).
- Pavilions, kit, etc., often suffer damage and vandalism when batsmen feel that they have been unfairly given out; players often use racist, misogynous and homophobic language in the 'locker room'.
- Conversation topics such as one's own sexuality, worries at work, discussion of one's favourite poet, fears about imminent divorce or symptoms of a long-term illness are unwelcome on the square (and perhaps later in the pavilion?).
- Captains of international cricket teams have been found guilty of 'throwing matches' or 'spot fixing' for a betting syndicate and subsequently have been banned from playing, disgraced and 'lost face'.
- Throwing at the batsmen with the aim of injuring the player is seen as unacceptable; tampering with the ball or taking performance-enhancing drugs in cricket is seen as cheating.
- The use of video technology to review decisions has raised important questions about the reliability of umpires' decision-making.

CONCLUSION

This chapter has provided an introduction to the psychology of leisure. As the discipline has developed historically, psychology has drawn unevenly on natural scientific methods and more recently on social science techniques of data collection in order to explain (and possibly predict) why human beings act as they do. Over the decades, schools of psychological theory and research traditions have held sway. The chapter has touched upon behaviourism, psychoanalytic perspectives, existential psychology and the 'new' social psychology of leisure. Given the structure of the book with its emphasis on the person's life cycle, the primary focus here has been on play, childhood and the construction of gendered identities.

5

GROWING UP AND GETTING OUT

THIS CHAPTER

- Analyses moral panics and adult fear of 'youth'
- Outlines major social theories in relation to mass media, normality and deviance
- Introduces key concepts of generational analysis and of generational time or epoch
- Explains key ideas in relation to feminism, black cultural studies and queer theory in respect of understanding youth and youth subcultures.

MORAL PANICS AND THE GENERATIONAL FEAR OF YOUTH

A good point at which to begin making sense of young people and leisure is to revisit the ideas of Stanley Cohen, writing in the early 1970s, and in particular his concepts of moral panics and folk devils. Drawing on the work of American symbolic interactionists and in particular on labelling perspectives on deviance, he highlighted the role of mass media in defining and stigmatizing categories of youth. The focus of academic attention was less on the behaviour of young people themselves but rather upon the responses of parents and authority figures towards young people. In so doing, there was evidence of an orchestration of moral outrage and social reaction against troublesome and disorderly youth. At that time newspapers and television journalists were key agents, or moral entrepreneurs, in agenda setting and framing explanations of youth behaviour. In an interesting and now sadly neglected book, *Law and Order News*, Steve Chibnall (1977) argued that Britain in the late 1960s and

70s witnessed the creation of a 'violent society' wherein youthful rebellion was fused with growing fears about crime and industrial disorder. Chibnall interviewed crime reporters and characterized core values which informed their view and understanding of crime and society.

5.1 Law and order news

Steve Chibnall's *Law and Order News* (1977) argued that 'newsworthy' crime stories were driven by six key values.

- **Dramatization** – making a crisis out of a drama.

- **Titillation** – teasing the reader with the darker side of leisure.

- **Sensationalization** – 'hyping', 'sexing up' salacious aspects of stories.

- **Personalization** – when a social phenomenon is identified with a specific (vilified) individual. For example, in the mid-1980s the famous miners' strike in England was strongly associated with the leader of the National Union of Mineworkers, Arthur Scargill. More recently, global terrorism was reframed as a battle between the US President and the al-Qaeda leader Osama bin Laden.

- **Novelty** – 'new' angles are worked and reworked on 'old' stories (e.g. sightings of Elvis Presley, of the Loch Ness monster or of Madeleine McCann).

- **Simplification** – complex issues, e.g. drugs, street robberies, AIDS, paedophilia, banking fraud, etc., can be explained away as the work of a single 'bad apple'. For instance, Sir Jimmy Savile was depicted as a cunning and evil predator on young people, whereas subsequent revelations suggest that TV personalities in the past were comfortable about initiating sex with juveniles – male and female.

These key values have shaped the writing and the rewriting of news stories – of deviance or the sudden death of a celebrity figure. In such instances journalists use a standard recipe for framing and reworking stories. See, for example, the death and legacy of Princess Diana, Gary Speed or of Amy Winehouse ... or for that matter, any other youthful media personality, male or female who dies suddenly, perhaps by their own hand. What exactly happened? Were they mentally depressed or struggling with failing relationships or careers? Were alcohol and drugs involved? If not, why not? Who were the witnesses and key stakeholders at the time? What do other celebrities say or 'tweet' about the tragedy? How have television, publishing media, film and 'the establishment' dealt with sudden death? And so forth?

In a later work, Stanley Cohen and Jock Young (1981) mapped out complex and selective processes as journalists in the mass media manufacture 'news' and newsworthy stories. News narratives simplify, trivialize, personalize and dramatize so that stories become morality tales where the good are rewarded, the weak are saved and evil is duly exposed and punished. This missionary narrative is most clearly expressed in how the media frame and capture drug use, particularly among young people. Jock Young (1974) argues that mass media present a consensual view of society, a shared view of reality which supports the status quo, but one which carries a twin and contradictory system of values – *formal* work values and *subterranean* leisure values. Formal values are related to modern employment and industry and this can spill over so that one works hard to realize oneself in leisure. But as Tony Blackshaw (2010) argues, leisure also offers a critical space in which individuals can exercise their 'leisure imaginations'. C. Wright Mills (1970) has captured this with a shrewd metaphor of people selling their souls to capitalism during the working week and buying back pieces of themselves at the weekend through relaxation and leisure. Individuals must produce in order to consume and consume in order to produce. Hedonism is closely tied to a compelling ethos of hard work, industry and productivity, that is, 'working hard and playing hard'. Pleasure can therefore only be purchased legitimately through the credit card of work and work provides the income for people to explore leisure choices.

As we have seen in Chapter 3, leisure and pleasure must be earned; they are a reward for working hard. So 'normal' people work hard, live in happy nuclear families, belong to close-knit communities and have a mundane or relaxed concept of religious experience. Extremists are labelled as radical Muslims, Jehovah's Witnesses, feminists, gays, anarchists or communists. Mainstream ideologies address the individual as just an ordinary subject getting on with his/her life in a taken-for-granted world of 'common sense'. These ideologies speak to the 'hard-working families' so beloved by contemporary politicians. Within that message normality is straightforwardly equated with middle-class values, whiteness and masculinity. Activities such as drug taking subvert both the dominant work ethic and labour productivity; for example, people in the 1960s were encouraged to 'drop out', to experiment and 'turn on' with drugs such as cannabis and 'mind-expanding' drugs such as LSD, which were superseded in the 1970s and 80s by 'rave' drugs such as ecstasy, amphetamines and speed. From the media's consensual point of view, such drug taking is morally wrong, especially amongst the workless such as students, black minorities, the unemployed and welfare dependents in inner-city neighbourhoods. Indeed, drug use becomes racialized and drugs problems and policy initiatives centre on largely 'black' inner cities, while turning a blind eye to high levels of alcohol abuse, tobacco and prescription addictions, among other problems in society. Vulnerable groups may drift into soft drug use, but this will inevitably lead to hard drug use and state welfare and drug dependency. From the mass media's standpoint no one chooses to take drugs, to be a drug user in a recreation or leisure context, so individuals must have been tricked or coerced into using drugs by 'drug pushers'. The model for drug use clearly distinguishes between the 'drug user' and the 'drug pusher', although Young's research in Notting Hill (1974) argued that people usually moved easily between the two roles – supplying drugs to networks of friends when they had supplies and buying from others when they did not. From the media's standpoint, drug taking must be deviant, unhealthy and unpleasurable. By the same token, sex leads to sexually transmitted diseases (STDs) such as chlamydia, gonorrhoea and syphilis, LSD to madness and paranoia, whereas cannabis or 'pot' leads to dependency and, further down the line, inexorably to heroin addiction. Consequently, there has been much political debate and media concern during the late twentieth and early twenty-first centuries when successive UK Labour Home Secretaries, Jack Straw, David Blunkett and Charles Clarke, approved a change in the designation of particular drugs, for example when cannabis was reclassified from a Class B drug to a Class C drug. Possession of cannabis for personal use was no longer seen by police as an arrestable offence as front-line officers and press officers acknowledged that drug use and abuse was a complex problem and police priorities must lie elsewhere. Nevertheless, the mediatized version of the world of drugs is populated by four types of people: (1) the *sick* (who can't help it); (2) the *innocent* (who are corrupted); (3) the *wicked* (who are corrupt); and (4) the *normals* (who must be praised and rewarded). From this moral standpoint, the media prescribe a clear policy on what must be done to solve the 'problem', 'crisis' or 'epidemic'. What makes Young's argument especially interesting is that he suggests that, for complex occupational reasons, police are susceptible to media stereotypes and police arrests and policy interventions 'amplify' the drugs problem. Policing reduces supplies of drugs and such actions lead to a 'self-fulfilling prophecy' in that criminal gangs, happy to meet the shortfall, gradually move in to sell both soft and hard drugs in local communities.

So, one major unintended consequence of police actions and interventions can be to generate or at least contribute to the very crime waves special patrols have been constituted to eradicate. There is madness in the method. The relationship between primary deviance and secondary deviance (i.e. between undetected and often normalized deviant behaviour and that which appears in official crime statistics and crime surveys) is a complicated field much debated by politicians, policy makers and academics alike. Some writers demand a stance of 'radical non-intervention' in policy (see Schur, 1973), suggesting that deviance is best left alone as its cure is often more damaging that its cause. So, troublesome youths become even more damaged by spells of incarceration in youth jails, subsequent release and unemployment, and become transformed into hardened criminals, or, at least, are much more likely to commit further crimes. Even the language used to describe troublesome youth must be deployed with due care and attention. Some commentators suggest the word 'gang' should not be used to describe the behaviour of anti-social youth as it serves to sour adult–youth relations further and cloud most appropriate interventions to help juvenile delinquents. Indeed, research found that young people, although deep in trouble with law and order agencies, rejected the word 'gang' as it signified a level of criminality that they felt did not accurately describe their own behaviour. For some, decriminalization is a realistic policy demand as intervention perversely only serves to amplify deviant behaviour and criminality.

As a result (see Figure 5.1), young people provide a potentially rich reservoir of potential stories for media to tell. Philip Abrams (1982) has argued that historical sociology has approached youth through two major lines of inquiry which he has framed as the *barbarian question* and the *Dracula question*. The barbarian question asks how savage infants become 'normalized', socialized into the culture of society. Secondly, the Dracula question asks how children become deviants. Parental fears of the next generation allude to both barbarian and Dracula questions and, when things go wrong, parents are keen to lay the blame at someone's door.

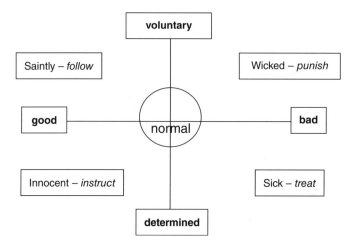

Figure 5.1   Drugs and the mass media

As Chas Critcher (2003) has argued, moral panics often rub against fault lines of class, race, gender and generation. In the 1960s youths were the devils themselves, as mods and rockers, hippies, punks and football hooligans. By the 1990s the media's gaze had refocused on youth as victims of devils in relation to alcopop sales, child abuse and the predatory behaviour of paedophiles. More recently, mass media have reasserted their proclivity to define young people as the problem.

There is, apparently, a new generation of young 'folk devils' who live unhealthy lifestyles – they eat fast foods, they drink too much alcohol, they smoke, they take recreational drugs, they have unprotected sex, and stay glued to television, the Internet and video games. Consequently, young people are often accused of slipping into a life of excess and this appears at an increasingly younger age, as newspapers bemoan the fact that 9–12 year olds have started to adopt consumption patterns that were previously attributed to and associated with 'teenagers', while, in their turn, 'tweenies' are now mini-adults with mobile phones, bank accounts and a penchant for shopping. However, when it comes to adopting healthy adult lifestyles, young people resist physical activity such as playing sport, working out through fitness and exercise regimes, cycling to school or even taking part in any kind of outdoor recreational activities and adventure, which are generally seen as 'boring'. Health educationalists are understandably pessimistic about the prospects for this cohort of teenagers, presently sustained by poor diets, having weak cooking skills, choosing passive leisure interests and exhibiting physical exercise patterns which are inadequate to secure any long-term health benefits.

Mass media have a crucial role in setting political agendas that define youth behaviour as throwing up (metaphorically and literally) problems that demand and even 'cry out' for policy solutions. Moral panics emerge among older generations when deeply held core values are threatened. There is immediacy to each social issue that demands attention.

5.2 A brief history of moral panics

Here are some examples of 'moral panics' that have worried adults and troubled mass media over the years.

What core values are threatened in each case?

What policy responses or solutions were suggested to deal with the problem?

- **1950s** Rock and Roll dancing ('jiving') and damage to cinemas during the showing of films featuring rock 'n' roll singers; Teddy boys and Saturday night disorder

- **1960s** Easter-time fights between teenage gangs of 'Mods' and 'Rockers' at Brighton and other seaside resorts

- **1970s** Peace Movement/Flower Power protests; hippie music and 'alternative/travelling' lifestyles

- **1980s** Crowd violence at football matches; football hooliganism; racism and 'race riots' in deprived inner cities

- **1990s** 'Clubbing': city-centre and street-corner 'binge' drinking; 'ecstasy' and recreational drug use; alcopops and youth street life

- **2000s** Internet pornography; gun crime, shooting and gang culture; child obesity and 'poor' eating habits

- **2010s** Child sexual abuse, 'grooming' and paedophilia

Heated debates about underage alcohol abuse among teenagers and 'binge drinking' among young adults, particularly students, provide clear examples of contemporary media outrage, exactly at a time when the government in the UK has liberalized licensing laws. It seems that all the lessons from nation states elsewhere, such as Ireland, are not so much ignored but rather are cast as myopic or irrelevant. The real costs and benefits in health and public disorder of 24-hour licensing seem distorted or suppressed by powerful interests from the brewing and entertainment industries, eagerly supported by local chambers of commerce, local government and even police authorities. The government knows best in so far as it can point to the need to liberalize drinking times and simultaneously showcase legislative measures to deal with particular problems should they arise. Consequently, in 2003 the 'New' Labour government introduced Anti-Social Behaviour Orders (ASBOs) to give police powers to disperse youth groups and deal with troublesome behaviours in residential neighbourhoods, inner-city communities and city centres. Certain public spaces can be designated alcohol-free zones and there are neighbourhood wardens and community support police to administer on the spot fines to miscreants. These policy issues are complex and policy outcomes can often fly in the face of common sense and media-orchestrated panic. Certainly, with the introduction of new UK licensing laws, many city-centre areas have surprisingly witnessed a decrease in arrests, violence and disorder, but other districts have experienced a distinct rise in night-time A & E hospital admissions. Public health professionals lobby the government and supermarkets to introduce a minimum cost threshold for a single unit of alcohol to discourage alcohol consumption, but the present coalition UK government has resisted taking this measure.

5.3 Alcohol and young people

What does 'drinking sensibly' mean to you?

What measure constitutes a 'unit of alcohol'?

What are the recommended weekly levels of alcohol consumption for adult men and for women?

What do health professionals define as 'binge drinking'?

How much is alcohol estimated to cost the National Health Service in any year?

What percentage of UK Accident and Emergency patients are there because of alcohol-related difficulties incurred over the weekend?

By the age of 16 what proportion of teenagers have three or more binge drinking sessions per month?

How many units of alcohol are older people (say, those over 60 years of age) recommended to drink in an average week?

As one would expect, social scientists and leisure scholars have cast a critical light over the claims of both government and mass media about the changing nature of youth, physical activity and their leisure lifestyles. To particularize this expectation, first, one would expect social scientific research, at the very least, to be able to contextualize the issues and moral panics that absorb the mass media, and to provide historical commentary and social analysis of contemporary youth and leisure networks. Second, one would expect some detailed empirical research and data in order to ground generalized claims about modern youth leisure lifestyles and highlight the diversity of youth experiences and identities in what postmodernists claim as these 'new times'. Third, one expects some semblance of value freedom to the extent of recognizing the need to engage with the diversity of ideological traditions and policy positions in relation to youth policy and practices.

Thus, to take a leading example of a writer who embraces these three objectives, through detailed historical analysis of newspapers, Geoffrey Pearson's book *Hooligan* (1983) examined the social construction of the 'law and order' myth. In Pearson's view, sustained debates about young people and 'law and order' reflect tensions that exist and persist between generations. Throughout the nineteenth and twentieth centuries, there were recurrent waves of nostalgia breaking every thirty years or so, as older generations voiced respectable concerns about the waywardness of next or new generations. Thinking about youth has historically been problem-centred and has subsequently focused on youth as a challenge for policy, demanding adequate education, management and control. Class relations were central to Pearson's overview, as middle-class media, especially newspapers, created myths about social cohesion and law and order in past communities and past times, while roundly denouncing contemporary working-class youth as 'hooligans'.

Particular fear and despair has always centred on the urban street life of young men and their apparent membership of gangs – especially in relation to violence, drug abuse and criminality. Girls have been defined as presenting less of a problem in relation to law and order. Troubles with girls have historically been less visible, confined to the private rather than the public sphere; for example, moral panics have related to teenage pregnancies and eating disorders. Pearson humorously and lucidly reconstructs the history of respectable fears about hooligans down the ages. He discovered a remarkably continuity – a history of crime and violence, of class struggle and of nostalgia, with each generation successively bemoaning the decline of 'the British-way-of-life'. As each older generation was fearfully criticizing its affluent, violent and barbarian youth, it looked back some twenty or thirty years to the tranquil times of 'law and order', when respect for the family maintained the traditional way of life. Yet each generation suffered 'law-and-order' crises: of the Teddy boys of the 1950s, the Edwardian hooligans of the early 1900s, the young garrotters in the 1860s, the artful Chartist dodgers and unruly apprentices of the nineteenth century, and so on. The demand for 'law-and-order' and 'short sharp shocks' to be administered to the young were signs of weakness as they were ample testimony to the failure of society to induce consent in the next generation, especially during the transition from school to work and employment. Pearson suggests that moral panics are generated to resist democratic movements in industrial society – for instance, Chartism in the 1840s, the Reform Bill in the 1860s, 'socialist agitation' in the 1890s, and so on. He concludes 'The inescapable reality of the social production of the most poor and dispossessed is the material foundation to these hooligan continuities' (Pearson, 1983: 236). In his final chapter Pearson demystifies the nature of crime statistics and points to the historical blindness of the 'law-and-order' myth to what actually happened (which is more terrifying than the myth allows).

YOUTH, GENERATION AND LIFESTYLES

This section explores the concepts of age cohorts and youthfulness, in order to provide an understanding of some aspects of current leisure lifestyles. Each generation grows up in, experiences and makes sense of its own historical setting or context, which, in turn, is shaped by distinctive economic, political, social and cultural formations. Yet, as Pearson (1983) has argued, each generation periodically voices essentially identical fears about its young people. There is a recurring moral panic about youth that amplifies worries about their physical fitness, moral degeneration and a possible social breakdown of 'the British way of life'. Current media anxieties over childhood obesity, fast foods, eating disorders and unhealthy lifestyles are simply the latest chapters in this long history of concern.

It is useful therefore to adopt some kind of historical perspective, as outlined by writers such as Pearson and the late Philip Abrams (1982). To understand present youth leisure lifestyles one needs to explore the changing collective experiences of generational cohorts and how these are expressed over a lifetime. This requires some Durkheimian analysis of the 'conscience collective', that social solidarity which crystallizes at distinctive historical junctures. Durkheim's work (1982) on deviance stresses the functions of social rules and rituals, the effervescence and celebration of shared experience and memories. Peer pressure and shared historical experience are crucial contexts and resources for individuals growing up and growing old together, producing a distinctive 'spirit' or 'zeitgeist' for every age. Each generation inherits both material and cultural resources from the previous generation and in modernity each generation must endeavour to win some cultural space from its parents and from the past.

HYSTERICAL SOCIOLOGY AND HISTORICAL SOCIOLOGY

Hysterical sociology is often one of anxiety, nostalgia and social control. It is part of mainstream social reaction when unsettling changes appear on the horizon. Nevertheless, whether driven by media hysteria or more detached academics, much theorizing has focused upon the predicament of working-class youth and their relationship to wider society and to law and order. One Marxist account of youth relations found its clearest expression in the work of the Centre for Contemporary Cultural Studies at Birmingham University, under the aegis of Stuart Hall in the 1970s (Hall and Jefferson, 1976). A succession of authors sought to make sense of what Bernice Martin (1981) termed the 'expressive' cultural revolution of the 1960s and the spectacular subcultural styles of mods, rockers and hippies in both the UK and USA. Brake (1980) has argued that such research suggests a partial and distorted view of youth, a celebration of masculinity and one to be found primarily within the white English working class. This concentration reflects not only the biographies of male white researchers in the 1970s but the central Marxian 'problematic' of class structuration and working-class resistance to middle-class cultural hegemony.

The doyen of the CCCS, Phil Cohen (1975), argued that youth subcultural styles were not only based in material class conditions but were also a reaction and response to parental cultural styles as well as dominant ideologies. Ostentatiously grounded in leisure, youth subcultures provided 'magical solutions' to the problems and contradictions of growing up in the class-divided society of the 1960s. These solutions were class based, mediated by distinctive commodities, mass entertainment and popular culture. The precise focus of subcultural concern varied with lifestyle, sexual relations, political radicalism, drug use, deviance and criminality. Brake (1980) identified three main strands in 1960s youth culture: the bohemian (those concerned with alternative lifestyles); the delinquent (those organized around identity-giving deviance, such as football hooliganism); and the political (those engaged in political critique and resistance – protesting against the 'poll tax' (in 1990), perhaps, or environmental pollution, or nuclear power or excessive air travel). The subsequent racialization of inner-city 'problem youth' was fully explored and theorized in Hall et al.'s (1978) definitive work on the amplification of black street crime in *Policing the Crisis: Mugging, the State and Law and Order*. This groundbreaking work synthesized discourses about moral panics, labelling perspectives on deviance and demonization, with an empirical case study of media, policing and criminal court outcomes.

Not all were convinced that class relations were central to understanding youth and the experience of adolescence. Class has been problematized further by gender divisions and not least by race and ethnic identity. Other writers developed black cultural studies and radical feminist approaches to understanding youth within the Centre for Contemporary Cultural Studies (see, for example, *Resistance through Rituals* (Hall and Jefferson, 1976) and *The Empire Strikes Back* (CCCS, 1982)).

YOUTH STUDIES: LEARNING TO GROW UP

The problems of growing up male and working class and living under capitalism were probably best explored by Paul Willis in his widely-cited

Learning to Labour (1977). The book focused on white working-class 'lads' and their resistance to the middle-class ideology of education and schooling; in the research this ideology is encoded and symbolized by 'the lobes', or school conformists. The lads who occupied centre stage in the book shared an 'anti-school' culture that rejected schooling, exuded masculinity and embraced a factory-floor culture of aggression, sexism, solidarity and the celebration of hard physical labour power. The lobes were pro-school, were located in higher GCSE streams, valued paper qualifications, careers advice and 'girlie' paper work. The 1980s saw Willis (1988), drawn into the local policy implications of youth unemployment and the 'new vocationalism'. He coined the phrase 'the frozen transitions of youth' to describe the social condition of youth unemployment in Wolverhampton. For Willis the three major institutions of industrial Britain had lost their rationale and direction – family, school and work no longer functioned. These three structures, that traditionally processed the life stages of children from 0 to 5 at home, from 5 to 16 at school and from 16 onwards at work, functioning as an escalator carrying young people to work, to an adult wage and into consumer society, had simply broken down.

In a more positive vein, Willis (1990) articulated ideas about the changing nature of youth and youth studies in *Common Culture*, a book that revisited issues of human agency, culture, class and consumption. Willis' concept of 'grounded aesthetics' heralded a postmodern argument and twist, in that commodities were now not so much functional objects but rather were of symbolic significance. Young people creatively used commodities, as documented in his earlier book about motor bikers (Willis, 1978). Applying Wittgenstein's dictum that meaning is use, young people had diluted and subverted capitalist commodities, thereby producing their own symbolic universe, for example punk rock and street fashion, etc., a much weaker form of class 'resistance' than earlier suggested by the CCCS (see Hall and Jefferson, 1976).

This symbolic creative capacity of younger generations to win cultural space from those older than themselves was the hallmark of Dick Hebdige's (1979) influential analysis of punk style, although his analysis was grounded in the 1970s rather than the 1960s. Spectacular subcultures, in Hebdige's view, fabricated a distinctive style of their own, a form of resistance via bricolage. Mods, Rockers, Hippies, Punks, all managed to knit together specific forms of language, music, dress sense, dance and place to constitute a meaningful whole, a distinctive style. Translated into Anthony Cohen's (1985) cultural anthropology, they had created their own imagined 'symbolic community', mapped out by symbolic boundaries with insiders and outsiders. As Barker (2000: 169) puts it, 'punk was not simply responding to the crisis of British decline manifested in joblessness, poverty and changing moral standards, but *dramatized* it'. Such ambivalence about symbolic boundaries was developed in Hebdige's later work, *Hiding in the Light* (Hebdige, 1988). Teenagers want to be noticed but certainly not recognized or supervised by a parental generation.

MY GENERATION: THE WHO?

One of the central themes of this chapter is to explore the historical context in which generational identities are forged. The generational cohort of post-war 'baby boomers' became teenagers amid the growing affluence and consumerism of the UK in 1960s. In sharp contrast, their parents' formative teenage years had been spent in the 1930s and 40s, in times of austerity, deprivation and poverty. So the 1940s and 50s adult generations developed the political will to lay the institutional foundations of the welfare state for their children. Their social reformist legacy was funded both by social insurance and progressive taxation policies, which resulted in the expansion of educational opportunities, pensions and health care. If the 1940s generation were Aesop's proverbial ants, the 1960s teenager generation embraced the grasshopper lifestyle. If we stretch the metaphor horribly, as we shall see later, the grasshopper teenagers of the 1960s became parents in their turn and produced a 1980s and 1990s youth generation of butterflies, who have to survive the risks of a more precarious environment.

Much ink has been spilt about the 1960s, but most writers agree that the times were not so much revolutionary as assuredly radical – they saw the emergence of student power, shifting sexual and racial power relations and, not least, media and cultural revolutions around music and consumption. For the purposes of this chapter, it is useful to adopt the concept of 'liminality' – that is, a state of transition or disorientation. The culture of the 1960s could be so described, because that period witnessed a generation of youth that challenged and redrew cultural boundaries, that pushed cultural norms, rituals and rules to their limits.

Bernice Martin (1981) has explored the concept of liminality fully, by drawing on the cultural anthropology of Mary Douglas (1970), with her key concepts of group (how clearly defined an individual's social position is as inside or outside a bounded social group) and grid (how clearly defined an individual's social role is within networks of social privileges, claims and obligations), to understand the 'expressive' cultural revolution of the 1960s and its particular impact on staid 'respectable' working-class culture. The iconoclastic rock group The Who expressed this aggressive invasive style in their clothes, lyrics, loud electric sounds, 'live' concerts with finales in which guitars and drum sets were smashed up, and in their films and rock operas such as *Tommy* and *Quadrophenia*. For example, in 'The Kids are Alright' and the iconoclastic 'My Generation' Pete Townshend, the doyen of the 'Mods', challenged established authority figures for '*putting us down*', and suggested to parents '*Why don't you all fffff... fade away and don't try and dig what we all say?*'

Youth in the 1960s had the collective experience of shaping and being shaped by liminal processes in affluent times. Importantly this youth cohort has carried that existential propensity with them into later life. Traditional life stages and family cycles have been undermined by subversion and challenged by rejection. The 1960s teenage generation became rebellious parents in the 1970s, restless middle-aged divorcees in the 1980s/90s and atavistic born-again pensioners after the turn of the millennium. Sustained by the feminist movement, many have set about challenging marriage, assumptions about child care, and conventional sexuality and gender roles. As one consequence, the constraints of 1950s respectable working-class culture have been diluted. Flexibility in work patterns has changed the sexual division of labour. Most importantly, white working-class culture had to come to terms with issues of race and ethnicity, embodied in what Sivanandan (1990) terms the (often migrant or imported) 'reserve army of labour'. This flexible stream of labour power has been sucked into an expanding UK economy to solve skill shortages and to take on poorly paid jobs and working conditions rejected by mainstream labour. Consequently, it has less power in terms of trade-union organization and citizenship and this is reflected in poorer pay, blocked job opportunities and insecurity of employment. When recession hits, migrant workers are usually the first to experience unemployment and deteriorating conditions of work and pay. Media and mainstream opinion affirm the relative powerlessness of migrant labour by conveniently turning a blind eye to changing patterns of employment in tourism and hospitality, the construction industry, domestic service and public transport. It is a minor inconvenience if the latest wave of East European economic migrants display poor English language skills, yet righteous moral outrage surfaces when routine exploitation makes national news, as with the deaths of 21 Chinese cockle pickers in Morecombe in 2004 or periodic exposés of sex tourism and prostitution in London.

In stark contrast to Pete Townshend's wish 'hope I die before I get old', the 1960s cohort refused to move gracefully into middle and old age in the manner of their parents. They have carried their rebellious edge forward, their thirst and taste for liminality, their deconstruction of stereotypes, as they seek to rewrite traditional boundaries of middle age and explore longevity, becoming that oxymoron, the 'young old'.

The central argument proposed here is the importance of experiential continuities in history and in generation. This position, incidentally, directly contradicts that adopted by other philosophers. For example, Merleau-Ponty's (1964) *Sense and Non-Sense* posits 'the liquidation of the self' into several role players; at different stages of our lives we are different persons that 'accidentally' inhabit the same body. Different selves get woven together retrospectively into a 'false biographical unity' (cited in Featherstone, 1995: 60).

GRASSHOPPERS, ANTS AND BUTTERFLIES

The 1960s post-war teenage generation had grown up in affluence and was restless to explore new tastes, new tourist destinations, new consumption styles and, later on, new patterns of early retirement. By the 1980s this generation of post-war baby boomers had rejected the fiscal disciplines of social reformism and its growing burden of welfare spending. Politically an important segment of this generation opted for the New Right discourse of choice and consumerism and settled for a less expensive and less intrusive residual state. While they themselves had grown up in a world of free dental, nursing and health care, final-salary, inflation-proof pensions and publicly funded education, they were not prepared to make similar collective financial provision for the next generation. They had further benefited as property owners from rising house prices, and, according to Hutton (1995), the top 40% of the population were wealthy from the one-off windfalls of 1980s privatizations. They had therefore both the cultural and economic capital to be interested in postmodernity and engage with 'new times' as they took on the Internet, mobile phones, globalized TV, fads in diet and lifestyles, along with a restlessness manifested in make-overs, moving house, and the acquisition of second holiday homes in the UK or abroad.

In the world of leisure and sports studies, figurational sociology makes much of the functional interdependence and growing democratization of social and cultural networks. Divisions of class, gender and race are held to become more egalitarian and the distance between generations becomes less pronounced. Rather than 'dancing in the light', 1980s and 90s teenagers find themselves dancing in the shadows of their parents. Forty and 50-year-olds are now buying more music albums than teenagers and determining chart success. Equally, videos seem to be an antiquated waste of money whereas DVDs are perceived as investments. Stated simply, middle-aged groups now have the material and cultural capital along with the demographic weight to be leisure trendsetters and market heavyweights. Their tastes in clothes, music, holidays, and so on, provide an important backdrop to the choices available for young people growing up in the 2000s. Traditional icons of youthful rebellion and style are now subverted and consumed by the middle-aged. Take, for example, Willis' favourite, powerful motorbikes; driving one of these now carries dangerous consequences in increasing road accidents for the elderly. Gender and sexual stereotypes also face scrutiny. Critics are challenging the gay press's preoccupation with male youth or advertising's disregard for older role models in placing products.

There is therefore some irony in the fact that the political New Right – led in the UK by Margaret Thatcher – found so much fault with the permissive revolution of the 'swinging 60s'. This 'grass/shopper' approach to recreational drugs and consumption undermines serious work, so valued by past generations of parents and grandparents. The satiric assault on tradition – the subversive interest in liminality, in progressive education, in alternative lifestyles and sexual identities, in the deconstructing of British identity, in alternatives to the institution of marriage, while turning a blind eye to the changing nature of communities and to spiralling rates of crime … all are now blamed on the baby-boomer children of the 60s. Yet in the decades of adulthood and middle age, this same (now parent) generation has also presided over the election of three Conservative governments and New Labour neo-liberalism. These governments consistently supported New Right ideas of what Hall and Jacques (1983) term 'authoritarian populism' which set its face against the expansion of public expenditure and welfare rights. Likewise, politicians like Mrs Thatcher championed personal liberty and an opposition to state interference – a stance which many see as conflicting with an opposition to, for example, the use of recreational drugs.

This more individualized 'grasshopper'-like approach, of enjoying the abundance of the present (provided essentially by the ant-like endeavour of their parents), together with a marked collective reluctance to invest long term in material infrastructure for following generations, has been highlighted most by environmentalist criticisms. Green thinking (whether of light or more radical dark green hue) has pointed out that grasshopper lifestyles are generationally unsustainable. Whether it is a question of mobility, lifestyle, landscape or biodiversity, things should change and change both globally and locally. Yet there is no sign that the 1960s teenage generation are prepared to abandon their cars, holiday homes, cheap mass tourism by airplane or consumerist lifestyles.

This hyperactive 1960s cohort was simply not ready to settle down into existing conventional patterns of class, gender or 'race'. Post-colonial patterns of immigration provided new and different historical challenges in the 1960s from those faced earlier in the nineteenth and twentieth centuries. All in all, the old institutional solutions conceived by past generations – the vision of self, life course, family and community, of work and of religion, simply seemed no longer appropriate. Sexual revolution in the form of widely available contraception and more carefree attitudes to sex challenged gender power relations, and feminism raised questions about patriarchal processes in public and private spheres. The next generation of 1980s and 1990s 'butterflies' in some ways became less important. They were suspended or delayed or reduced by smaller family size, as the large demographic bulge of the baby boom chronologically grew older. But socially and culturally, as we have seen, this was resisted. In some ways the 1960s cohort were reluctant parents – in the sense that they put their demands for self-expression and identity alongside the needs of their children rather than subsuming themselves in their traditional roles as parents. It was not so much that the next generation of children was the future; but that they as the parent generation were reluctant to be sidelined and felt they had a crucial role to play.

This reluctance of the 1960s 'baby-boomer' generation to act their chronological age is pervasive. Media commentators discovered that old people, the 'bus pass' generation, were in denial, as marketeers identified a new generation of 'OAP youth'; vox pop surveys suggest that 55–64-year-olds feel that they are no older than 40, whereas those over 60 feel they have a brain age of 46, grannies want to dress like their grandchildren, and pensioner membership rates at gyms continue to expand. It is the middle aged and elderly who have accepted the message about exercise and healthy lifestyles. This ageing population has resulted in the usual policy problem of young people being overshadowed by policy concerns of the old – who will look after us in our old age? Who will pay for our pensions? Who will pay for expanding respite and long-term residential care? Such tensions impose pressure on key institutions such as the NHS. What should NHS priorities be over the next decades as generational cohorts have different interests? Should the NHS prioritize spending on paediatric research into obesity, IVF treatments or diagnostic approaches to Alzheimer's disease?

GENERATION X: THATCHER'S CHILDREN

Youth studies, therefore, benefit from paying closer attention to age cohorts and historical contexts and processes. Conflicts between generations are reworked on different material and cultural battlegrounds, orchestrated by shifts in commercial investment, labour markets and public policies. The post-war generation of 'baby-boomers' grew up as teenagers protected by the welfare state of the 1950s and 60s, enjoyed full employment in middle age and have taken retirement on relatively generous state and occupational pensions. Their children, and particularly their grandchildren, will not share this collective provision. Indeed, the 1960s generation of 'grasshoppers' has, as we have already observed, spawned a 1980s/1990s generation of 'butterflies'. Writers have used a variety of terms to try to capture this generational shift: Thatcher's children, the X generation, the 'cool' generation, and so on. But all labels fail to capture the plight of this next generation of young people who are growing up, to use Beck's term, in a 'risk society'. Awaiting them is a general distrust of politics, public policy and the collective solutions of the past. For them the only certainty is that life is growing more uncertain and unpredictable.

Researchers working in the Institute of Popular Culture at Manchester Metropolitan University closely documented growing trends of individualism and consumerism in the 1990s. There is a tinge of nostalgia as Steve Redhead (1993, 1997), a founder member of the centre, surveys the fabrication of 1980s rave culture in contrast to the expressive authenticity of 1960s sub-cultural styles. He and many others (see e.g. O'Connor and Wynne, 1996) argue that 'authenticity' in youth cultures is less possible now that cultural industries have permeated youth forms and are crucial resources in, for example, the production of garage/house music. There is also a critique from Sarah Thornton (1995) and Jim McGuigan (2002) to the effect that cultural resistance is everywhere and what one has now are markers of distinction and taste. Sarah Thornton (1995) stresses the centrality of the media in the construction and classifications of tastes.

The butterfly generation who were growing up as teenagers in the 1980s and 1990s are now in many cases depressed and mentally 'stressed out' about their lives. Experts are keen to point to a thousand reasons for children and young people to be cheerless in the noughties. They are simply self-indulgent, left too much to their own devices, growing up in self-organizing cellular families, eating fast foods, left in front of their own TV, with no shared family meals and an absence of clear timetables and bedtimes. It therefore should come as no surprise that as teenagers they live their lives solely in the present, as short-run hedonists. Recent surveys document young Britons having the highest rates for hard drinking and unprotected underage sex. When faced with self-funding in higher education and flexible credit arrangements, why plan and save for the future? What chance of lifelong careers and property ownership? Why then worry about deteriorating state support and the disappearance of final salary occupational pension schemes, when so many are being encouraged to be warehoused in university student culture, in 24-hour licensed cities, where active weekend lifestyles are essentially drinking to get drunk, and with young women just as eagerly embracing ever higher rates of smoking and binge drinking?

BLACK YOUTH

As Benedict Anderson (1991) argues, nation states are best understood as 'imagined communities' which share landscape, language and history, with mass media as key institutions drawing symbolic boundaries to delineate 'insiders' and 'outsiders'. According to Eric Hobsbawm and Terence Ranger (1983), European nation states historically created distinctive 'invented traditions' in the nineteenth century and these, by their very nature, exclude foreigners. As a consequence, politicians, media and interest groups can draw selectively on such nationalist traditions to celebrate 'belonging', conversely marking out for special attention those who do not belong or confirm to nationalist values and behaviours.

5.4 Nation states and identities

(See Hobsbawm and Ranger (1983) *The Invention of Tradition*.)

Nation States in Europe (see e.g. UK, France, Germany, Italy).

During the period 1850–1914 'Metropolitan' elites set up invented traditions to bind people in a nation state, often based in the capital city, for example London, Paris, Berlin, Rome and to unify regional differences, for example between North and South, West and East.

   State institutions of nationhood and identity:

- military – e.g. marches, displays, ceremonies, parades
- monarchy – rituals, procedures, appearances
- government – public parks, statues, squares, expositions, fairs, ceremonial events
- education – national schooling and curricula, physical education
- sport – stadia, spectacle, international competitions and the Olympics
- leisure – national pastimes, festivals, ethnic and folk traditions

What sorts of things/events/dates do **you** consider to be typically 'English'?

What sorts of things would tourists/foreigners define as central to 'English' culture? And what of 'Scottish', 'Welsh' and 'Irish' culture?

In the post-war period, there have been periodic moral panics about 'race relations', leaving black youths culturally defined as the subordinate 'Other'. In a sense, primarily because of skin colour, they are perceived as aliens who can never be 'one of us'. In the words of post-colonial theory (see Aitchison, 2000; Spivak, 2006), they are the 'subaltern other' whose voices have been silenced. 'White' mainstream culture ignores the material inequalities and discriminatory practices that shape the lives of each new immigrant population. Indeed, Stuart Hall (1992) argues that we define ourselves by stressing what we are not. One cannot understand one's own culture without contrasting it to the 'Other'. As Paul Gilroy (1987) suggests that 'There ain't no black in the Union Jack', and one must acknowledge a 'double consciousness' in that black people are both inside and outside white culture. Yet Bhikhu Parekh (2000) opened up a debate about what exactly it meant to be 'British' at the beginning of the millennium with a report that argued that any versions of Britishness that ignored the presence of diverse black and Asian communities were racist. One outcome is that black and Asian youth look towards the black diaspora – taking inspiration from US black music such as blues, soul, rap and garage, and black radicalism such as Rastafarianism or Islamic fundamentalism. Linda Colley (1992) has argued that the 'English' are not Catholic, are free from the tyranny of absolute monarchy and are white and civilized. Within conservative ideology, foreigners do not share the same instincts, do not belong to our 'tribe', they can never be part of our blood, families, kinship or community. However, this view hardly impeded the imperial projects of European nation states that set out to 'civilize' the rest of the world, while appropriating, controlling or administering their scarce resources. It is hardly surprising that patterns of migration to the UK have drawn upon colonial roots and routes to recruit black Afro-Caribbeans, Indians, Pakistanis and Bangladeshis to mop up the unskilled work of an increasingly affluent UK economy during the post-war period. The waves of immigration, and subsequent tensions between host nations and local communities also find their expression between first, second and third generations (Sivanandan, 1990). The current moral panic about black youth gun and drugs crime and murder, as well as the supposed isolation and extremism of Islamic youth in Britain, worries both white and black parent generations. Hence, it should come as no surprise that all politicians, especially members of UKIP, are keen to reassert some form of British culture on the UK population, but such aspirations are diluted by the forces of globalization and, not least, the Iraq war. During the 2000s, asylum seekers are feared and economic migrants, with the enlargement of the EU in 2005, are stereotyped and stigmatized.

CONCLUSION

Postmodern analysis implies that individuals can choose to be youthful and engage in distinctive exercise regimes and make active leisure choices. This chapter has argued that it is essential to take a generational perspective emphasizing the historical, material and cultural contexts of each generation and how such spaces and identities are negotiated and constructed between different generations. Postmodern analysis celebrates the diversity of individual experience and choice in relation to work, family and leisure lifestyles. Such analysis demands that traditional collective experiences of class, gender and race in the UK are deconstructed and hence that more attention is paid to the individual. Indeed, Giddens suggests that one major feature of postmodernity is that we are all forced to choose, whether it be work, intimate relationships, leisure, diet or exercise regimes. However, an equally rich tradition is to be found in using historical sociology and generational continuities of time. Figure 5.2 provides a starting point to think about the significance of age cohorts marching through history at different speeds and at different times (see overleaf).

However, there is one final caveat – the need to acknowledge problems of aggregation and naïve stereotyping of generational cohorts. Similar debates have arisen about interpreting the north–south divide when seeking to account for broad changes in UK Census data. The UK government's response to claims of high regional variations is to highlight differences within regions which are said to be more pronounced than inter-regional difference. Indeed, there are still important resilient continuities of class, gender and racial division. These, along with the inter-generational and intra-generational differences described here, continue to drive to historical processes and outcomes.

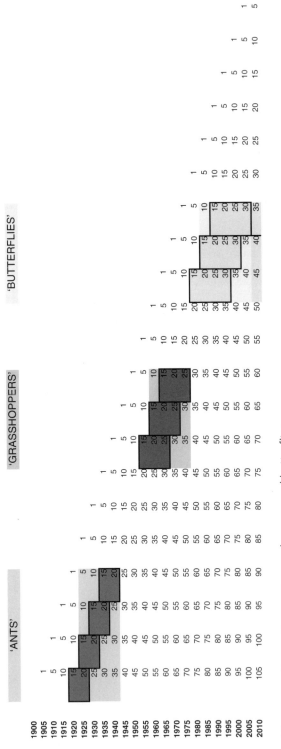

Figure 5.2 Generations: ants, grasshoppers and butterflies

6

STAYING IN AND SETTLING DOWN

THIS CHAPTER

- Evaluates the contribution of Robert and Rhona Rapoport's analysis of leisure and the family life cycle
- Discusses the formation of couples in the establishment phase of the life cycle and home-based leisure
- Introduces the concepts of delayed and accelerated transitions into adulthood
- Focuses on the emergence of young adults as leisure consumers, drawing on Tony Blackshaw's arguments about the leisure imagination and on Bauman's view of liquid modernity
- Provides a case study of young adults who develop serious leisure within 'extreme sports' and alternative lifestyles.

This chapter explores two sister concepts – the family life cycle and the life course. The growth of home-based leisure and individualization has been partly captured in social theory by the nuclearization thesis. This mode of social analysis established itself in the 1970s, the decade when the generation of 'baby boomers' were twenty-somethings. According to that thesis, people are choosing more diverse and privatized leisure lifestyles. This chapter develops the arguments of the previous chapter about young people 'growing up' by examining how transitions into adulthood, into occupational careers and into the roles of parents and parenting are becoming less clear and pre-determined. Institutional changes, specifically in patterns of work and education, as well as more complicated family relationships and networks, have resulted in increased ambiguity and ambivalence. The chapter begins to deal with some of the issues that surround postmodern culture and change by looking at Zygmunt Bauman's conceptualization of liquid modernity. These themes are developed further in Chapter 8 in which middle age and moral panics regarding mid-life crises are discussed.

During the 1970s, in Britain and elsewhere, there emerged a strong policy agenda based on the idea of leisure needs. Staff in the newly established leisure services departments could define their own professional expertise through identifying, researching and satisfying these emergent needs. Just as social policy experts debated how to deliver selective or universal benefits according to factors of income, housing, health and education, leisure services and leisure researchers started to debate the nature of leisure needs in terms of how they could best be satisfied within target populations and realized in local communities.

Stephen Mennell (1979) draws up a threefold distinction between *manifest*, *latent* and *real* needs in the realm of culture, with each order of need generating different research strategies. Manifest needs refer to existing demands for culture in terms of sport, recreation and leisure. These can best be measured by surveys of participation, economic consumption and expenditure. In sharp contrast, latent demands can only be explored through the collection of more qualitative data, in the pursuit of which researchers encourage respondents to discuss new opportunities for leisure, often with the help of cultural support from animateurs who encourage individuals and target groups to consider new leisure forms and contexts. Such cultural animation asks individuals to take on new challenges and to experiment with leisure forms that were previously ignored or not considered, for whatever social, economic or political reasons. This newly interventionist policy position taxed the professional confidence of leisure specialists and it required a degree of political consensus, both over what might constitute 'leisure needs' and how those needs might be satisfied through public policies. Mennell's final category of 'real needs' also proves to be problematic. There is a marked absence of consensus about the concept of 'real' needs, as differing perspectives in academic disciplines such as psychology, sociology and political sciences argue that because of the machinations of unconscious drives, ideology or mass media propaganda, ordinary people may not be aware of their real needs and consequently may persist in actions and behaviours which are deemed contrary to their own short- or long-term interests. So, in terms of leisure choices, experts in healthy lifestyles can produce substantial clinical evidence that risk taking – for example, smoking, drinking alcohol, consuming illegal drugs, unsafe sex and abnormal eating behaviours – can all run counter to an individual's interests. For some experts, individuals cannot be relied upon to recognize their 'real' needs and, thus, to make the right choices.

LEISURE AND THE FAMILY LIFE CYCLE

It is precisely this policy context of leisure needs that characterized the research by Robert and Rhona Rapoport (1975). It is usual for academic collaborations to overlap with personal friendships and academic partnerships but quite rare for authors to be husband and wife. This coincidence may in part explain the authors' central interest in marriage and family life – a topic previously neglected by leisure theorists. The Rapoports focus on the family life cycle and they argue that there are distinct stages within married and family life which are determined by biological and psychological needs. The brevity or longevity of what one might term the 'domestic age' or household arrangements offer an interesting lens through which to view leisure choice. People build lifestyles that offer experiences they value upon the social relationships by which they are surrounded. Families offer diverse resources and 'natural' taken-for-granted relationships for leisure, and key stages in the family life cycle bring different demands and opportunities to grandparents, parents and children alike. For writers such as John Kelly (1983), following Joffre Dumazadier, families offer opportunities for 'semi-leisure', as people are constrained by reciprocal familial obligations (unlike in 'pure leisure' which entails more freedoms), but they do provide 'the immediate community' (Kelly, 1980) for leisure experiences which are valued not so much for the activities that people are engaged in *per se* but rather more for the sociability of others with whom they share leisure.

6.1 Shakespeare's Seven Ages of Man:

All the world's a stage

And all the men and women merely players:

They have their exits and their entrances;

And one man in his time plays many parts,

His acts being seven ages.

At first the infant

Mewing and puking in the nurse's arms

And then the whining school boy

...

Last scene of all

That ends this strange eventful history,

Is second childishness and mere oblivion

Sans teeth, sans eyes, sans taste, sans everything

(Continued)

(Continued)

Do you agree with William Shakespeare in his play *As You Like It* that there are seven major life stages?

What do you see as the main stages in people's lives?

When do they usually start and finish?

Are there exceptions?

Will your life course run through the same stages?

J. M. and M. J. Cohen *The Penguin Dictionary of Quotations*. Harmondsworth: Penguin Books 1960, p. 311.

The Rapoports' research involved collecting data from 30 middle-class, dual career families, and they were particularly interested in how people balanced work, family and leisure commitments throughout the family cycle. These three planes of work, family and leisure intersected in ways that changed during the life cycle. From their qualitative interview data, they posited four key distinctive phases or stages within the family life cycle demarcated by marriage, birth and career opportunities. As much feminist research testifies (Deem, 1986; Green et al., 1990; Wearing, 1998), marriage and child care have more significant impacts on women than men. Men carry on their leisure lives, whereas women often struggle to manage domestic work and careers, and once children are born, women almost invariably take responsibility for child care – and accommodate this either by stopping work or by working part-time, as well as taking major responsibility in organizing daily child-minding and baby sitters for 'nights out'. Women also face the responsibility for organizing the care of elderly parents, but that pressure usually appears later in the life course and the implication of this for leisure will be dealt with in Chapter 9.

6.2 Life stages and life interests

Life stage	Preoccupations	Interests
Adolescent (13–19)	Quest for satisfying personality	Experimentation
Young Adults (19–25)	Social identity Attachment to work, sexual relations, marriage	Privatization of interests – Family centred Sexual relations Marriage

Establishment (25–55)	Satisfying life investments	Children leave – wife works
Old age (56–?)	Establish personal integration/work/family less important	Leisure central

What adjustments, if any, would you make to the above typology of the family?

Explain the degree to which this model relates to your own experience and that of your friends?

What principal changes do you think have taken place in family life since the original research was completed in the 1970s?

How might increasing diversity in households and family structures undermine the Rapoports' arguments?

LEISURE CONSUMERS

One central debate in UK sociology during the 1970s was about the nature and extent of privatization – an increasing preoccupation with the private and the personal – in family life. Many studies documented the changing nature of work family and local communities. It was suggested that the collective organizations of working-class life – extended families, trade unions, working men's clubs and the Labour Party – were in decline. According to some commentators, as we shall explore in the next chapter, social-class membership and ties were weakening and dissolving as individual identities became less likely to be determined solely by class of origin. Individuals were not solely defined by their work or occupation but more by their leisure and lifestyle. The world of class and production seemed less relevant as people had more economic resources and turned their attention towards leisure and consumption. This theme of individualization will be explored in more detail in the next section where we see how social theorists have become more interested in difference and diversity, and also in the final chapter which traces the debates, chiefly in the early 1970s, over the emergence of a leisure society. It will be argued that social identities that are constructed around the importance of sexuality, gender, ethnicity and racial categories have come to dominate mass media attention, marketing and leisure consumption.

In the 1970s the 'privatization thesis' was that young people, particularly in the working classes, were beating a retreat from the public world of traditional networks and instead investing more of themselves in the private worlds of home-building and family life. At that time social theory in the USA and Europe focused on the 'nuclearization' thesis that suggested that couples with two children (usually captured by the statistical average of 2.2 children per modern family) were much better suited to the spatial and social mobility patterns of modern industrialism. Traditional families, with their extended family obligations and loyalties, tied young people down, closing off opportunities for individual advancement and choice. Young people had to be cosmopolitan, open to an urban and increasingly global pattern of life, rather than endure the village and neighbourhood localism of their parents and relatives.

Peter Berger and Thomas Luckmann (1968) offered a powerful and compelling analysis of the nuclear family as offering 'a haven in a heartless world'. Here, two strangers with different biographies and separate experiences meet and embark on a long-term relationship, in the process redefining and repositioning themselves as a 'couple'. Thus the nuclear family provided an intimate private space wherein its members could be, and could see themselves as a couple or, in these modern times dominated by business discourses, as 'partners'. Such are the ambivalences and sensitivities about committing to or, more darkly, being trapped in, lifelong relationships that some choose to qualify their relationship commitment with an adjective, such as 'present', 'current' or 'long-term' partner. As one may expect in a 'celebrity culture' (Rojek, 2001) rich individuals insure themselves against things going wrong and seek to avoid financially damaging marriage break-ups by entering into pre-nuptial legal contracts.

In similar vein, Erving Goffman (1971b) developed an insightful analysis of how social relations in public treat heterosexual couples as representing the norm. Singles, never-marrieds and divorcees are (or were, at the time of Goffman's writing) out of place in leisure spaces such as bars, restaurants, cinemas, hotels, and the like. Goffman argues that for women this is a pressing problem and they often seek to give off signs that they are in fact not alone but waiting for someone – so, saving seats, intermittent glancing at watches or the clock, gazing at exits for a purported new arrival should all be read as clues to ward off predatory males who regardless may still seek to engage unattached women in conversation, with the offer of a drink, and maybe more.

Setting up nuclear families is a risky business as a great deal is invested in the idea of romantic love, marriage and happy families. The ideology of love and intimate family relationships is amplified at Christmas time , although the reality of travelling home, present giving, meeting up and spending the holiday with family and Christmas dinner itself are all very likely simply hard work for the majority. Getting Christmas over or getting over Christmas is a pressing existential problem. Despite the chasm between ideology and reality, sharing domestic work, coping with career ups and downs, buying property, choosing furnishings and going on holidays may be opportunities to consolidate this social construction of reality. But all these realities, including leisure lives, have to be negotiated, lived and managed. Clearly having and rearing children helps to consolidate this long-term project and provides the major momentum and focus for the two adults who are now young (and not so young) mums and dads.

In the UK and elsewhere, the emphasis on couples and nest building was in the 1960s in no small part fuelled by the growing availability of disposable income to be spent on home ownership and the purchase of domestic goods. It was also driven by a manufacturing and service sector keen to develop niche markets in lifestyle consumption. After the austerity of the post-war years and relentless rationing, vividly described by the social historian David Kynaston (2007, 2009) the 1960s and 1970s witnessed a sustained growth in home ownership and leisure-related spending. This was accompanied by the idea of affluent workers (Goldthorpe and Lockwood, 1969) and changing gender roles (Young and Willmott, 1973), as it was suggested that men were becoming more home-centred in their thinking and likely to be spending more time there, becoming more involved with domestic work, DIY and child care. The slogan of 'we're all middle class now' implied not only that class divisions had melted away but that everyone now aspired to middle-class tastes in home and car ownership, leisure lifestyles and mass media consumption.

Car ownership and travel became *sine qua nons* of this newly emerging affluence and, for most, they were ingredients essential to the new leisure lifestyles which included excursions and holidays, both at home and abroad. Indeed, for some historians of leisure, the post-war period signified the weakening of local community ties and the emergence of a new generation enjoying higher rates of geographical mobility and wider horizons than previous generations. This 'hyper-mobility' as writers such as John Adams (1999) termed it, was experienced mostly by young adults and it was typified by the explosion of cheap 'low cost' airlines such as easyJet, Flybe, Jet2 and Ryanair. These airlines all flew, for example, to Spain and Greece, to tourist destinations which rebranded themselves as key venues and niche markets for 'club culture', 'raves' and holiday excess. Indeed, this holiday atmosphere was recreated in student cities in the 1990s with the emergence of vibrant student music scenes, often flourishing in unlikely old industrial northern cities such as Manchester, Leeds, Newcastle and Sheffield.

Day excursions, mini-breaks, holidays abroad, eating out and dining at home were now the province, and to the taste of, the vast majority of the population, see Roberts (2004). The closely-knit working-class community portrayed by Richard Hoggart (1957), Alan Sillitoe (1960), Young and Willmott (1957), and many others in the 1950s and 60s, had been dissipated by new housing patterns in cities, by mass production and generally by the mass consumption of media culture – TV, cinema, records, and so on. The 1960s 'countercultural' revolution in both USA and Europe challenged and transgressed the boundaries of class, gender and race. However, despite the claims for political and personal change, many social researchers found resilient continuities in class, notably in restricted social mobility and hierarchical personal relations. Feminists challenged the idea of 'new men' and doubted that a more egalitarian sexual division of labour was now being observed. The 'affluent worker' research, led by John Goldthorpe and David Lockwood (1969), has been reassessed by many writers interested in social class and industrial sociology (Eldridge, 1980). Marketers and advertisers sought to develop brand loyalty with concomitant interest in buying 'white goods' such as washing machines, fridges and freezers as well as black goods such as radios, television sets, record players and tape recorders. In the 1970s this area of consumption seemed to point up a traditional sexual division of labour about such purchasing decisions, with women taking on the choice of white goods while men concentrated their attentions and conversations around the more expensive hi-tech and prestigious black goods.

6.3 Consuming gender and leisure goods

Think about the following list of consumer and leisure goods and services.

- Alcoholic drinks
- Bicycles
- Body tattoos
- Cars
- Children's clothes
- Cinema and film DVDs
- Earrings
- Fitness classes
- Jeans
- Laptops
- Leisure centres
- Mobile phones
- Motorbikes
- Newspapers and magazines
- Shoes and trainers
- Sports broadcasting
- X-box games

In what ways do business providers seek to differentiate between men and women in the marketing of these?

Are any of the commodities or services 'gender free'?

How important, for instance, is colour in differentiating between 'male' and 'female' leisure goods?

What are the traditional boundaries between male and female leisure?

How have these boundaries changed over the past 30 years?

Does it make any difference if the leisure experience is located in voluntary, commercial or public sector organizations?

DELAYED AND ACCELERATED TRANSITIONS

As we have argued in the previous chapter on youth, each generation seeks to establish its own distinctive identity or at least to win some distinctive space from the parent generation and from that generation's cultural issues and historic concerns. The emergence of privatization and the weakening of local community ties were in part imposed by changing work patterns during the 1960s, 1970s and 1980s. This occurred primarily because of shifts in the international division of labour from West to East and also in response to the impact of global patterns of migration on the UK. With declining primary industries and the relocation of manufacturing industry to the developing 'tiger' economies in Asia, many regions in the UK, particularly the Midlands and in the North, suffered exceptionally high rates of unemployment. The restructuring of the UK economy, with its growing dependence on financial and other service sectors in the South East, resulted in high local rates of youth unemployment. Some academics and policy makers designated these drastic changes in patterns of employment as playing a significant role in causing the 'youth crisis'. For Paul Willis (1988), the young unemployed were suddenly trapped in 'frozen transitions' because of the functional and systemic breakdown of three major building blocks of industrial capitalism. These three blocks, forged in the nineteenth century and fine-tuned in the twentieth century, were the nuclear family, primary and secondary education and paid work. The three institutions functioned as an industrialized escalator from childhood, through adolescence and into adulthood. With no paid employment and no work, the youth cohort was going nowhere and enjoyed few resources to break into affluent consumer culture and leisure consumption. This cohort, then, entered into a period of enforced leisure, but with few leisure opportunities. Previous generations had waited or had been made to wait patiently for adulthood. The counter-cultural youth of the 1960s had wanted the future and they had wanted it 'now'. The youth of the 1980s felt that they were being denied even the present.

Another, newer and more disruptive force for change during this historical period was state-sponsored immigration. This saw the growth of what Sivanandan (1990) has called a 'reserve army of labour', composed of migrant workers who were encouraged by the British government to come to Britain in times of growth in the UK economy yet were usually among the first to experience unemployment and exclusion in times of recession. In large urban conurbations, first traditional white working-class communities, and later middle-class communities, were transformed by new patterns of migration as Afro-Caribbean, Pakistani, Indian and Bangladeshi male workers and later their families established themselves in London, the East Midlands and West Yorkshire. Substantial research about 'race relations' was completed during this period (Banton, 1967; Miles and Phizacklea, 1979; Rex, 1970, 1973; CCCS, 1982), and policies to combat institutional racism in education and work, community hostility in leisure spaces, housing discrimination and personal prejudice were enacted.

Significantly, these new Commonwealth migrants also introduced cultural difference and diversity, particularly in family relationships and structures. As we have seen in the previous chapter, one response to this emerging difference and diversity was a moral panic, often about 'law and order', orchestrated by the mass media and with a distinctive focus on the differing lifestyles of 'black' single parents or tightly knit extended 'Asian' families. The paradox for welfare policy and social work institutions was one of managing inequality and difference. Through the lumping together of 'black' and 'Asian' families for policy convenience, the issue became framed as a straight choice between integration and separation. The matter was thus rendered in stark and increasingly racist terms: should these 'foreigners' be integrated into mainstream 'white' culture or should they retain their distinctive 'black' religious and cultural practices. One solution demanded equal opportunities to encourage and enable migrants to assimilate; the other championed anti-racist policies and policing to make mainstream power structures accept diversity and difference.

During periods of change, schooling and education were designated as crucial mechanisms for managing transitions into work and developing the necessary skills to become competent adults. Indeed, as we shall see in the final chapter on leisure futures, one major new challenge for academics was to provide a curriculum appropriate and relevant to 'the leisure society'. In the UK, the 1970s cohort of young people experienced the consolidation of a comprehensive school system and an increase in educational opportunities for young men and women. The raising of the school leaving age in the UK from 15 to 16 in 1972 and the substantial growth in higher education resulted in a much large proportion of young adults going off to university, supported by state educational grants. In the UK, unlike most other EU states where young people gravitated towards local universities, more and more young people spent at least three years away from home. The conventional transition into adulthood, traditionally secured by full-time work, was therefore delayed for many and meant that young adults had more time and space to establish their own personal identities and future career directions. For many too, the shift into Rapoports' second stage of 'young adults' was delayed and this permitted individuals scope to explore and experiment with their identities, sexuality and lifestyles. The very idea of settling down was questioned by the mass media, particularly those agencies committed to what writers term the 'counter culture', and individuals were exhorted to 'do your own thing', a slogan later condensed by the transnational sport goods corporation Nike to 'just do it'.

It seems clear that during the 1980s and 1990s one institutional response to the problem of Willis' 'frozen transitions' was to postpone adulthood for many young people by extending the time they spent in education. Politicians, policy makers and educationalists welcomed the development of new universities and colleges. City planners in university towns developed university sites, student halls of residence and designated student quarters where recreational drug and alcohol use (and abuse) were deemed a normal weekend diet for those involved in student lifestyles. Indeed, student lifestyles around city-centre pubs and a vibrant club culture scene were often the centre piece of re-imaging postmodern cities in the UK (see Bramham and Spink, 2009; Spink and Bramham, 1999, 2000).

With this expansion in the number of higher education places in the 1980s and 90s, particularly in the 'new' universities (generally the former British polytechnics, made into universities in 1992), there was a body of right-wing opinion that suggested that the bulk of students were simply playing at university for three years or hardly working for a degree. A clear dividing line was drawn, or was perceived to exist, between elite universities that offered real university education and degrees (such as London, Oxbridge and the 'Russell' group), whereas the emerging 'virtual' universities in new places such as Brighton, Derby, Coventry and Southampton offered, in the then contemporary press parlance 'Mickey Mouse' degrees, featuring subjects such as the widely decried 'Media Studies'. However, the old polytechnics in traditional university cities towns such as London, Oxford, Liverpool, Nottingham, Manchester, Leeds and Sheffield, renamed themselves often as city or metropolitan universities and quickly mirrored traditional universities by appointing Professors, building research expertise and developing postgraduate courses, with governing bodies appointing new Vice Chancellors on salaries and with remuneration packages often well in excess of their more traditional university counterparts.

For critics, those students embarking on new multidisciplinary degrees and courses were simply gaining 'useless knowledge' with no clear vocational destination, despite the latter never being the hallmark of traditional university education (students studying Classics at Oxford or Cambridge are seldom rebuked for doing degrees that have no job relevance): these young people were simply being provided with three years' purposeless leisure at the state's expense. Philosophers such as Roger Scruton dismissed as useless degrees in such fields as sport, media or football studies. Such courses, he argued, were simply warehousing young people. The time spent at university was said by right-wing spokespeople to be a waste of time and public money. The 'New' Labour government's commitment, made by Prime Minister Tony Blair at the Labour Party conference of 1999, to have at least half of the teenage population in higher education by 2010 was seen as a misguided attempt at large-scale social engineering and a convenient means of concealing large-scale youth unemployment. It is worth mentioning that Roger Scruton's opinions stand in sharp contrast with other philosophers. For instance, Bertrand Russell celebrated the importance of what he described as 'useless knowledge', that is knowledge achieved by the sheer love of learning rather than applied knowledge used as a means to an end. This argument was developed by Bertrand Russell in 1932 and has since been reprinted in the Routledge Classics series with the title, *In Praise of Idleness* (2002). The second chapter in that collection of essays is called 'Useless' Knowledge. Russell questions passionately, and with eloquence, the value contemporary society has placed on a utilitarian theory of knowledge, that is, on the need to know things in order that we may achieve some practical outcome or purpose. He maps out the potency of natural sciences in gaining knowledge in order to predict and to control nature and so generate new technologies in medicine, engineering and industry but, paradoxically, such technologies also generate negative consequences and unpredictable outcomes. Indeed, in this regard, Russell pre-empts some of Ulrich Beck's arguments about the risk society by over half a century. By the 1990s Anthony Giddens (1999) and Ulrich Beck (1992) were emphasizing that science and technology had generated unforeseen damage to the natural environment and nobody in government or elsewhere appeared to be in control: people were living in a 'runaway world'.

Two generations earlier Bertrand Russell had sought to defend the notion of learning at leisure. He stressed too that historically the English education system has valued a traditional and, ultimately, 'useless' curriculum, cherished in grammar schools and old universities; such institutions value the sheer *joie de vivre* in learning and in a 'classical' education. Abstract knowledge is simply an end in itself. Russell argued that such 'useless' knowledge leads to human self-awareness, a transcendence of self-interest, of power and all things practical. He argued, perhaps more controversially, that totalitarian impulses have been fuelled by ill-educated drives to control, bully and dominate, whereas we should pursue knowledge to celebrate both culture and leisure.

So, for some philosophers and sociologists, leisure is grounded in culture and self-expression and self-exploration. However, not all have shared in these new found freedoms of education. The constraints of class, race and gender have meant that comparatively few have experienced substantial social mobility and, perversely, social and political events of the 1980s and 90s meant that many experienced frozen transitions because unemployment or underemployment simply tied poor people to their existing social positions and lengthened their years of dependency and debt. Some young women too became parents at the adolescent stage and there were media panics about teenage pregnancies and single parenting. Some unhappy teenagers may have used pregnancy to escape the constraints of their own family of origin and from the point of view of the mainstream media, this accelerated transition was another luxury funded by state welfare and housing benefits and there was growing moral panic about single parenting. This was followed up by a demand that absent fathers contribute financially (and perhaps emotionally) to the support and maintenance of their offspring. This led to the passing of the Child Support Act of 1991 and the setting up of the Child Support Agency to administer it two years later.

HYPERMOBILITY AND RESTLESSNESS

Zygmunt Bauman is not insensitive to such massive inequalities of experience as characterize modern life. In a prodigious series of books, articles and, just as importantly, interviews (1992, 2002, 2005, 2006, 2007) he has outlined what he sees as the emergence of a new kind of society or, more accurately, a new sociality of individuals. In solid modernity, according to Bauman, an individual's identity is *fixed* by family and reinforced by growing up and working in the networks of face-to-face relationships that characterized local neighbourhoods. The individual was firmly grounded in these local communities, and bound, furthermore, into the cohesive institutional structures represented by the agencies of the local and national state. Identity in solid modernity is fixed and, to illustrate this, Bauman deploys the metaphor of the traditional Victorian family photograph, often taken by a professional photographer. This photograph worked to freeze any significant event such as a christening, wedding or graduation; it was then framed and displayed prominently on the mantelpiece, the hall walls or in the family photograph album.

6.4 Photographing people and places

Drawing on Susan Sontag's work, Jenny Hockey and Allison James (2003: 7) argue that even the family photograph betrays not only the decline in the importance of family networks but also the process of ageing.

> 'To take a photograph is to participate in another person's (or thing's) mortality, vulnerability, mutability. Precisely by slicing out this moment and freezing it, all photographs testify to time's relentless melt' ([Sontag] 1978: 15). In its overarching claim to be a representation of the real, the photograph fixes us, so providing us with a sense of continuity. Simultaneously, however, its claim to realism helps to remind us of time's passage and the instability of the moment captured by the lens.

What are Hockey and James saying here?

Would you agree with such an analysis of family photographs and the nature of photography?

How does this measure up to John Urry's (1990) analysis of the 'tourist gaze'? In the book of that title he argues that holiday makers and tourists gaze upon iconic places, buildings, landscapes (etc.) often including family and friends and so collect authentic records of people and places visited.

Think of the variety of reasons why you (and your family members) take photographs.

How do you feel about the photos taken when you were a baby, and at primary and secondary school?

However, in what Bauman in his earlier work cast as postmodernity (but has more recently defined as liquid modernity), the individual's identity is far more open and flexible. He and other contemporary sociologists question the very concept of the life cycle with its fixed divisions and predictable cyclical phases or stages, preferring the more unrestricted concept of 'life course', where career pathways and family relations and friendships are negotiated, managed and, to a degree, open-ended. Young adults avoid long-term commitments to others; relationships are contingent, ambivalent and sustained 'until further notice'. To capture this difference and fragility, Bauman persists with the photographic metaphor. For him the postmodern identity in the 1990s and onwards is captured by video camera and videotapes: it is erasable. The problem for people in solid modernity was often how to escape a fixed identity designated by class, or gender or race, whereas in liquid modernity with its emphasis on flexibility and the gaining of new skills, the challenge is to stabilize identity, to secure some kind of permanence in a somewhat chaotic, risky and unpredictable existence. In later works Bauman drives that metaphor further as most photos, certainly by young people, are now taken on mobile phones. The mobile is the icon of postmodern times or liquid modernity; it captures the individual's own identity, a repository of contacts – friends to text and family members to call on – as well as providing global access to Internet forums and chat groups, Twitter, Facebook and so on ... all immediately accessible but always at a distance. Paradoxically, this digitalized technology overcomes what Giddens terms 'time space distanciation' but yet the individual remains alone and isolated.

RESTLESSNESS AND TRAVELLING LIGHT

Over the last few decades, social theorists have become concerned with the specific and burgeoning area of leisure activity that is travel and tourism. As we have seen, postmodern life and times have been characterized by restlessness, by the individual's desire to visit new, often exotic places and to take in new sights and experiences. Zygmunt Bauman draws a clear distinction between the journeying, expeditions and tours of the past and the holidaying, travel and tourism of contemporary times.

It is via the use of metaphor that Bauman (1996) contrasts personal identity, past and present. If the modern 'problem of identity' was about how to construct and stabilize identity, the postmodern (or 'liquidly modern') problem is to avoid fixation, remain flexible and 'to keep options open'. In solid modernity, Bauman sees people as pilgrims through time, struggling with eternal persistence of the soul: people search for a trail through the desert which is both placeless and boundless. Life becomes a pilgrimage – a search for the truth, a distinctive time and place away from home where one can discover oneself and God's presence. Hence the religious quest for salvation and spiritual fulfilment: the Protestant work ethic created an inner desert of delayed gratification. Within this form and other versions of religious belief, one's existential quest is to know that one is on the way to heaven to join God's elected few and avoid damnation in hell.

For the wealthy UK aristocracy in the nineteenth century this journey would be recast as the 'The Grand Tour of Europe' wherein young men, but sometimes also young women, often accompanied by their mentors and would-be chaperones, could sample the comforts and freedoms of hotel life, while visiting important tourist destinations in France, Italy and Switzerland, and so gain experience of the 'other' or 'the foreign' in terms of classical antiquity and the Renaissance in art, food, culture and landscape. Hence, the pilgrim is the metaphor for identity building in modernity. By contrast, the stroller, the tourist and the vagabond jointly offer the postmodern metaphor of resisting the horror of being fixed. All these roles in liquid modernity are at leisure or at the very least not tied directly to paid employment and work disciplines.

For Bauman, the pilgrim's successor is Baudelaire's 'stroller' or Benjamin's 'stranger' – these are people *in* but not *of* the crowd; similarly tourism is a marginal activity. The tourist searches everywhere he goes *in* but his home is elsewhere. So, as one 'strolls' whether in city-centre arcades, out-of-town shopping malls, countryside parks or seaside promenades, the individual only fleetingly captures experiences, glancing at sights – perhaps important historical sites. One is blasé and distractedly pays attention to people and places, but, more importantly, one is perhaps noticed, one is on display, viewed by others but one is essentially self-contained and alone, just going about or at least minding one's own business. Through postmodern eyes all is ephemeral, transient and transitory. So in leisure one can explore and experiment with identities just as one can surf the Internet, visiting many websites and choosing to register, log in and become a member and so construct different identities or avatars. The dark side of this urban anonymity, this world of urban strangers, is an unexpected encounter with the 'urban other' (Taylor et al., 1996) or in Bauman's terms the vagabond – in the past master-less individuals who roamed from local parish to parish and whom poor law officers were keen to 'move on' lest they sought relief and became a burden on the rates. So, for Bauman, vagabonds are marginal people and are, in a sense, homeless. Poor people live on the margins of capitalist society and consumer culture. Liquid modernity thrives on simulation, ambiguity, deception and ambivalence. One would expect that these processes are even more powerful in virtual reality rather in the material world. On websites on the Internet, identities are not always what they appear or purport to be. There is always the danger of misrepresentation as some adults may choose to 'groom' children for their own dark pleasure. There is also the fear of the unknown as Internet bloggers or 'trolls' threaten rape, violence and murder against other Facebook or Twitter users.

6.5 Pilgrims, strollers and vagabonds

How useful are Bauman's ideal types of the *pilgrim*, the *stroller,* the *vagabond* and the *tourist* in understanding the following leisure experiences:

- Young people, usually students taking a 'gap year' before or after college or university – does it make a difference if this involves periods

(Continued)

(Continued)

of paid work, voluntary charity work, visiting far-flung relatives or attending important mega-events, for example rock concerts, music festivals, sporting competitions (e.g. Rugby and Football World Cups, Tour de France, the Olympics, etc.)

- A newly married couple on honeymoon

- Taking a holiday on a cruise ship

- Tackling an endurance event/challenge overseas single-handedly, for example a marathon/Audax cycle event, long-distance walk, rock climbing or a triathlon

- Shopping for new clothes – for oneself or a present for others, for example birthdays, Christmas, christenings, etc.

- A self-catering week in a holiday cottage

- A skiing holiday with 'mates'

- A city mini-break

- A summer month in one's own holiday home

- A celebrity millionaire spending a week under cover for a TV documentary

EXTREME LEISURE AND LEISURE LIFESTYLES

The recurring message of Chris Rojek's book, *Decentring Leisure* (1995), is one of the profound social change that accompanied the transition from industrial capitalism to post-industrialism. In this particular book his preferred terms to denote this seismic economic and cultural shift are Modernity 1 and Modernity 2. Whereas Modernity 1 is about rational productive work, state bureaucracy and ordered leisure, Modernity 2 is about the phenomenology (subjectivity) of individual experience and the individual's restless quest for pleasure and self-identity. In *Leisure and Culture* Rojek (2000) suggests a shift from ritual to performative culture. Societies must organize time and space for social and economic survival yet they have surplus energy and unused resources. At the heart of Modernity 1 are poverty, inequality and scarcity and the individual's role as a disciplined worker, *homo faber*, whereas abundance, conspicuous consumption and transgression lie at the heart of Modernity 2 wherein the individual is recast as a creative and playful *homo ludens*. In the final chapter, Rojek raises the question of whether leisure is an individual or a societal need. The productivist view is that, as *homo faber*, an individual should have the right to work. Alternatively, the postmodern thrust of the *homo ludens* emphasizes the importance of exploring play, learning and culture in the leisure society. Another recurring theme in Rojek's book stresses the processes of de-differentiation. De-differentiation features as a central concept in postmodern thinking which suggests that rigid traditional cultural boundaries are fragmenting and haemorrhaging: for example, the divisions that separate high and popular culture, and also those between work and leisure. Traditional elite forms of opera or art may become popularized, just as old industrial buildings can become tourist and leisure spaces and work offices become more relaxed, pleasant and computerized. With digitalization and computerization, people can work hard at 'working out' in their leisure time and also 'chill out' and relax during more flexible work hours. Few professional workers in service sector jobs have to face up to the discipline of clocking on and clocking off. This relaxation of work discipline has a downside, as such workers are expected to be flexible, to attend breakfast meetings and to work long hours at night or over weekends in order to meet organizational and project deadlines.

The de-differentiation of the boundaries between work and leisure gain significance in research into young adults with a taste for extreme sports or what Belinda Wheaton (2004) terms 'lifestyle sports'. Such activities celebrate the postmodern condition in that they tend to be individual pursuits, often demanding hi-tech equipment, stylized commodities, enhanced physical fitness and performance skills, risk taking and, most importantly, they are defined as central to the individual's self-identity. So, in answer to the Goffmanesque existential question, 'Well, who am I really?' the reply to one's self and others is immediately, 'I'm a rock climber, athlete, sky diver, snowboarder, mountain biker, surfer or fell runner'. In Modernity 2 work and occupation no longer determine or signify one's personal identity but rather what the individual chooses in leisure time. These activities constitute 'serious leisure' and the bedrock of personal identity, as is the case, for example, with women rock climbers where women can really be themselves when they are rock climbing (see Dilley and Scraton, 2010). Indeed, Wheaton suggests that lifestyle sports draw upon subaltern or subordinate subcultures and have the potential to challenge cultural traditions, particularly a gender order characterized by hegemonic masculinities.

Given the postmodern taste for restlessness and transgression, Rob Shields (1992) argues that these sports are liminal, denouncing or resisting institutionalization, regulations and commercialization. However, in late capitalism, these processes are hard to resist as niche market entrepreneurial firms seek to commodify sporting forms and equipment with brand names and distinctive exclusive products: surfing and skateboarding would be good examples here. Bespoke commercial websites, often celebrity endorsed, as well as social network sites such as Facebook and Twitter, feed off and develop interest in lifestyle sports. As yet few detailed empirical content analyses have been completed on this plethora of webs (what some cultural researchers now refer to as 'netnography'), but one only needs to look at Sheldon Brown's (2001) website or search the Internet for 'cycling' to gain an insight into the diversity and intensity of these subcultural sites (see http://www.sheldonbrown.com/home.html). Nevertheless, work and paid employment are often chosen to facilitate the leisure interest in extreme challenges such as mountain biking, rock climbing, surfing, paragliding, and so forth. Extreme sports often operate with strong subcultures which celebrate the playfulness, enjoyment and ecstasy of peak experiences (which are denied or crushed by routine everyday life). The postmodern condition of restlessness, the search for excitement, stimulation and challenge are central to these pursuits.

6.6 Extreme sports

Belinda Wheaton has written extensively on these extreme or lifestyle sports. She argues that they exhibit the following characteristics.

Extreme sports:

- are recent
- emphasize 'grassroots' participation
- involve the consumption of new objects and technologies (e.g. longboards in surfing)
- demand commitment in time, money and lifestyle and in terms of collective expression
- generate a participatory ideology that promotes fun, hedonism and self-actualization
- are practised predominantly by white middle-class Western 'youth'
- are usually individualistic in form and attitude
- are non-aggressive yet involve risk and danger
- take place in outdoor spaces and are 'liminal' without fixed spaces or boundaries. In the 1980s, these activities were also termed 'whizz sports' or Xgames. Participants such as skateboarders challenged urban planners and the preconceived functionality of architectural design in car parks, pedestrian shopping centres, and squares. Equally, BASE jumpers choose antennas, skyscrapers, bridges and cliffs for free-fall parachute jumping.

What experiences have you of any of the extreme sports mentioned above?

What arguments can you offer to support Lincoln Allison's (2001) claim that lifestyle sports are postmodern revivals of 'amateurism' in sport?

CONCLUSION

This chapter has explored current debates in social theory about the nature of the family life cycle, leisure and the life course. It has been suggested that the growth of home-based leisure and individualization has been partly captured in social theory by the nuclearization thesis and more recently by the emergence of a fragmented postmodern cultural condition. In addition, this chapter has developed the arguments of the previous chapter about young people 'growing up' by examining how transitions into adulthood, into work and into the roles of parents and parenting have become less clear and pre-determined. Institutional changes, specifically in patterns of work and education, as well as more complicated family relationships and networks, have resulted in increased ambiguity and ambivalence. The chapter has begun to deal with some of the issues that surround postmodern culture and change by touching on Zygmunt Bauman's conceptualization of liquid modernity. These ideas are developed further in the Chapter 8 which discusses middle age and moral panics about mid-life crises.

7

DIVIDED LEISURE: LEISURE AND SOCIAL CLASS

THIS CHAPTER

- Introduces key ideas of class, culture and identity
- Discusses Thorstein Veblen's concept of the leisure class and conspicuous consumption
- Examines the contemporary debate about 'chavs'
- Explains Pierre Bourdieu's ideas of cultural capital and competence
- Explores key concepts underpinning the social divisions of gender, race and sexuality.

LEISURE, SOCIAL DIVISIONS AND IDENTITY

People are often uncomfortable with talk of social division. Many of us, indeed, would prefer to think that crucial cleavages in society such as social class are a thing of the past. A difficulty here is in recognizing clear markers of social class. It was easier in the 1930s when upper-class males sported top hats and working men wore cloth caps. Today clothing such as jeans is common to all groups, even presidents and prime ministers. However, some writers, while acknowledging the difficulty of identifying social class, have argued powerfully that it remains. For instance, George Orwell once wrote: 'Whichever way you turn this curse of class-difference confronts you like a wall of stone. Or rather it is not so much like a stone wall as the plate-glass plane of an aquarium; it is so easy to pretend that it isn't there, and so impossible to get through it' (Orwell, 1986–87: 145).

Two things should be clearly understood before reading this chapter. One is that leisure is contoured by social division. That's to say, middle-class people, generally speaking, have different leisure opportunities and experiences than the working class; male leisure usually differs from female; black from white; gay from straight, and so on. The other – a corollary of the first – is that leisure can never be seen simply as a matter of *access* – to pubs, parks, squash courts, or whatever. Leisure experiences are crucially bound up with life chances and identity. This chapter explores the ways in which academic debate has progressively taken these considerations into account. We begin with the most influential theory of social division in intellectual history – Marxism.

MARXISM, CLASS AND LEISURE

Marx wrote principally during the middle of the nineteenth century and was one of a number of thinkers – radical or conservative – to grapple with the problems perceived to arise from the growth of industrial society. Some of these thinkers were concerned primarily with the problem of social order and of how it could be maintained. A particular concern here was with the huge agglomeration of people in the expanding industrial cities across Europe, and the threat, at times, of social and political unrest that these large populations posed. We can date the increased currency of the terms 'the masses' and 'the working classes' to this period and much of the social philosophy written, then and since, represents a longing for, and a romanticizing of, the supposedly more organic rural communities of pre-industrial times.

One thing seems fairly certain in relation to the transition from the country to the town and that is that this brought about a sharper division between work and leisure. As the Marxist historian E.P. Thompson suggested, life in the countryside had been regulated by the weather and the seasons; in the factory life of industrial capitalism it was regulated by the clock (Thompson, 1967). Karl Marx, in his early writing, envisaged a socialist society in which people would be liberated from the strict division of labour imposed by capitalism and the relationship between work and leisure would be fluid. In this society, he wrote in 1845, it will be: 'possible for me to do one thing today and another tomorrow, to hunt in the morning, fish in the afternoon, rear cattle in the evening, criticise after dinner, just as I have a mind, without ever becoming hunter, fisherman, shepherd or critic' (From Marx's *The German Ideology* of 1845, quoted in Tucker, 1972: 124).

There was, however, no sign of this liberated society in the mid-nineteenth century. Instead, as the working week was gradually reduced – initially with the granting of Sunday as a free day – policy makers sought to promote what they called 'rational recreation', pastimes, in other words, that would in their view improve members of the lower classes as people. The aristocracy and gentry, by contrast, were an established *leisure class* and the history of the nineteenth century is one of accommodation between the landed class, the rising capitalist middle class and the emergent proletariat. There are two vital considerations here: the widespread concern that *commerce* and the *profit motive* would threaten the social bonds that were perceived to hold society together, and the notion that democracy would bring political power to those either ill-equipped to exercise it or bent on radical transformation of society. These twin considerations gave rise to a preoccupation with *culture*. A landmark here was Matthew Arnold's *Culture and Anarchy*, first published in 1869. Culture, wrote Arnold, 'seeks to do away with classes; to make the best that has been thought and known in the world current everywhere; to make all men live in an atmosphere of sweetness and light ... ' (Arnold, 1960: 70). This notion survived strongly into the twentieth century and was associated in Britain with the Cambridge University lecturer F.R. Leavis (1895–1978) who sought to identify the best in English literature and to foster an intellectual elite that would teach and sustain what he called the Great Tradition (Leavis, 1948). He insisted on a sharp distinction between good and bad in culture and was a severe critic of 'mass culture', typified for him by television and Hollywood films.

7.1 Elite culture

Do you think there is still an 'elite culture'? If so, what does it consist of?

What is 'mass culture'? Suggest whether or not it is socially beneficial, and why.

Think of your favourite book, music album, TV programme and film. Make a case *for* and *against* each of these being taught as a set text for GCSE.

It is perhaps surprising, then, that left-wing commentators on culture should write out of sympathy with Leavis, and from similar assumptions. For instance, philosophers of the 'Frankfurt School' in Germany in the 1930s wrote of the corrosive effects of modern mass culture, media and materialism. One of them, Herbert Marcuse, wrote in 1950 that people now recognized themselves only 'in their commodities; they find their soul in their automobile, hi-fi set, split-level home, kitchen equipment ... ' (Marcuse, 1972: 22). Similarly, as we observed in Chapter 5, the left-wing American sociologist C. Wright Mills argued a year later that 'Each day men sell little pieces of themselves in order to try to buy them back each night and week end with the coin of "fun"' (Mills, 1951: 237). And, in his largely autobiographical book *The Uses of Literacy* (1957), reflecting on his working-class childhood in Leeds between the wars, the English academic Richard Hoggart argued that commercial and/or Americanized popular entertainments were weakening the culture of his own class of origin.

Hoggart was one of a number of writers who saw working-class culture as a culture in its own right, based on collectivism, solidarity and a sense of 'us and them'. It was socialist, perhaps, or it carried a strong commitment to democracy and resistance. Another was the highly influential Raymond Williams. Williams was paradoxically a follower both of Marx and of Leavis, having written for the latter's journal, *Scrutiny*. His intellectual work tried to reconcile these (apparently contradictory) impulses: there was 'high culture', he argued, and there was a broader culture, embracing a whole way of life and a 'structure of feeling' based on 'lived experience'. (This idea was present in Williams' work from the mid-1950s but is developed most notably in his book *Marxism and Literature* – see Williams (1977).) This theorizing was important for at least two reasons. First, Williams convinced many Marxists that culture should not now be seen straightforwardly as part of a society's 'superstructure' – determined by the economic base of that society: allowance had to be made for people's subjectivity. Second, he came to question the notion that an elite, 'high' culture was indispensable to a civilized society; in 1958, he condemned the 'extraordinary decision to call certain things culture and then separate them, as with a park wall, from ordinary people and ordinary work'. (This quote is taken from Williams' essay 'Culture is ordinary'; it is reprinted in Ben Highmore's *The Everyday Life Reader* – see Highmore (2002: 94).)

The work of Hoggart and Williams was a vital factor in the growth of Cultural Studies in Britain and Hoggart became the first director of the Centre for Contemporary Cultural Studies (CCCS) at Birmingham University in 1964. The centre's work tended, expectably, to concentrate on the study of class cultures and, within that framework, to investigate the widely decried leisure activities of working-class youth. Teddy Boys, Mods, Skinheads, football hooligans and others – the successive foci, as we saw in Chapter 5, of moral panics in the wider society – were analysed as *subcultures* within working-class life, waging a symbolic battle against destructive social change. Another important piece of research, by CCCS member Paul Willis, explored the antipathy of working-class lads towards their secondary schooling and their positive, masculine embrace of unskilled labour (Willis, 1977).

Working-class (usually male) youth were seen, not as passive recipients of the passing of traditional jobs and industries, but, as Williams had prescribed, as enacting their own structures of feeling – in this case, mounting 'resistance through rituals' (see Hall and Jefferson, 1976). The centre's analyses were increasingly influenced by the work of the long-forgotten Italian Marxist Antonio Gramsci (1891–1937) whose principal writing had been done while he had been imprisoned by Mussolini's fascist regime. The CCCS did, however, also include studies of the specific problems faced by females (see, e.g, The Women's Studies Group, 1978) and ethnic minorities (see, e.g., CCCS, 1982), thus reflecting the growing movements in the wider society for feminism and anti-racism. This work, while clearly progressive, posed two clear (and related) problems for the development of the Marxist analysis of leisure and culture. One was that gender and 'race' self-evidently cut across class. The other was that the social movements fighting sexism and racism (and their academic spokespeople) were organized around *identity* and the politics of the personal. This, by definition, entailed giving a voice and a validation to previously ignored minorities and not dismissing their experiences as (to adopt the popular Marxist concepts) mere 'alienation' or 'false consciousness'. A good example of the difficulties that could arise here is the work of CCCS researcher Janice Winship on women's magazines. Addressing the conventional feminist socialist view that these magazines merely demeaned women and boosted capitalists' profits, Winship declared that she enjoyed reading them:

> That didn't mean I wasn't critical of them. I was (and am) but it was just that double edge – my simultaneous attraction and rejection – which seemed to me the real nub of feminist concern. Many of the guises of femininity in women's magazines contribute to the secondary status from which we still desire to free ourselves. At the same time it is the dress of femininity which is both source of the pleasure of being a woman – and not a man – and in part the raw material for a feminist vision of the future. (Winship, 1987: xiii)

7.2 Women's magazines

Find at least four women's magazines, each aimed at a different section of the women's magazine market.

Suggest in what ways, if any, they might contribute to the secondary status of women that Winship refers to.

Similarly, suggest in what ways, if any, they might be a source of 'the pleasure of being a woman – and not a man'.

Similar problems faced those wishing to accommodate issues of 'race' within the new Cultural Studies. In the elite national culture that Leavis had sought to protect and Williams subsequently to question, there had been no black voices. Nor had black people featured very strongly in Hoggart's reminiscences of working-class Leeds. These absences were acknowledged by the British-Guyanese CCCS researcher Paul Gilroy when, with massive irony, he borrowed a line from a racist chant for the title of his first book: *There Ain't No Black in the Union Jack* (Gilroy, 1987). In the book Gilroy recognizes the same type of difficulty as that faced by feminist researchers:

> Feminist critiques of Marxism have emphasized the political privileges attached by it to work outside the home and the way it has devalued labour performed in the private sphere. They point towards the same critical conclusion even when, as in some socialist feminist writing, a reconstruction of class theory is proposed. If class analysis is to retain a place in explaining contemporary politics in general and the relationships between black and white workers, citizens, neighbours and friends in particular, it must be ruthlessly modernized. (Gilroy, 1987: 19)

Black experience, in other words, could not, any more than female experience, be reduced to the workings of capitalism, nor embraced by any theory predicated solely on social class. And besides being spread, as females were, across the class structure, racialized groups differed, according to Gilroy, in their degree of assimilation into the national culture: those of African descent he perceived to be more marginalized – 'despite the unifying tendencies of racist activity which regards the racial characteristics of both "Pakis" and "niggers" as being equally worthy of hatred' (Gilroy, 1987: 39).

But if these (wholly understandable) theoretical difficulties had caused the class-centred analysis of Cultural Studies to falter, a decisive reassertion of the neo-Marxian approach and of the importance of class in relation to leisure was published by two other alumni of the CCCS in the mid-1980s. This came in the form of *The Devil Makes Work*, a landmark book in the field published by John Clarke and Chas Critcher in 1985. The title played with the old Protestant aphorism 'The devil makes work for idle hands', a sentiment that condemned all leisure activity, but the book itself confronts the proliferating (and opposite) view that prevailing 'leisure activity patterns' were 'the outcome of untrammelled individual choice' (Clarke and Critcher, 1985: 145). Clarke and Critcher thus challenged the growing political orthodoxy that class no longer mattered (that 'we are all middle class now' or, as Margaret Thatcher suggested two years later, that 'there is no such thing as society. There are individual men and women and there are families': these famous words were uttered in an interview with *Women's Own* magazine and published on 31 October 1987), while trying at the same time to accommodate feminist and anti-racist critiques. Yes, women had different (and more restricted) access to leisure than men and, yes, black communities had different leisure patterns to white, but both female and black leisure were ultimately contoured by class (see Clarke and Critcher, 1985, Chapter 5, in particular: 145–180).

CULTURAL STUDIES AND THE CONTINUING DEBATE OVER CLASS DIVISIONS

A number of writers have pursued this theme of the continued importance of class, usually with new inflections to take account of economic and technological changes. The leading social theorist Scott Lash, for example, looks at classes in relation to the emergence of important new information technologies. He argues that classes persist, but not in terms of collective organizations, or even communal forms in relation to the mode of production, but rather in relation to modes of information. There are, in his view, three classes: those who manipulate information at the 'sharp end' (financiers, business experts, IT gurus); those who work with Information and Communication as part of their work and in consumption; and those who are excluded, the underclass or 'information poor' (Lash, 2002).

Perhaps the most influential writer to explore the relationship between social class and leisure, however, was the French sociologist Pierre Bourdieu (1930–2002). Bourdieu is probably best known for analysing class in relation to the concept of *cultural capital*.

There is a certain irony that British Cultural Studies turned to Italian Marxism when starting to map out a new problematic around class, hegemony and modernity. Anxious to distance themselves from the bleak structural Marxism of Louis Althusser, other French writers tended to be overlooked or to be less influential or inspirational than one would expect. For example, while British Cultural Studies became immersed in the work of Gramsci, Pierre Bourdieu's work was busily addressing the relationships between class and culture in France. However, Bourdieu (1984) has had a profound influence both on figurational sociology and on postmodern studies of cultures of consumption. Both perspectives seek to distance themselves from Marxism and class analysis, yet for Bourdieu class is now widely seen as central to any understanding of culture.

Perhaps Bourdieu's ideas were less influential in shaping British Cultural Studies than they might have been because his major work *Distinction: A Social Critique of Taste* (Bourdieu, 1984) arrived late on the scene, being published in 1979 and translated by Richard Nice in 1984. As the title of his book implies, Bourdieu sought to challenge conventional wisdom, which argued that aesthetic judgements were expressions of some detached, universal disinterested discourse. Art and culture were not separate from economic or social factors, but rather expressions of both status struggle and class hierarchy. Stated simply, classes sought to distance themselves from others by expressions of taste. Cultural forms were hierarchically graded and coded; classes expressed themselves in their mastery and consumption of high and low culture:

> To the socially recognised hierarchy of the arts, and within each one of them, of genres, schools and periods, corresponds a social hierarchy of the consumers. This predisposes tastes function as markers of 'class'. The manner in which culture has been acquired lives on the manner of using it. (Bourdieu, 1984: 2)

Bourdieu's work sought to engage with the four formations of modernity – the economic, the political, the social and the cultural. Traditional Marxist analysis had located class divisions in inequalities of capital, property and income; selling labour power at the point of production was central to understanding class position and class consciousness. Bourdieu argued that just as there were markets for accumulation and display of economic capital there were also markets for accumulation and display of cultural capital. Thorstein Veblen's theory of the leisure class (Veblen, 1994) had already suggested that economic elites displayed their material wealth and gained status by conspicuous consumption. Bourdieu argued that other classes may similarly value cultural

goods and services, seeking to demonstrate cultural competence in their consumption of high culture. Bourdieu immediately offered a synthesis of the
economic and the cultural in modernity by dividing classes into those who
possessed economic and cultural capital and those who did not.

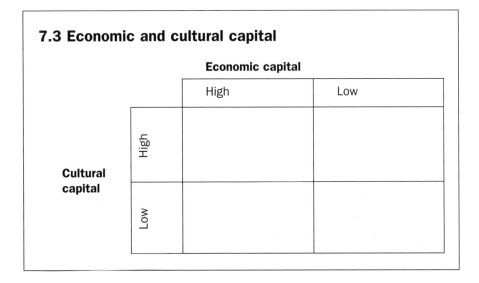

7.3 Economic and cultural capital

Bourdieu's analysis shifted attention away from the economic towards the
cultural, as classes sought to differentiate themselves from others in matters of
taste. It was, in his view, a question of class and of distinction:

> Tastes (i.e. manifested preferences) are the practical affirmation of an
> inevitable difference. It is no accident that, when they have to be justi-
> fied, they are asserted purely negatively, by the refusal of other tastes. In
> matters of taste, more than anywhere else, all determination is negation;
> and tastes are perhaps first and foremost distastes, disgust provoked by
> horror or visceral intolerance ('sick making') of the tastes of others. ...
> The most intolerable thing for those who regard themselves as the posses-
> sors of legitimate culture is the sacrilegious reuniting of tastes which taste
> dictates should be separated. (Bourdieu, 1984: 56–57)

Postmodern analysis, as we will see later in this chapter, argues that within late
modernity these localized class cultures are no longer relevant or at least
become increasingly de-differentiated, more flexible and less significant in everyday life. But, for those in sympathy with Bourdieu's analysis, examples of the
'visceral intolerance' he talks about are not hard to find. There is, for instance,
the widespread media scorn for 'chavs', a signifier for coarseness and bad taste
but, in the opinion of one recent author, simply a synonym for 'working class'
(Jones, 2011). Witness also the packaging in the United States of 'trailer trash'
distress for popular television programmes such as *The Jerry Springer Show*.

THE MEANING OF 'CHAV'

In the UK the word 'chav' seems to be at the heart of much contemporary conversation about social class, and often heated debate now surrounds the use of the word. In this section we chart some of the social progress of the word and present as many sides to the debate about its use as possible. At the online Oxford Dictionaries the word 'chav', as a noun, is described as 'British, informal and derogatory' and it refers to 'a young lower-class person typified by brash and loutish behaviour and the wearing of (real or imitation) designer clothes'. It dates no further back than the 1990s and probably derives from the Romany word 'chavo' meaning 'boy' or 'youth'. The word is sometimes said to have originated in Chatham, Kent, and to be a shortening of that name (http://www.urbandictionary.com/define.php?term=chav (accessed 11 November 2013)).

Samples of the deployment of this 'informal and derogatory' term can be found at sites such as Urban Dictionary, a populist platform where people contribute their own definitions of words. Here the word 'chavs' is described as applicable 'loosely to every culture with a nasty, thieving element' or as the dregs of human existence. They live merely to piss everyone else off with their love of crap clothing and manky gold jewellery. They have taken the wearing of tracksuits and baseball caps to a new level of pikieness. Chav girls (or chavettes) commonly sport the Croydon Facelift (hair pulled back in a bun so tight that it pulls their faces tight) with at least 6 dangly faux-gold earings [sic] in each ear. Also often seen pushing a pram round shopping centers [sic] while chain-smoking and wearing fake burberry or nasty velour tracksuits. (Taken from *theurbandictionary.com*: http://www.urbandictionary.com/define.php?term=chav&defid=566598 (accessed 15 February 2014).)

Together, these characterizations place 'chavs', geographically and socially. They are seen as sitting on the bottom rung of the class system and are identified with travellers – 'pikies' is another term for travellers. They are seen as residing principally in the London hinterland: the outer suburbs (such as Croydon) and the overspill towns of the Thames estuary in Essex and Kent. They are identified by their purported laziness, criminal tendencies and most importantly, their brash attire.

'Chavs' now have a prominent place in popular culture. For example, the BBC's sketch-based comedy show *Little Britain*, shown between 2003 and 2006, featured a recurrent character called Vicky Pollard. The garrulous and ignorant Vicky, played by a man in drag, was seen by many as a 'chavette' stereotype. A number of websites invite discussion of the 'worst chav town' in Britain and there is also a Twitter site for this purpose. There are spoof guides to 'chav' culture, such as *Chav! A User's Guide to Britain's New Ruling Class* (Wallace and Spanner, 2004).

In April of 2006 the Princes William and Harry attended a fancy dress party dressed as 'chavs'. Two years later Prince Harry's girlfriend Chelsy Davy, an undergraduate at Leeds University, followed suit, attending a party 'wearing the stereotypical uniform of the chav: a baseball cap turned to the side, a white Adidas tracksuit jacket and plenty of 'bling' jewellery – including gold hoop earrings' (Kay, 2008).

But perhaps the most vivid presence in British popular culture of a person styled as a 'chav' was that of Jade Goody (1981–2009) who came to public notice as a contestant in the 'reality' TV show *Big Brother* in 2002. Goody, the dental nurse from Essex, was initially vilified in British tabloid newspapers for her lack of sophistication and racist remarks, but won huge public support for her stoicism in the face of terminal cancer, much of which was shown on television. Coverage of her death boosted circulation among the British popular press (Luft, 2009). The Prime Minister, Gordon Brown, paid tribute to Goody at her passing and celebrities such as David and Victoria Beckham sent flowers to her funeral.

From time to time other public figures have been identified as 'chavs-made-good' – among them the singer Cheryl Cole, footballer Wayne Rooney, Katie Price (aka 'Jordan') and Michael Carroll, winner of nearly £10 million on the UK National Lottery in 2002 (de Castella, 2011). Carroll had 'King of Chavs' painted on the side of his van.

All this talk of 'chavs' – most of it derisive – has sparked an often angry debate in the British media. In an article of 2011, the liberal journalist Polly Toynbee condemned the use of the term 'chav', arguing that 'wrapped inside this little word is the quintessence of Britain's great social fracture. Over the last 30 years the public monstering of a huge slice of the population by luckier, better-paid people has become commonplace.' She further suggested that: 'Fostering the loathing of a feral underclass allows public resentment to be diverted from those above to those below' (Toynbee, 2011).

In his book on the subject, the left-wing columnist Owen Jones agreed with Toynbee that the word had become assimilated into daily discourse – he recalled being at a dinner party where a guest observed innocently 'It's sad that Woolworth's is closing. Where will all the chavs buy their Christmas presents?' – and went on to suggest that talk of chavs was a shorthand way of demonizing the working class (Jones, 2011: 1).

The sociologist Imogen Tyler agreed:

> Being identified as 'chav' not only means having the place you live, the way you speak, the clothes you wear, your culture, habits, and lifestyle subject to perverse misrepresentation, mockery, and derision but also actively blocks your social mobility. In the final instance, the cumulative effect of disgust at chavs is the screening of the disenfranchised white poor from view; they are rendered invisible, inaudible or, like Vicky Pollard, laughably incomprehensible. (Tyler, 2008: 32)

But right-wing writers were unapologetic in their contempt for 'chavs'. In *The Times* James Delingpole wrote:

The reason Vicky Pollard caught the public imagination is that she embodies with such fearful accuracy several of the great scourges of contemporary Britain: aggressive all-female gangs of embittered, hormonal, drunken teenagers; gym slip mums who choose to get pregnant as a career option; pasty-faced, lard-gutted slappers who'll drop their knickers in the blink of an eye ... these people do exist and are every bit as ripe and just a target for social satire as were, say, the raddled working-class drunks sent up by Hogarth in Gin Lane. (Delingpole, 2006)

Five years later, and in response to Toynbee, *Telegraph* columnist Ed West was similarly defiant:

Of course when upper-class partygoers dress up as chavs it has a class-mocking undertone, in about the same way that tarts and vicars parties have an anti-clerical undertone, but the word itself has little to do with snobbery. Working-class people use it all the time, understand what it means and, if anything, dislike chavs more than anyone. Why? Because they have to live with them. Being a chav is not about being poor, or unskilled, or any of the traditional markers of the proletariat, but about attitude, and in particular one that lacks civic-mindedness and civility. (West, 2011)

7.4 The debate about 'chavs'

Julian Fellowes, the creator of the popular period TV drama *Downton Abbey*, complained that it was not 'chavs', but 'posh' people who suffered the most derision in contemporary Britain, claiming that 'poshism is the last acceptable form of discrimination' (White, 2011).

The provocative blogger Brendan O'Neill expressed scorn for both these positions, arguing in 2011:

In many ways, of course, the rise of toff-hatred and chav-attacks speaks to the very real, objective decline of two major classes: the old conservative ruling class and the powerful working class. .... into the vacuum left by the demise of the old right and the old left, assuming political and intellectual influence almost by default, come the value-lite middle classes, the modern-day cultural elite, who are spectacularly intolerant of both the well-spoken class above them and the chippy class beneath them. (O'Neill, 2011)

- In 'chav' mythology, 'chavs' seem to live around London and the Thames estuary. What do you think is the significance of this?

- 'Chavs' are deemed to make bad leisure choices – the baseball hats, the cars with furry dice hanging off the rear view mirror, the 'bling' jewellery, the 'trackie' bottoms and so on. Why do you think these choices are seen as bad?

- Drawing on *Little Britain* clips available on the Internet, make a case *for* and *against* the Vicky Pollard character.

- What does West mean when he claims that 'chavs' lack 'civility?

- How valid is the argument that scorn for 'chavs' constitutes the 'demonization of the working class'?

- How accurate is the suggestion that we have seen a decline of the two major classes in British society?

Bourdieu developed a range of interlocking concepts which have reframed some of the main concepts of social theory. The key concepts of role, identity, socialization, status groups and cultural institutions and processes were now recast within a class perspective, using formulaic short hand: '[(habitus) (capital)] + field = practice'. For critics of Bourdieu this was achieved by a literary sleight of hand, involving nothing more than a change in terminology, with the concept of class completely disconnected from its economic ties and the explanatory power given to it by Marxism. But Bourdieu's analysis needs further elaboration and there has been a wealth of supporters, both Marxist and non-Marxist, keen to map out his contribution (see Jarvie and Maguire, 1994; Murdock, 1978; Rojek, 2001).

Bourdieu argued that classes had separate tastes and general dispositions and these were embedded in fields of practice. Each of these fields constituted a distinctive way of life, or a class *habitus*. Individuals were born into a class habitus and this shaped both their conscious and their unconscious tastes. For Bourdieu habitus permeates individual choices and attitudes; tastes in music, exercise regimes, preferences in food and cooking styles, holidays, sports, films, and so on, can be related back to class habitus, upbringing and education. Bourdieu does not simply assert these interrelationships in theory but uses them to classify and interpret survey data on consumption patterns collected in 1963 and 1967/68 as expressions of cultural capital and cultural competence.

Thinking about class tastes and the importance of patterns of consumption (rather than production) opens up important debates about the changing nature and composition of classes and not least about the processes of usurpation and emulation amongst status groups. For Bourdieu, education and educational accreditation are decisive mechanisms that differentiate, symbolize and consolidate tastes and establish status and distinction. The length and character of education develops and consolidates class dispositions and cultural knowledge, which in turn express themselves in different patterns of cultural consumption. Rather than the rise of the proletariat, Bourdieu points to the rise of the intelligentsia, a new middle class of educated professionals who accumulate and display high cultural competence but are less successful economically. Clearly, in Bourdieu's terms, working-class groups lack both economic and cultural capital and are defined within existing classificatory schemata as 'vulgar', wallowing in popular or 'low' cultural forms. Bourdieu's work modernizes Marxist perspectives in so far as it shifts analysis away from economic production, work and labour power and directs it towards cultural consumption, leisure and taste. This is in line with much contemporary social theory. Paul Gilroy, for instance, said recently:

> ... my fundamental problem with Marxism has always been what could be called its productivism. Even in the times when I tried to translate my own thinking into a more Marxian vocabulary, I was very clear about the tyranny of productivism and that side of Marx which, I think as Adorno says, wanted to turn the world into a big work house and to look at human social development through the relationship between self-making and labour. (These remarks are taken from 'Cosmopolitanism, Blackness, and Utopia', a conversation between Paul Gilroy and Tommie Shelby posted on the website *Philosophy in a Time of Terror*, 23 October 2010: http://philosophyinatimeoferror.wordpress.com/2010/10/23/interview-between-tommie-shelby-and-paul-gilroy-class-post/ (accessed 19 July 2011). The exchanges were originally published in *Transitions* in 2008.)

However, although the Frankfurt School long ago pursued an interest in the commercialization and commodification of culture and the role of cultural industries, Bourdieu rejects their pessimistic view of alienated labour and designations of mass tastes as 'false needs' confected under consumer capitalism. Bourdieu maps out class differences in cultures, habitus and dispositions, thereby suggesting some kind of cultural autonomy for classes. He is at pains to point out, and at very great length, that cultural categories and systems of classification are, by their very nature, fields of struggle and contestation. Dominant classes seek to impose and secure hierarchical systems of classification and categories, which privilege their own particular habitus, dispositions, taste and manners. Such classificatory schemes maintain distinctions as natural or self-evident; social sciences must generate an appropriate epistemology, research methodologies and techniques of data collection and analysis that lay bare class hierarchies and class dispositions. Consequently, Bourdieu's use of empirical data to connect disparate and unexplored cultural fields in relation to the body, eating, cooking, film, TV, music, and so on, is in no way incidental or arbitrary. In his work Bourdieu is determined to challenge bourgeois social science paradigms, which, because they are grounded in notions of individual free choice, serve to disengage individuals from the very structures, classificatory frameworks and fields that shape their lives.

Bourdieu's influence survives strongly in social theory, and the importance of class has been reasserted by writers such as Beverley Skeggs, who in 2004 wrote:

> class is so ubiquitous, one wonders why all the energy, anxiety and aggressive denial is put into proving that the working-class either does

not exist or, if it does, is worthless. Class struggle is not just about collective action ... it is also about the positioning, judgements and relations that are entered into on a daily and personal basis. (Skeggs, 2004: 173)

It is also evident in a significant piece of research on social class published in 2013 by a team of sociological researchers, including academics from France and Norway and led by professors Mike Savage of the London School of Economics and Fiona Devine of Manchester University (Savage et al., 2013). The research was aimed primarily at an academic audience but gained wider currency through a collaboration with the BBC, who popularized its main findings ('Huge survey reveals seven social classes in UK', http://www.bbc.co.uk/news/uk-22007058 (accessed 15 October 2013)).

Two aspects of this research are crucial to thinking about leisure and class in contemporary societies. One is that the team confirm a widening of the gulf between the social classes in Britain today. They propose a new, seven-class model to replace previous three- or five-part typologies. At the apex is an elite, wealthy and heavily self-recruiting, making it quite remote and separate from the rest of society; at the base is the 'precariat'. In between are two strands of middle class – the 'established' and the 'technical' – and three sections of working class – 'new affluent', 'traditional' and 'emergent'. The precariat – a term coined by London University professor Guy Standing (see Standing, 2011a, 2011b) – is composed of working-class people who are subject to poverty and, when they have work at all, precarious working conditions: 'flexible' work patterns, 'zero hours' contracts and low wage 'McJobs' in call centres or care homes, on check-outs, driving vans, and so on. (The existence of a precariat is not universally accepted. See, for example, Choonara (2011).)

Secondly, the team adopt and develop Bourdieu's concept of cultural capital in their study. They distinguish between 'highbrow cultural capital' – familiarity with, interest in and access to classical music, stately homes, museums, art galleries, jazz, the theatre and French cuisine – and 'emergent cultural capital' – video games, social network sites, the Internet, playing and/or watching sport, spending time with friends, going to the gym and attending gigs. The precariat scores low on both these indices – predictably, perhaps, since most of the activities cited are quite expensive – and we are left to wonder what constitutes the leisure life of the lower working class. We can say with reasonable certainty, though, that it is heavily restricted to comparatively inexpensive pursuits such as watching television. Recent research has shown that in the early years of this century: the proportion of children living in a family that could not afford to take a holiday away from home had risen; so had the number (and proportion) of children whose parents could not afford to let them have friends round for tea; likewise the number of children who were too poor to pursue a hobby and the number of children living in single-parent families without access to a car. (Dorling, forthcoming; for further information on the findings of the Economic and Social Research Council project 'Poverty and Social Exclusion', go to: http://www.poverty.ac.uk/)

LEISURE, SOCIAL THEORY AND THE POLITICS OF IDENTITY

As we have seen, explanations of culture based upon social class could not wholly satisfy scholars seeking to show the importance of gender and 'race' to the understanding of social and political life. There's little doubt that these (and related) theoretical currents reflected important political changes in Western societies during the period since the Second World War. These changes, broadly speaking, have entailed the decline in class politics (as evidenced in a generally decreasing support for major political parties at election time) and the corresponding rise of a new politics. This new politics was based on identity and derived from the new social movements of the 1960s that campaigned for the rights of women, ethnic minorities, gay people and the disabled (or, perhaps on 'single issues' such as abortion, nuclear weapons, the environment, the death penalty or animal rights). In Cultural Studies these changes have manifested themselves, *inter alia*, in theories of gender, 'race' and sexuality. Generally speaking, there has been a trend away from approaches that concern themselves with social class or economics and towards a preoccupation with identity and selfhood. A major influence here has been the French social theorist Michel Foucault (1926–1984) the thrust of whose work (Foucault, 2006 [1961], 1975, 1990, 1992, 1998) is that institutions, almost irrespective of their specific nature, have a dehumanizing effect on the individual, whose task it then becomes to resist institutionalization in all its manifestations. Foucault was one of a number of French intellectuals who embraced, but then in the wake of the political upheavals of 1968, rejected Marxism, seeking instead to validate more personal, identity-based interpretations of the world, such as feminism and anarchism. This Foucault called 'the insurrection of subjugated knowledges' (Foucault, 2003: 7). This whole development has brought Cultural Studies closer to debates about leisure, since leisure is, for most people, the social domain in which identity is forged and expressed. There has, needless to say, been less concern with class culture, solidarity or the patterns of perceived resistance among working-class youth. The new emphasis has been upon individuals, their identities and their quest to become who and what they might want to be. Gilroy's impatience with 'productivism' has, in other words, been increasingly accommodated.

In the field of gender studies this meant a greater recourse to *social constructionism* – that's to say the assumption that, contrary to Freud, who once said that biology was destiny, the typical roles that males and females assume in any society are the product of culture. There is, in any event, a wide variety in the ways that males and females behave; there are *masculinities* and *femininities* and these are *socially constructed*. In the mid-1990s the Australian academic R.W. Connell summarized this transition. He noted an article in a local Sydney newspaper which suggested that women were more likely than men to stop people in the street to ask directions. This was 'simply because the sexes think differently'. If pressed on the question of sex differences, he wrote, psychologists and journalists would probably appeal to biology. They might recall research on sex differences in bodies and behaviour, brain sex, hormonal differences and genetic coding. These too have become staple media stories. If [the newspaper] went in for investigative journalism and the writer stepped across Parramatta to Sydney University, she would find that these views of masculinity and femininity, uncontroversial in the biological sciences, are fiercely contested in the humanities and social sciences. On those parts of the campus, academics talk about 'sex roles' or 'gender relations', and speak of masculinity and femininity being 'socially constructed' or 'constituted in discourse'. (Connell, 1995: 4–5. The last term, borrowed from Foucault, means that something becomes real simply by being described as real in language and conversation.)

Connell goes on to discuss a range of masculinities, some of them 'marginalized and subordinated' (Connell, 1995: 164). A number of these masculinities are prominent in recent popular culture and leisure lifestyles – notably the 'new man', the gay man and the jauntily heterosexual 'new lad'. Each of these is recognized and catered for in the market – the 'new man' with an expanding range of male cosmetics and 'metrosexual' exemplars such as David Beckham; the gay man with a multiplicity of goods and services defined as 'pink' and spaces defined as gay, such as the Gay Village in Manchester; and the 'new lad' with a clutch of unapologetic comedians, TV programmes like *Men Behaving Badly* and *Top Gear* and magazines such as *Loaded* (see Whelehan, 2000).

In relation to 'race' and ethnicity, notions of culture have been opened up to take account of vital factors such as migration, the dismantling of empires and globalization. Central to developments here has been the concept of 'hybridity'. In imperial times, this was a derogatory term for the offspring of inter-racial unions; such people were seen as unfortunate, or suspect – as with the 'half-breed' characters in cowboy films. More recently it has been used to take account of the patterns of migration and settlement of the late colonial and post-colonial periods and their effects on the forming of identities. An influential writer here has been the Jamaican intellectual Stuart Hall, a founding member of the Centre for Contemporary Cultural Studies and later Professor of Sociology at the Open University. By the early 1990s, Hall, now taking account of non- or ex-Marxist writers such as Foucault, had turned his attention to black culture and how it might now be understood. He argued that this could be done in two ways. The first way saw 'black' as a unifying term: through the adverse experiences imposed by slavery and colonialism, black people had sought a 'oneness' (Hall, 1990: 223), based on the black diaspora – the enforced uprooting and scattering of black people around the world. This perspective had been adopted for political reasons – to provide the basis for black resistance and emancipation. Now, though, in the post-colonial era and with subsequent patterns of migration and settlement, it was necessary to promote a more nuanced approach to black identity, one that indeed recognized a range of black *identities* based on the varied cultural traditions, histories and experiences previously subsumed under the word 'black'. This new lens could be trained both backwards towards societies of origin ('how different', Hall wrote, 'Martinique is from, say, Jamaica' (Hall, 1990: 227)), and also forward towards rising generations of children born, say, in Britain to Caribbean or Asian families who were developing their own cultures and senses of self. 'The diaspora experience as I intend it here is defined, not by essence or purity, but by the recognition of a necessary heterogeneity and diversity; by a conception of "identity" which lives with and through, not despite, difference; by hybridity' (Hall, 1990: 235). That's to say, adds Hall, we should acknowledge transformation and difference, or, citing CCCS writer Dick Hebdige, 'cross-overs' and 'cut-and-mix' (Hall, 1990: 236).

7.5 UK leisure patterns and immigration

In what ways have British leisure patterns been influenced by the post-war immigration of families from the Caribbean and the Asian sub-continent?

In what ways are the leisure patterns of the children of those families likely to have differed from those of their parents?

Another key development in the now long road towards the studying of identities and culture has been in relation to sexuality. Political initiatives to combat prejudice and discrimination against homosexuals date back to the nineteenth century, but a concerted social movement did not emerge until the late 1960s and, specifically, the riot that resulted from police harassment of the Stonewall gay bar in New York's Greenwich Village in 1969. This incident, in the wake of the widespread political tumult of the previous year (anti-Vietnam war demonstrations, feminist activism, hippie happenings, etc.) provoked much academic work on homosexual culture and, among other things, popularized the terms 'gay' and 'straight'. Much of the theorizing of same-sex attraction has been directed to show that it was, once again, socially constructed and not an illness or a biological pre-disposition, as mid-twentieth century conventional opinion held it to be. (See, e.g., Rose and Rose, 1982a, 1982b; see also Weeks, 1981 and Plummer, 1981. For a fuller catalogue of relevant academic work during this period, see Gough and Macnair, 1985.) In recent times, often through the increasingly pervasive influence of Foucault, this theorizing has seen the emergence of queer theory – an area of academic debate which has flourished particularly since 1990 and the publication of *Gender Trouble* by the American philosopher Judith Butler (Butler, 1990). Butler, in common with a range of queer theorists, challenges the conventional vocabulary in which social relations are discussed as 'hetero-normative', as, in other words, assuming heterosexual desires to be the only normal ones. Queer theory not only challenges

the 'binary' distinction between 'gay' and 'straight'; it casts doubt on the valid-
ity of the very categories of 'male' and 'female'. This means that the ideas of
'gender' itself, and likewise 'identity', are called into question. These facets of
the self, it is now argued, can never be seen as fixed: human beings are too
complex for that.

7.6 Gender, identity and leisure culture

In what ways may the questioning of this binary distinction between 'gay'
and 'straight' have influenced post-war leisure culture?

With this train of academic thought, theory has travelled still further away
from the idea of people as members of collectivities and, thus, from the notion
of culture itself. For many contemporary theorists, drinking at the well of post-
structuralism, people are really neither this, that nor the other; they are only,
following Foucault, 'constituted through discourse', and attempts to categorize
them ignore their individuality and their complexity.

CULTURE AND THE POSTMODERN

Contemporary societies are widely held to have become 'postmodern' and to
have acquired a 'postmodern' culture. This means that they have moved on
from 'modernity' which entailed societies dominated by industrial production,
technology, science and rational thought towards a society based on the production of services, the predominance of mass media and commercial popular
culture and characterized by challenges to grand theories or 'narratives'. One
clear consequence of this has been the fading of any distinction between high
and low culture. The Leavisite concept of a 'great tradition' of literature and
the arts, propagated and protected by a cultural elite, has been virtually aban-
doned. (A good explanation of postmodern culture is to be found in Strinati
(1992) and in McGuigan (1999).) This means that although, as Bourdieu
argues, some class-based taste groups might look down on others, previously
privileged authors, composers and other creative artists have no prior claim on
the popular imagination. In the postmodern popular cultural marketplace,
William Shakespeare is no better (and no worse) than *Coronation Street*,
Neighbours or *Harry Potter*; Bach no better (or worse) than The Beatles,
Michael Jackson or Eminem; Picasso no better (or worse) than the graffiti
adorning some inner-city landscape; and so on. In the words of the American
rock and roller Chuck Berry, 'Roll over Beethoven' (Berry, 1956).
    One clear and important implication of this trend has been seen in the realm
of media culture: the mass media – particularly television – have been subject

to substantial deregulation in countries such as the United States and Great Britain. Requirements on broadcasters to provide programmes of a certain type or specified quality have been relaxed and a great array of commercial channels has become available. On television, talent contests, soap operas, sport, quizzes, cookery, reality shows, comedy, gardening and home improvement programmes proliferate; programmes about politics and current affairs do not. There has been a heightened concern, especially in the popular press (now competing with the Internet and the 24-hour news channels to supply news) to report the activities of celebrities – those people 'known', in the words of the American writer Daniel J. Boorstin, for their 'well-knownness' (Boorstin, 1963: 67). Chris Rojek notes that, although the status of some celebrities is *ascribed* (for example, royal figures such as Princess Diana or the Duke and Duchess of Cambridge) the status of the great majority is achieved – based, usually, on the fulfilling of talents and social progress from some humble beginning. Rojek adds the element of *attribution* to the mix, arguing, with Bourdieu, that most contemporary culture is *mediagenic* (generated by the mass media) and that celebrities are in large part produced by the media and are not the spontaneous expression of the popular will (Rojek, 2001: 16–18). Rojek recognizes that the very fact of achieved celebrity 'drives a wedge between [the celebrities] and their audience' (Rojek, 2001: 190). On the one hand, celebrities represent the reward that can accrue to gifted people in an open society; on the other hand, and by the same token, the admirers of a celebrity could see themselves as failures, having failed to make similar progress in that same society. This explains the ambivalent 'Build them Up/Knock Them Down' attitude towards celebrities manifested by both the popular media and the public. Thus, a legion of admirers might buy a female celebrity's albums or watch her films but still enjoy newspaper gossip about her drug-taking or photographs of her on the beach, revealing her cellulite or body tattoos. Proprietors of such newspapers have claimed a democratic purpose for this sort of reportage. When the *News of the World*, the British newspaper most preoccupied with the surveillance of celebrities, closed in July of 2011, the paper's owner, Rupert Murdoch, claimed that it had been 'in the business of holding others to account' (http://www.bbc.co.uk/news/uk-14074704 (accessed 26 July 2011)). In an age when membership of political parties is in decline, turn-out in elections is falling and popular 'Mock the Week'-style disdain for politicians is rampant, celebrity, then, could, for good or ill, be seen as a substitute for democracy.

For cultural conservatives this onrush of postmodern culture has been part of a process of 'dumbing down'. For broadcasting executives, it has been a matter of giving the public what it appears to want and a fact of life in the increasingly global media marketplace. For those on the cultural left – the inheritors of Raymond Williams – and on the parliamentary left – the Labour Party – debate has come to centre on the need for choice and plurality in the media marketplace. The argument was given unexpected impetus in the

United Kingdom in the summer of 2011 with the eruption of the phone-hacking controversy, wherein private detectives working for the *News of the World* were said to have illegally intercepted voicemail messages on the phones of thousands of celebrities and others. This jeopardized the British and American media businesses of the paper's owners, News Corporation. But a greater number of owners in the British media marketplace would not necessarily bring a greater diversity of media content, for two reasons. First, a huge amount of money would be required to launch, say, a new newspaper and, under current political circumstances, this is only likely to come from a wealthy entrepreneur or group looking to promote a pro-business, pro-celebrity formula. Second, most writers, commentators and politicians have come to see people primarily as *individuals* and as *consumers*, making choices in the marketplace.

Some of the most influential radical writing on culture is pessimistic in this regard, seeing a drastic narrowing of consumer choice through the growth of globalization. The best example here is the American sociologist George Ritzer's work on 'McDonaldization'. Ritzer argued that the four key business characteristics of the global fast-food chain McDonalds were efficiency, calculability, predictability and control, and that these principles were now being generalized to cultures around the world. The company perceived this as rationalization. Ritzer insisted it was the opposite: 'Most specifically, irrationality means that rational systems are unreasonable systems. By that I mean that they deny the basic humanity, the human reason, of the people who work within or are served by them' (Ritzer, 1994: 154).

8

TURNING POINTS

THIS CHAPTER

- Deconstructs the notion of a 'mid-life crisis' and explores destandard-izing processes in everyday family life, for example new dependency relations when caring for self and others – children, step-children and grandparents
- Examines the importance of both racial and gender identities in middle-age
- Provides a case study of people who change places and identities, for example transsexuals
- Introduces the concepts of 'emotional intelligence' and the 'leisure imagination' which feature in recent leisure studies debates.

This chapter develops some of the themes of earlier chapters with respect to change and continuities in people's lives. For some commentators these are seen as risky new times in human history; prior confidence in science and technology wanes as they both fail to provide acceptable solutions to the problems faced by human kind living in a fragile global bio-sphere. In the past modern science could claim to predict and control reality; as Zygmunt Bauman has argued, to know things is to disarm them, but now industrial capitalism has generated and continues to generate long-term and unforeseen environmental consequences. Indeed, the world is just too full of invasive and unknowable stuff. New technologies derived from digitalization such as the Internet and mobile phones have meant that physical spaces have become, in Bauman's terms, 'frontierland' and 'extra-terrestrial'; there are no protective boundaries around people's lives. Whether the issue is climate change, work opportunities, financial transactions, breaking news stories on celebrities or terrorist attacks, we all have daily reminders that we live in a global age. To quote Bauman directly (2002: 48):

Since we hear occasionally that what other people do and what happens to them somehow affect the life we live and the chances of living life the way we would like it to be lived, we guess that we may be travelling, all of us, aboard the same superjumbo jet; yet what we don't know is, who – if anybody – is sitting in the pilot's cabin.

This chapter remains focused on the lives of the generation of post-war 'baby boomers' because, in the first decades of the new millennium, the noughties, this generation achieved 'middle age' in the life course. The restlessness and liminality they experienced in their teenage years have been carried forward, reasserting themselves as this cohort face up to middle age and negotiate transitions such as retirement from work. But as a generation they are well placed, both materially and culturally, to experience uncertainty and also be agents of changes that commentators cast broadly as constituting the 'new times' of postmodernity.

> To live in the universe of high modernity is to live in an environment of chance and risk, the inevitable concomitants of a system geared to the domination of nature and the reflexive making of history. (Giddens, 1991: 109)

One of the important arguments of Chapter 5 on youth and youth cultures (see p. 106–7, My Generation: The Who? section) was that the cohort of post-war 'baby boomers', that is, teenagers growing in adulthood in the 1960s, challenged many of the moral codes and cultural constraints surrounding racial and gender identities. They were not prepared to accept the more conservative attitudes and behaviour of their parent's generation towards sexual relationships, marriage, deviancy and drug taking. They were no longer grounded in the safe claustrophobic institutions of modernity. In many ways the Left in politics in the UK, France and the US won new cultural battles over sexuality, family life, cultural taste and national identity, whereas the Right won the economic war over markets and state regulation and intervention.

The 1960s was a period of substantial national and global economic growth, in marked contrast to the austerity of the post-war period, which continued throughout the 1950s; but subsequent decades after the 1960s were also a period of substantial political and cultural changes. If the 1960s witnessed radical rather than revolutionary changes, it should hardly be surprising that, over the next decades, many traditional institutions such as the family, trade unions or imperialist regimes and projects were dismissed as old fashioned, irrelevant or simply unjust. Class, gender and race hierarchies could no longer hold sway over people's lives. The tradition of segregated gender roles, embedded in the sexual division of labour, with men working in the public sphere and women remaining in the private world of housework and child care, was dissolved by increased educational and employment opportunities for women, not forgetting the politics of the feminist movement. Equality legislation, such as the British Equal Pay Act of 1970, sought to extend employment opportunities irrespective of gender and racial identities. Pushing at the boundaries of cultural rules and regulations would be seen by those defending the status quo of traditional family, nation and empire as subversive and traitorous, whereas for women and racial minorities such transgressions would be seen as just one step towards equal opportunities and equity in policy thinking. For conservative commentators, accelerating rates of illegitimacy, abortions and the rise in sexually transmitted diseases were read as clear indicators of marriage breakdown and moral laxity, and was indicative for some pundits of a corrosive misplaced gender war. The conservative discourse of the Right suggested that cultural change and transgressions had simply gone 'too far'; 'political correctness' had gone mad, flying in the face of 'ordinary common sense' wherein one 'calls a spade a spade'. It is all so obvious: coloured/black people are 'johnny foreigners', homosexuals are 'poofs/nancy boys', all feminists are ugly 'butch lesbian/ dykes' who cannot attract men and a disabled person is a 'spaz'.

It was probably inevitable then that these cultural changes would have unforeseen and unintended consequences. During the 1990s the media recorded and amplified changes in sexual, marriage and family relationships. Media discourses focused upon the failure of 40- and 50-year-old men and women to settle down into monogamy and staid old age. Contrary to the earlier predictions of Robert and Rhona Rapoport (1975) with their static stable view of the life cycle, middle-aged men and women were cheating on their husbands and wives, divorcing, scooping up their disparate children and, undeterred, embarking on new marriages and new lives. With rising divorce rates and more equitable marriage settlements between partners, the material circumstances of the middle-aged depended in part on whether the individual was among the growing cohort choosing 'serial marriage'. Income divisions between social classes became more confused as remarriage stretched incomes and property ownership across the social class divides. People might be trapped in a loveless marriage but that was financially more comfortable than divorce and/or re-marriage.

The media simplified or recast these changes as the 'male menopause' or 'male middle-life crisis', with husbands often trading in old wives for younger women. The language of the times changed too and traditional hierarchical terms such as husbands and wives, sanctified by the religion, became translated into more egalitarian or transitory terms such as 'partner' or, more humorously, by the BBC celebrity Terry Wogan referring to his long-term wife as 'the current Mrs Wogan'. So, meeting new people in leisure settings became more unpredictable and embarrassing as new couples, in their fifties, referred to their new companions as a 'friend' or the infantilizing 'girlfriend' or 'boyfriend'. Equally, relatives from the previous marriage on both sides struggle to keep up with the blossoming new relationships and query, 'Well, which one is he/she with now?' or more pointedly refer to previous spouses and fail to remember or catch the name of the new partner. Market analysis started to be interested in 'bean pole' families, with individuals casting off wider kinship ties of the extended family as they embarked on remarriage and untangling the labyrinth that new partners and their children brought.

For sociologists, the task was to explain the diversity of personal and family relationships. The 'breakdown' of the family and changing gender relationships were heralded by Young and Willmott's (1973) argument of the symmetrical family with its central proposition that husbands and wives were becoming equal partners in terms of paid employment, domestic work, home ownership and leisure choices. The lifestyles of the middle classes (suggested by the Rapoports) would, it was assumed, gradually percolate down to the working classes. The symmetrical family would become the archetype for modern family life. Yet, at the very time this model of stratified diffusion was proposed, it was immediately challenged, in part as feminists suggested that women were still not equal partners in work, domestic responsibilities and particularly in leisure (see Deem, 1986; Green et al., 1990).

The flexibility with which the middle-aged cohort approached lifestyles in the 1990s has led some sociologists to write about the wholesale restructuring of institutional rules and regulations, positing a new sort of social order and disorder. It is as if society has lost its grip on people's lives and individuals are cast adrift from the constraints of family, community and social class. Rather than being bound into the traditional extended families and communities of 'solid' modernity, people settled in 'beanpole' families with little contact with wider kinship networks, given divorce and subsequent remarriage. Even marital relationships were now seen as flexible and not necessarily permanent – as Bauman argues, in 'liquid' modernity, relationships resist long-term binding commitment. In postmodernity, individuals are always looking for exits from relationships and proceed cautiously 'until further notice'. As we have already seen, some have embraced these changes and celebrate the coming of postmodernity and the importance of life politics and individual identity.

RACE AND GENDER IDENTITIES

In the UK, the middle-aged cohort of post-war baby boomers has not only grown up and matured during a gender war of changing sexual relations but most people living in cities have also experienced racial and ethnic difference in a post-colonial era. The pervasive confidence in white racial superiority was diluted and challenged by new patterns of migration, education, employment and inner-city housing. Gender relations and traditional hierarchies became transmogrified by more complex diverse forms of extended, nuclear and single-parent families. Living singly, cohabitation and shared households added further complexity to people's lifestyles. However, racial and ethnic stereotypes abounded in academic work and popular media. Ambivalence thrived as commentators both celebrated and questioned diversity: from traditional extended patriarchal families, to single mothers and same-sex couples. Traditional ideas about 'the family' were deconstructed and subverted by more diverse households and living arrangements. For the mass media different household structures became synonymous with racial and ethnic stereotypes of the 'Other'. For some politicians Asian families were celebrated as close-knit extended families, bound together in hard work and strict Muslim religious behaviour, while social work media experts bemoaned the tight or tighter parental and community control over the next generation who appeared 'Westernized' and more attuned to, if not integrated into, mainstream culture in terms of dress, language, leisure, sexual relationships and in a more secular outlook. On the other hand, Afro-Caribbean families were cast as dysfunctional, with young black men generically demonized as unemployable, drug users/dealers or violent criminals, disregarding their commitments to sexual partners and their children. Although conventional wisdom defines adolescence as a time both of change and experimentation, the middle-aged cohort in the 1990s were challenged to negotiate some sort of terms with their own complicated lives. As we shall see in the next chapter on ageing, the bulk of this middle-aged cohort had to come to terms with the care of their own very elderly parents and the pressing demands of their own children and grandchildren.

During the 1990s, the growing demand for 'political correctness' (i.e. the elimination of sexist and racist discrimination) was testimony to the black and the women's movement finding a voice and gaining a more confident presence in institutions open to public gaze. But changes in attitudes and behaviour, even within the public sphere of front-line policing, were hard won, as is illustrated by the entrenched and recalcitrant racism revealed in the Metropolitan Police's handling of the murder of Stephen Lawrence in 1993 and by the policing practices and media accounts of public disorders such as those witnessed in 1989 at Hillsborough or in London in 2011. Even harder, therefore, is the challenge to renegotiate and redraw gender roles and responsibilities within changing boundaries of racism and ethnic cleavages. Such struggles and tensions are made light of in situation comedies, whether in the US or the UK.

The tensions between the middle-aged parent generation and their children, the next generation, have been highlighted, simplified and distorted through the lens of 'Westernization' when discussing racial and ethnic minorities. Academics felt that black and brown youth was caught 'between two cultures' and young people were therefore experiencing some kind of identity crisis. However, during the 1980s and 1990s this crisis of identity plagued the middle-aged generation and societies came under siege, to borrow a phrase from Zygmunt Bauman (2002). This is a time during which the certainties of previous institutions such as careers and work, families and friendships, public service and state welfare were all subject to seismic change from growing individualization. Because of globalization and the new politics of neo-liberalism which emphasized consumer choice and freedom, 'solid modernity' gave way to newer more flexible, more ambivalent social arrangements – what Bauman termed 'liquid modernity'. Rather than binding us into a social order of external obligations and commitments, to institutions such as the family, work, local community and religion, such traditional ties were loosened or actively untied by the nation state and globalization. Rather than looking outwards, individuals, particularly of the middle classes, turned their attention inwards, towards themselves and, following Friedrich Nietzsche, their being (*Dasein*) in the world. The distinctive focus of their attention became their own bodies and they began to pursue personal projects to shape their own bodies in line with their own predilections and leisure interests as well as the ubiquitous advice from 'experts' in the media. During the 1990s and 2000s there was no shortage of advice in the form of handbooks, TV programmes, DVDs and podcasts to help individuals choose their own diet, clothes, exercise regimes, the internal décor of households ... indeed, their whole lifestyle.

8.1 Lifestyle and generations

The notion of lifestyle sounds somewhat trivial because it is often thought of solely in terms of a superficial consumerism: as suggested by glossy magazines and advertising images. But there is something much more fundamental going on than such a conception suggests: in conditions of high modernity, we all not only follow lifestyles, but in an important sense we are forced to do so – we have no choice but to choose. A lifestyle can be defined as a more or less integrated set of practices which an individual embraces, not only because such practices fulfil utilitarian needs, but because they give material form to a particular narrative of self-identity. (Giddens, 1991: 81)

Advertisers and marketeers are interested in identifying and developing the wants and needs of niche markets or market segmentation. Markets can be divided into demographic, class or psychological characteristics. Marketeers want to develop the desires of consumers and broadly label them to denote their distinctive tastes.

What do you think the leisure tastes of the following categories might be in terms of household consumer durables, holidays, restaurants and leisure pursuits (e.g. cycling, walking, and outdoor pursuits)?

- 'Mature': elderly, 75–90-year-olds
- 'Baby boomer': newly retired, 60–70-year-olds
- 'X-generation': thirtysomethings, 25–40-year-olds
- 'Neets': teenagers and young adults, 16–24-year-olds

What do you make of these sub-divisions sometimes identified amongst the X-generation, i.e. what lifestyles do they evoke?

- 'Kippers': kids in parents' pockets eroding retirement savings
- 'Chav': working-class youth
- 'Dinky': double income, no kids yet
- 'Student': living in student accommodation/flat away from home

How many TV comedy programmes can you think of that deal with these different age groups and their lifestyles?

What issues/problems confront the main characters?

What makes them funny, or not?

BODIES AND IDENTITIES

With growing individualization, a substantial proportion of the middle-aged people now therefore turn their attention and interest towards their own bodies as an expression of who they are. The attempt to maintain or achieve a lean, muscle-toned body for example, becomes an important indicator of one's personality and personal worth. For the past two or three decades, the sport and exercise industries have not been slow to respond to a growing demand for accessible and attractive exercise classes to keep middle-aged men and women attractive and in shape. Originally housed in austere and regulated local authority leisure centres, sport and physical exercise was once seen as part of the citizen's right to leisure and healthy lifestyles. However, the commercial sector has increasingly developed niche markets in the fitness business and encourages exclusive spaces for more wealthy 'members' to 'work out' in their free time. As one should expect in these new times, the choices of activities are diverse, whether it be Tai Kwando, aerobics, Pilates or spinning classes, but participants can also enjoy relaxing, eating and drinking with fellow club members as a just reward for all that hard work in the gym. Indeed, inspired by Pierre Bourdieu's concept of class tastes and lifestyles, Derek Wynne's study (1998) highlights the different interests, involvement and networks among the sporting and the socializing groups that visit the private leisure centre on an exclusive middle-class estate in the Manchester area of the UK.

The German social theorist Ulrich Beck (1992) has stressed the importance of the individual taking centre stage as the nation state retreats in its collective endeavours, shunning policies of citizenship and welfare. With the neo-liberal political agenda which celebrates market forces free from regulation, politicians in the nation state no longer feel that they can afford nor indeed offer collectivist policies. The individual is therefore thrown back on his/her own resources and he or she must shoulder responsibility and take decisions. There is no dialogue between public issues and private troubles; a discourse that Charles Wright Mills (1970) cherished as a fundament of the 'sociological imagination'. The historical processes of society provide the context and the resources for individuals to live out their lives; history ties individual biographies to society. But with civil society in retreat and the state busy dealing with institutions plagued by insecurities and uncertainty, individuals are increasingly left to their own devices. In policy terms, it is said that 'there is no alternative', since previous collective solutions based on welfare provision and the assumption of citizen rights are now regarded as disempowering and as promoting dependency. So the nation state has outsourced its most demanding functions (in economic, environmental and social/cultural formations) to non-political deregulated market forces. Even 'law and order', the heart and discipline of the nation state, experiences both privatization and a sustained dilution of any semblance of local democratic control. Private companies such as G4S and Serco, for instance, now drive prisoners to and from court and apply electronic tags to their legs when they are out on parole.

Drawing on Beck's ideas on risk society, Zygmunt Bauman argues, 'How one lives becomes the *biographical solution to systemic contradictions*' (Beck quoted in Bauman, 2002: 68). But this is no easy matter in 'liquid' modernity: 'More often than not, control over life is the way in which the story of life is told, rather than the way in which it is lived' (Bauman, 2002: 69). So, if individuals have to find their own way in the world as the collective paths of class, gender, race become harder to decipher, it is not so surprising that individuals start looking inwards for a narrative of the self. And what easier way than to take control over ones' body and exercise regimen? There is no belief in a better tomorrow, no progressive optimistic vision of a good society. Despite Barack Obama's post-electoral tweet in November 2012, that 'the best is yet to come', what individuals hope for and pursue is different today. If everything else is out of control and uncertain, why not control one's own body through routines of diet and exercise?

So the baby boomers, now in, or a little past, middle-age are becoming more individualized and isolated, immersed in consumer culture. As Bauman says, we middle aged have fallen back on 'our own *doxa* – that subliminal knowledge, the foundation stone of perception sunk so deep that it seldom if ever rises to the threshold of attention; those thoughts we do not think *about* but *with*' (Bauman, 2002: 52). One uncontested and primary assumption of that *doxa* is that individuals are biologically grounded in their own physical bodies and, in the final analysis, the individual is responsible for taking care of his or her body. Healthy body culture and body maintenance is the royal road to resisting morbidity and securing vibrant longevity.

All people are trapped both existentially and physiologically within decaying bodies and these and our selves in turn are placed and positioned in cultural locations and historical contexts. Mainstream social theory, as well as debates about leisure and tourism, has recently taken a 'cultural' turn. There has been growing interest in drawing on work in cultural studies both to contextualize and to interpret human societies. This has meant a heightened sensitivity to geographies of space and place, as well as making sense of historical processes such as globalization. For example, post-colonial theories have sought to deconstruct the authoritative voice of the 'West' that has ignored or talked over what the Indian philosopher Gayatri Spivak (2006) has called the 'subaltern' voices of the 'Rest' or the 'Other'. So the cultural turn demands theory to be more sensitive to codes and representations of mass media, where social science must deconstruct articulated messages of ideology, particularly sexism and ethnocentrism. As we have argued, these mass media influences are central to understanding the production and consumption of lifestyles, changing tastes and shifting spaces.

Some social analysts have sought to challenge directly the natural categories of sex and race. One leading example here is Judith Butler (2006) with her view of 'gender performativity'. In her work Butler seeks to deconstruct essentialist biological categories of sexual difference by arguing that individuals are socially constrained to adhere to an impossible heterosexual gold standard of masculinity and femininity. Bodies become important signifiers in this gender game as both men and women struggle to display prescribed universal gendered bodies. Yet human experiences of sexual identity, of physicality, are more diverse than the conventional bipolar categories of male and female, masculinity and femininity, can encompass. Judith Butler has explored transsexuality as a site for 'gender trouble' to highlight her iconoclastic analysis of the body (Butler, 2006).

8.2 Gender trouble?

Take the following four famous people – a politician, a rock star, a tennis player and an artist. How and why have their lives (and media representations/coverage of all three) raised important questions about gender identities?

Margaret Thatcher

David Bowie

Martina Navratilova

Grayson Perry

However, it is no easy task to make sense of Judith Butler's work as it is not easily accessible to sociologists. It draws heavily on French psycho-analysis but this should be not so surprising as her primary aim is to make a strategic theoretical intervention into US feminist theory and provide a foundation for a Foucauldian shift in discourse to lay the firm foundations to 'queer theory' or 'queer studies'. Queer theory calls all labelling of sexual behaviour and identity (be it as 'normal', deviant', or whatever) into question. One element of Butler's theoretical influence has been writing about the concept of 'performativity', but she acknowledges that the exact nature of that influence is not clear:

> It is difficult to say precisely what performativity is not only because my own views on what 'performativity' might mean have changed over time, most often in response to excellent criticisms, but because so many others have taken it up and given it their own formulations. (Butler, 2006: Preface (1999), xv)

Butler's contribution rests on the strength of her resonance with Tony Blackshaw's (2010) insightful depiction of liquid modernity. Butler's body blow to sociological theory and analysis lies in her deconstruction of the solid concept of gender difference; she subverts the supposedly natural categories of 'man' and 'woman', of 'masculinity' and 'femininity'. Gender is only viable if people act out the gender order – the preconceived hierarchy and privileging of the masculinist *Weltanschauung* or world view, simultaneously discounting or denigrating the 'Other' as invisible or as feminine. So gender relations and Goffmanesque bodily deference and demeanour are not so much biologically predetermined and natural but rather are nurtured, socially constructed or pre-constructed from within (as 'radicals' such as homosexual men, lesbians, bi and transsexuals might see it) ultimately oppressive patriarchal categories and lifestyles. Gender trouble is not about a singular act or performance of gender roles. To quote Butler's, admittedly tortuous, prose:

> In the first instance, then, the performativity of gender revolves around this metalepsis, the way in which the anticipation of a gendered essence produces that which it posits as outside itself. Secondly, performativity is not a singular act, but a repetition and a ritual, which achieves its effects through its naturalization in the context of a body, understood, in part, as a culturally sustained temporal duration. (2006: xv)

'EMOTIONAL INTELLIGENCE' AND THE 'LEISURE IMAGINATION'

In this section we discuss the work of two influential contemporary leisure theorists. We show how their ideas express some of the existential questions facing postmodern lifestyles and how they may help us understand some aspects of today's leisure culture. Chris Rojek (2010a) in 'The labour of leisure' defines 'emotional intelligence' as a key to capturing leisure experiences, whereas Tony Blackshaw (2010), in his key concepts textbook *Leisure*, articulates the importance of the 'leisure imagination' to make sense of contemporary leisure. These ideas are at the heart of the debates which characterize the shifting foundations of contemporary leisure studies. Chris Rojek's (2010b) article on emotional intelligence and leisure was the centrepiece of Volume 54 Issue 4 of the *World Leisure Journal* and elicited several responses from key internationally recognized academics, including Tony Blackshaw.

The phrase 'shifting foundations' appears to be an oxymoron but it captures their arguments about seismic fundamental change shaping people's lives. It also echoes Marshall Berman's (1983) postmodern version of Marx's famous suggestion that life under industrial capitalism was such that 'All that's solid melts to air'. Berman rejected the notion of the postmodern, but instead argued that: 'To be modern ... is to experience personal and social life as a maelstrom ...' (1983: 345–346).

Since both Rojek and Blackshaw are determined to steer away from what they see as staid notions of structure, class and community, what implications do these two writers draw out for leisure in these 'new times'?

CHRIS ROJEK: THE LABOUR OF LEISURE

Chris Rojek is resolved to analyse leisure within the wider context of culture. His substantive contribution to leisure studies is twofold: it has been secured, first, by a distinctive mapping of shifting debates in leisure studies and, second, by raising new questions in order to open up new lines of scholarly enquiry. He was, moreover, one of the first writers to adopt postmodern perspectives on leisure. His later publications, as with any leading contemporary social theorist, have changed emphasis and he subsequently has sought to establish an 'action approach' to leisure. However, his work continues to reveal an interest in postmodern theory. For instance, to quote Tony Blackshaw:

> Here was a dramatic irony: by the mid-1990s, postmodernism had lost its magnesium-flare fame, but at the very moment some in sociology were gleefully driving a stake through its heart, Rojek was using it to give the study of leisure a blood transfusion. (Blackshaw, 2012: 2)

Chris Rojek's presence within leisure studies is one of increasingly explicit engagement with moral, political and environmental issues. He has consistently sought to develop a coherent sociology of leisure and has been a resilient player in developing debates about leisure studies as a field of study. His writing directly challenges most of the domain assumptions and conventional wisdoms embedded in this field of study. From the outset his work has been transgressive and subversive in questioning 'conventional wisdom' which associated leisure with free time and freedom. Both need to be contextualized and any quest for a universal theory of leisure is both illusory and idealistic; one cannot dislocate free time or quality of experience from its context. This is a position he reasserts in his latest leisure textbook (Rojek, 2010a) about emotional intelligence and emotional labour. Consequently, Rojek rides roughshod over philosophers and social theorists who search for any universal theory of leisure. In his view, as free-floating intelligentsia seeking to demarcate the essential features or characteristics of leisure, they all fall foul of Wittgenstein's criticisms of the fallacy of essentialism. Leisure, he argues, is shaped by history and there can be no 'timeless' theories of leisure. Leisure is a distinctive form of human experience and not a derivative of work. Nor is leisure necessarily 'good'; it need not, for example, be a site for the accumulation of pleasure or human freedom, as founding fathers of this sub-discipline seem to imply.

Rojek returns to explore yet again the iconic domain assumptions in leisure studies: voluntarism, freedom and choice. But he remains an iconoclast:

> One of the attractions of studying leisure is that it addresses people's free-time behaviour. Or to alter the payload of the term in a manner that is more apposite for the central arguments in the book, it explores what people plan and do when they believe themselves to be free. (Rojek, 2010a: 1)

Drawing on sociology's interest in the processes of individualization, clearly articulated in the works of Giddens (1991), Beck and Beck-Gernsheim (2002) and Bauman (2005), Rojek also takes inspiration from social psychology in deploying the concepts of emotional intelligence and emotional labour.

> Emotional intelligence and emotional labour are, I think, core concepts for the analysis of leisure forms and practice. This is because the display of credibility, relevance and competence in our 'voluntarily' chosen 'free' time activities speaks to others about who we are, what we hold to be valuable and how we can make a difference. (Rojek, 2010a: 4)

Karl Spracklen, another leading writer, questions Chris Rojek's confidence in 'emotional intelligence which he introduces without any critique or recognition of the strong arguments against the concept' (2011: 194). However, a specially commissioned edition of the *World Leisure Journal*, focusing on Rojek's work (in 2010) has been both gently and warmly received by various international authors. Rojek maintains that there are real differences in respect to freedom, choice and life satisfaction – these three he sees as qualities of citizenship enmeshed in cultural codes, rendering them attractive and desired characteristics in the conduct of life. Importantly, Rojek examines how they are represented in relation to power and 'governmentality', the latter a concept closely linked to Foucault's discourses about medicine, penology and the history of ideas. Rojek challenges the simple syllogism that less work means more leisure and more leisure means more freedom. Leisure is a regime not a vacuum for voluntarism. To quote his last lines:

> Leisure is a school for life. The end of schooling is to maintain and enhance competence, relevance and credibility. The successful attainment of this end requires perpetual emotional intelligence and emotional labour. Freedom is for the birds. (Rojek, 2010a: 176)

TONY BLACKSHAW

Tony Blackshaw (2010) is the other important sociologist working his way from the margins of leisure studies into the mainstream. Now he is truly centre stage, if not celebrated, as the sole editor of the *Routledge International Handbook of Leisure Studies* and writer of the important textbook *Leisure* which appeared alongside his *Key Concepts in Community Studies* in the same year of 2010. He burst onto the leisure scene with the publication of his PhD thesis, a very rare achievement in the academic press of the noughties, published as *Leisure Life: Myth, Masculinity and Modernity* (2003). The research, extensively quoted by Chris Rojek (2005) as an exemplar of good research, was in keeping with his commitment to an 'action approach' to understanding modern leisure practices. In his ethnography he revisited the working-class culture of his school contemporaries, now aged in their thirties, as they (in the sense of the word adopted by Phil Cohen) 'magically' recreated and restated their local class identity and their aggressive masculinity in their pub-based leisure lifestyle. The title of the original PhD resonated with, although never referred to, Paul Willis' (1977) decisive cultural studies work, *Learning to Labour: How Working Class Kids get Working Class Jobs*. Tony Blackshaw vividly recreates the world of working-class lads in the 1990s in Leeds as they 'steam', alcohol-fuelled, through the town centre, just as Willis captured in his research the secondary school leavers trapped in Wolverhampton in the 1970s. Although inspired by different theoretical perspectives, academic networks, locales and times, Paul Willis, driven by Stuart Hall and many others (including John Clarke and Chas Critcher) working in the CCCS at Birmingham University and Blackshaw by Zygmunt Bauman, working tangentially at Leeds University, both writers were stimulated or seduced by similar concepts and discourses of class and community in their incisive accounts of 'solid' and 'liquid' modernity.

Tony Blackshaw's explanatory footnote spelling out the meaning of *individualization* is worth quoting in full as it clearly outlines Bauman's view of 'liquid modernity'.

> The casting of society's members as individuals is the trademark of modernity. The major difference between 'solid' and 'liquid' modern individualization is that the former is *reflective*, mirroring the underlying tensions between individual agency and structural determinants of a modern society built on such differences as social class, gender, ethnicity and age (Lash 2002). With the emergence of liquid modernity, however, individualization has become *reflexive*. As Lash points out, reflexes are indeterminate and immediate and as a consequence of 'liquid' modern change reflexive individuals are those individuals who have to cope with living in an uncertain, speeded-up world, which demands quick decision making. Bauman argues that with the processes of change associated with 'liquid modernity', individualization ends up transforming human identity from a 'given' into a 'task'. (Blackshaw, 2010: 13, italics in original)

THE RISE OF THE 'LEISURE SOCIETY' AND THE DEMISE OF SOCIOLOGY

Blackshaw is keen to stress the difference between Bauman Mark 1, who made his name as a Marxist sociologist, and Bauman Mark 2, who in his later career has become noted as an iconoclastic thinker deploying literary metaphors to capture the *zeitgeist* of liquid modernity. Although rejecting a postmodern sociology but rather wanting to develop a sociology of the postmodern, Bauman, in an exploratory article of the late 1980s (1988) points to the growing forces driving these new postmodern times which he prefers to call liquid modernity.

In his earlier work, he emphasized globalization and flows of footloose capital that work to haemorrhage the body of the nation state as a container of power. Bauman has more recently (1999) argued that markets of capital and labour now function on a global scale with local working-class populations at the mercy of footloose global corporations and with workers more or less unprotected by the welfare state. The implications for people's lives are uncertainty and ambivalence. Ulrich Beck has stressed the emergence of a risk society. Both Beck in *Risk Society* (1992) and Bauman, particularly in *Society under Siege* (2002), spell out the implications for the sociological enterprise. These implications are catastrophic because sociology as a discipline emerged in the nineteenth century and it established its legitimacy as the handmaiden of the nation state in solid modernity. Sociology and its policy offerings now have been displaced, marginalized and threatened to make them redundant. In Bauman's terms (1987; 1992), sociologists working for the nation state or welfare state, were no longer *legislators*, confident social scientists managing and guiding cultural forms but merely *interpreters*, competing amongst the babble of experts trying to tell the world what was really happening.

The huge shift from solid to liquid modernity is laid bare in the political and cultural formations of modernity. As Stuart Hall has observed, with the neo-liberal project of the 1980s gathering pace, the capitalist state in the 'West', that is, in the USA and throughout Europe, is hollowed out, out-sourced and gradually privatized and deregulated (1992). Forms of 'governance', processes securing governability in civil society, no longer remain solely with the coercive authoritative nation state as the latter starts to hive off its functions to private companies, thus to commodify services and discipline citizens.

Bauman (1992) has argued that we live in divided societies as the top two-thirds of the population are seduced into lifestyle consumer culture while, in contrast, the bottom third, the underclass, are subjected to work discipline and surveillance. Society, the social, is no longer constituted as a singular universal safe public domain and has instead become diluted and fragmented. The inhabitants of working-class communities have therefore retreated into more private, consumer orientated and perhaps risky domains, such as satellite TV, drugs and the acquisition of tattoos. If the state and society is in retreat, individualization thrives. The key feature of liquid modernity is that class no longer has its tight grip on people's social and cultural lives and society is underdetermined: there are no longer any tried and trusted paths mapped out by class, race and gender. Individuals have to make sense of living in these new times. Life is no longer predestined nor given – the narrative of the self becomes ever more important as individuals seek a meaningful identity in these changing times. Individuals are free to choose and where else to try things out but in leisure? With deregulation and gradual subversion of the constraints of class, gender and race, happiness, supposedly, looms on the horizon for everyone. As Bauman stresses (2002) living is no longer about '*having*' material goods but more about '*being*' in the world. The cultural *zeitgeist* is one of experiencing authenticity, the singular and particular pursuit of happiness in Western capitalist societies. For those in the West, the traditional religious world view was that individuals had a 'duty' to obedience and deferred gratification in order to secure an afterlife. That historical consciousness dissolved, and now religious fundamentalism, particularly Islam in the East, offers a polar opposite to the individualistic hedonism of the West (Giddens, 1999). Bauman argues that these new times offer a counter view to Freud's theory of repression and submission to the 'reality principle'. Individuals now feel that they have the right to leisure and to be happy; today's trademarks are free time and the freedom to choose what to do. The relationships or community network that suit today may become tiresome tomorrow. It is a world of contingency and uncertainty.

> A liquid modern life, in other words, has no solid ontological status, something that is given, is inevitable, we are predisposed to, or firmly believe in. Some lives no doubt are more congealed than others, but anyone's *habitus* is just something that is until further notice. In other words, it seems to fit you as a person who chooses to live this kind of life rather than another. (Blackshaw, 2010: 88)

CONCLUSION

This chapter develops our approach to leisure theory by deconstructing the notion of a 'mid-life crisis' as experienced by the 'baby-boomer' generation in middle age. It explores the destandardizing processes in everyday family life as we look at new and emerging dependency relations when caring for self and others – children, step-children and grandparents. It complicates a simple reading of life in middle age by examining the importance of both racial and gender identities. In order to highlight flexibility and choice in lifestyles, which characterize these new times, we discuss transsexual people who change places and identities. The chapter concludes by tackling the concepts of 'emotional intelligence' and the 'leisure imagination' which feature in recent leisure studies debates.

9

HOME ALONE: DEMOGRAPHY AND AGEING

THIS CHAPTER

- Documents the changing demographic profile of the UK
- Outlines the key policy issues informing the politics and economics of old age
- Evaluates the new dependency relations between generations when caring for self, children and grandchildren
- Analyses the active leisure lifestyles of retired people
- Provides a case study of ballroom dancing.

DEMOGRAPHY

In the past 35 years the proportion of the UK population aged over 65 has grown by 31%, from 7.4 to 9.7 million, and the Office for National Statistics predicts this figure will double in the next 20 years and treble in the next 30 (Garfield, 2008). Life expectancy at the start of the nineteenth century was less that forty years; over the past half century life expectancy has steadily increased by two years each decade. In the UK life expectancy at birth presently now stands around 75 years of age for a male and 80 years for a female. Tom Kirkwood (2001) stressed that it was the death rates of the older age groups that showed the greatest decline. These groups, the 'old old' (people of 85 years plus) now constitute the fastest growing sector of the UK population. This shifting demographic balance has occurred because of declining birth rates and

growing longevity; therefore, the balance between the generations that constitute the UK population has changed significantly. This has prompted a seismic
reorientation of policy imperatives, with some commentators talking of a
'demographic time bomb'. The weight of the population has now gravitated
towards the 'young old' (60–80 year olds) and the 'old old' (80 years plus).

> Taking the human race as whole, just 1% of the world's population was
> aged 65 and above a century ago. This figure has already risen seven-fold
> and will rise to around 20% by the middle of the 21st century. Already
> in the UK today, 85% of newborns can expect to celebrate their 65th
> birthday. And those now reaching 65 can expect to survive 16 more years
> if they are a man and 19 if they are a woman. (Kirkwood, 2001: 2)

'YOUNG OLD' AND 'OLD OLD'

It is not simply that people are living longer but also that morbidity occurs
much later in the lifespan. Healthy lifestyles mean that older people can avoid
sickness and live independently and for longer than at any time in human history. Rather than dying from infectious diseases in infancy, people are now
more prone to die from conditions associated with old age such as cancer,
heart disease or stroke. Ageing comes about through the gradual build up of
unrepaired faults in the cells and tissues of the body rather than through some
active mechanism or instinct for death and destruction, as posited in Freudian
psychology. Indeed, Tom Kirkwood (2001) celebrates the triumph of public
health, medical science and health care in increasing human survival and longevity; he states 'science no longer dictates that our bodies have to wear themselves out and die according to some preordained plan' (2001: 2).

The significance for leisure of this success story is that the generation of 'baby
boomers', who were teenagers in the 1960s, have now reached retirement age
and beyond. Unlike previous generations, they can look forward to twenty to
thirty years of life, free from the constraints of work obligations and paid
employment. In the UK this generation are financially and culturally well
placed to pursue leisure lives, to develop their tourist gaze (Urry, 1990) and to
exercise their leisure imagination, as we have discussed in the previous chapter.
This is because, as Will Hutton (1995) has cogently and convincingly suggested,
the 'baby boomers' generation in the 1990s and 2000s benefited from early
retirement and severance pay, favourable voluntary redundancy settlements
and, most important of all, inflation-proof, final-salary pensions, buttressed by
the State Earnings Related Pensions (SERPS) introduced by a Labour government in 1978. In 1980, the Conservative government of Margaret Thatcher
disconnected universal pension entitlements from average earnings and prices,
thereby reducing the long-term financial burden on the nation state (Vincent,
2000). The same strategy was adopted more recently when the UK coalition
government of Conservatives and Liberal Democrats tied pension, universal
and work credits and benefits to a lower rate of inflation, as expressed by the

Consumer Price Index (CPI) rather than by the traditional, more generous measure of the Retail Price Index (RPI).

This seemingly innocent, technical and statistical sleight of hand has serious long-term policy and leisure implications. As a consequence, the baby-boomer generation has acquiesced to the present UK coalition government's austerity project by pulling the welfare ladder even further out of the reach of younger people. All their welfare blessings will be subsequently denied to the next generation who must face longer working lives and future pensions significantly downgraded to average earnings accumulated over a career lifetime. Nor must we forget that, in middle age, during the 1970s and 80s, politically influential factions among the baby-boomer generation not only refused to fund a universal welfare state but they themselves benefited substantially both from rising house values as owners of property and also, for those who took advantage of purchasing cheap shares in privatization sell-offs in energy, communications and transport during the 1980s, from stock market inflation. This long-term assault on the welfare state has been completed recently by a final ideological push on the part of the present coalition government on the very idea of state welfare. There has been a growing orchestration of anti-welfare discourse, particularly through the Department of Work and Pensions (Walker, 2013) that stigmatizes those on welfare and restates the importance of Victorian 'less eligibility' in state benefits: people need to work for a living and they are not entitled collectively to universal benefits as citizens. This could be the twilight of the welfare state as the neo-liberal discourse celebrates 'workfare', honed in the financial global crisis which gathered pace in 2008. Nevertheless, the 'young old' and even the 'old old' remain safe; they have secured in their working lives substantial economic resources from capital holdings and income flows to construct viable leisure lives in their retirement and therefore are much better placed than their parents were in the 1970s and than their own children will be when their time for retirement comes in the 2030s.

THE POLITICS AND POLICY FOR OLD AGE

The changing demographic profile of the UK population also carries significant political consequences. Political parties that fail to engage with the growing population of the elderly run the risk of failing to win electoral support of an older generation with a higher propensity to vote at local and general elections, given disaffection and indifference that 18–25-year-olds have towards mainstream politics. Certainly, older people have become conspicuously more politicized. In the United States in 1970, a church worker called Maggie Kuhn, angry that she had been obliged to retire at 65, helped to found an advocacy group for the elderly that later adopted the name of the Gray Panthers. In Britain, largely at the instigation of the retiring trade unionist Jack Jones, a National Pensioners Convention was established in 1979. Both organizations are still active.

The burden of taxation and current funding of inflation-proof pensions rests squarely on the shoulders of the younger generation of working age.

Because of the financial economic crisis facing the Western world, the neo-liberal policies of retrenchment and austerity have been applied most vigorously to public sector spending. Youth services, work training and education opportunities have been drastically cut back, whereas old-age pensioners may still enjoy universal benefits such as free public transport, winter heating allowances, free prescriptions, free eye tests and, for those over 75 years of age, exemption from paying the annual television licence fee. In previous years too, local authorities provided free access to swimming pools for those aged over 60 years of age. A third of public leisure centres are currently managed by charitable trusts, and they have developed leisure packages which are accessible, inclusive and affordable, for example Active Lifestyle programmes for the over 55s, and the more elderly have become a priority because of recent health policy initiatives (Birch, 2013). Socialists argue that universal welfare benefits such as child allowances, fuel and TV payments and travel concessions are essential to maintain middle-class commitment to the welfare state, to secure their belief that they have a stake in welfarism. Selectivity – for example, means testing – in benefit rights would carry a stigma and undermine feelings of charity and civil reciprocity. In the retreat of welfare altruism, neo-liberal market ideologies have gained ground over the decades as they connect economics with politics: market forces become linked to traditional liberal politics and translated into individual freedom and choice (Stedman Jones, 2012). The voices of taxpayers grow ever louder, demanding 'value for money', as they question public expenditure on collective services they may not use because they increasingly purchase education and health care from the private sector. A lot of this comes from the right-wing press (which is most of it) and right-wing pressure groups such as the Tax Payers Alliance, founded in 2004 and funded by firms like McAlpines and JCB.

9.1 Old age concessions

Imagine you are 75 years of age and the nation state offers you free eye tests, free prescriptions, a free TV licence, free public transport on buses/local trains and a £200 cash heating allowance.
Would you:

1 Accept them all or some?
2 Demand to pay the full costs of each item or service involved?
3 Donate all/some of them to a bespoke designated charity (e.g. recommended by Age Concern)?
4 Donate the monies involved to a charity of your own choice? Would it be a local charity (i.e. working on UK projects) or a global charity organization (e.g. Amnesty International, Wateraid, International Red Cross or Oxfam)?
5 Give the equivalent money to your grandchildren?
6 You are interviewed on local radio to explain your decisions, what reasons would you give for your choices?

However, recent media commentators and government reports (Select Committee on Public Service and Demographic Change, 2013) suggest that policy makers are sleepwalking into the future, ignoring the real challenges that an ageing population will present in terms of social care, access to new technologies, transport, mobility and quality of life. In the UK, current uncertainty about the precise future levels of government spending significantly affects long-term local authority strategies and priorities. Political leaders in the UK's major cities argue that local government functions will be reduced to waste disposal, as local authorities will have lost a third of their budgets by 2015. Radical and broader policy communities, often local authority led partnerships in the fields of youth services, libraries and community care will simply disappear (Taylor et al., 2013). The private sector too faces reduced business and revenue: for example, according to National Express figures, cuts in transport subsidies have meant 'Since the government withdrew concessionary fares for national travel in 2010 there have been 1 million fewer journeys made by the elderly and the disabled' (Topham, 2012).

THE ECONOMICS OF OLD AGE

It is hard to overestimate important divisions of class, race and gender in an ageing cohort in relation to health, leisure and the quality of life. As Joseph Rowntree remarked more than two generations ago, poverty increasingly exerts its grip over people's lives in old age. The injuries of class build up over one's life; one clear economic indicator becomes the level of wealth and income one can draw when no longer in paid employment. Women face a double jeopardy which is grounded in the loss of occupational pension contributions during childrearing years, thus diminishing their final pension. If one then factors in changing household patterns, divorce and remarriages, men and women's work and family life courses are no longer straightforward. These inequalities frame key questions about the economics of niche markets, access to pensions, gender and minimalist state income support.

It is therefore often misleading to speak of the 'silver pound' as signifying a single homogeneous market, not least because the present financial crisis has challenged the saving and consumption patterns of older people:

Average incomes for the over-55s have fallen by 4% over the past year while savings levels have dropped by more than a quarter, according to research by Aviva ... The report also highlights deep income inequalities among older people. One in five 55–64 year-olds enjoy incomes over £2,500 a month, or five times the earnings of the bottom tenth. (Collinson, 2011)

Moreover, there is not necessarily a linear relationship between chronological age and growing poverty in ageing:

One of the more remarkable findings of the report is that, on average, 65–74 year-olds have higher incomes than 55–64 year olds. Aviva said its quarterly tracking of income levels has found a consistent 'retirement bounce' at age 65, when payouts from state and company pensions lift incomes'. (Collinson, 2011)

But for a cohort still divided by class, race and gender, for some people, old age promises and carries little in the way of leisured lifestyles, as basic needs are not met.

The ICM survey of 1,000 people aged 65 and over found almost a quarter would sometimes not heat a bedroom or living room because of the cost; 10 per cent said they were always or often lonely; for all the talk of silver surfers, more than 70 per cent had never used the internet. (Garfield, 2008)

According to the ONS 2011 UK Census data, in 1973 9% of the adult population lived alone whereas that figure had increased to 16% by 2010. Isolation may not only result in loneliness and misery, it also carries health risks as the isolated elderly have a 26% higher death rate than statistically expected. It is this dark vision of old age that features in the stigmatizing stereotypes that abound in media and common-sense perceptions of the old. Old people are cast adrift or trapped in lifestyles that are struggling with and against disabilities such as Alzheimer's disease, stroke, osteoporosis and arthritis. Life becomes little more than survival, raising important questions about the quality of human life in modernity. However, for some researchers, leisure offers a space where those suffering from dementia and with problems of memory loss can challenge stigma and negative stereotyping of old age and the ageing process itself:

When diagnosed with dementia, older adults may experience increased stigma due to memory loss. However, leisure can be a space for resisting dominant ideologies, and older adults may use leisure to resist ageist stereotypes, leading to feelings of empowerment. Since persons with dementia experience increased stigma, leisure may be a space to resist stereotypical notions of dementia. (Genoe, 2010: 303)

Research in the USA documents that people suffering from dementias still want to be engaged in everyday life, maintain autonomy and retain family and friendship networks. Genoe (2010) again argues that leisure can be seen as resistance to power structures in society. Drawing on the work of Susan Shaw in Canada and Betty Wearing in Australia, she continues:

Leisure behaviours, interactions and settings can challenge the ways that power is exercised. Since freedom is encouraged through engagement in leisure pursuits, leisure is an ideal space for resisting existing power structures and ideologies. It is 'a space where there is room for the self to expand to beyond to what it is told it should be'. (Wearing, 1998: 146)

> Leisure discourse emphasises abilities and interests and right to time and space for enjoyment and freedom, ideally affording people the opportunity to do what they wish, instead of what is expected of them.
> (Genoe, 2010: 305)

Giddens (1979b, 1991) suggests that one important feature of modernity is the sequestration of human experience and trust in expert systems. Unlike in previous centuries, individuals are cut off from harsh realities of birth, puberty, sexual intercourse, illness and death. In the twentieth century, with growing importance attached to ideas of child care and child-centred education, the older generation, both biological parents and educational professionals, have consciously made more effort to protect children and young people from bearing witness to such physiological and psychological milestones in the human life course. These have now become very private matters: the latter two life stages are now invariably subject to the advice of experts and managed in segregated professional and organizational settings, such as geriatric hospitals, hospices and, not least, generic residential homes for old people. One great fear of becoming old is that of losing one's home and one's independence because of mental and physical frailty. The leisure lives of those in care become recast as therapeutic recreation with animateurs or helpers encouraging the elderly to take armchair exercises, to be entertained by visiting musicians, and to 'sing along' to tunes that were popular during the Second World War and the immediate post-war period. For the coming cohort rock 'n' roll songs will become favourites, followed by hits and dance tunes of 'the swinging sixties'. In the popular imagination, old people's homes are the epitome of Erving Goffman's (1961b) ideal type of a 'total institution' where the pain of imprisonment is living life in public and being managed collectively by staff. Nothing prepares people for residential institutions, cut off from the outside world; a decision to place an elderly relative into a care home is generally as traumatic for the carer (who usually, for whatever reasons is now unable to cope) as it is for the neophyte inmate. Added to this residential mix is the real fear of mistreatment and abuse. Indeed, according to a recent NHS survey, one in five elderly patients are not treated with dignity in hospitals (Boseley, 2013). This is more routine disregard than the occasional exposé of wholesale neglect and abuse that troubles the media, given that the elderly in care are surprisingly not protected by human rights legislation (Batty, 2005). The crisis in residential care was highlighted in June 2011 by the financial collapse of Southern Cross, a commercial care company responsible for running 750 homes and caring for 31,000 people. Commercial care companies have stepped in to take advantage of the decline of welfarism given the determined central state propensity to devolve and to privatize personal care for the elderly. However, such private companies have frequently been criticized for poor standards of care, provided by low-paid and under-trained and unqualified staff, despite government rules and regulations enforced by the Care Quality Commission. As in the Southern Cross case, local authority social services have to sort the future care problems out as the private company heads for liquidation.

WHO CARES? THE PROBLEMS OF AND FOR THE 'OLD OLD'

This chapter on ageing deals with important questions about the quality of life and the role that leisure may play in older people's lives. As argued previously, social analysis needs to capture the recursive processes of age cohorts routinely living out their lives in time and space. To stay with the word's etymological roots, the military metaphor for describing demographic groups as cohorts is just perfect, as each generation has to do battle with life, has to struggle to deal with the legacy of previous generations and at the same time, try to secure some kind of future for the next generation. We have suggested that the 'baby-boomer' 1960s teenage generation is best understood as 'grasshoppers' who have benefited from the collective welfare state, laid down in the 1950s by their industrious parent generation ('ants'), while offering a more fragile individualized risky future to their own children ('butterflies'). By refusing to grow up and grow old gracefully, the ageing post-war 'baby-boomer' generation are now casting a shadow over the next young generation with their existential commitment to liminality and consumption-driven leisure lifestyles and tastes. If changing rates of morbidity and longevity are factored into existing pension arrangements; the 'grasshopper' lifestyles of living and consuming in the present are unsustainable at current levels. The changing dependency ration between those in work and those economically inactive is gradually increasing, with the result that there is substantially less of the population gainfully employed than in previous generations. If this were not enough, the next generation faces a future with depleted natural environments characterized by overpopulation, global warming and pollution.

Although the baby-boomer generation appears myopic about the future and absent minded about their collective responsibility for sustaining the long-term material environment for the next generation, many individual women and couples, now themselves in their 50s and 60s, have been drawn into coping with the longevity of their own parents. Although the provision and organization of care for elderly parents, the 'old old' (85 years plus), is often solely the responsibility of women, the nature of funding of care and the quality of its provision involve the very elderly themselves, the family and relatives of main carers as well as the more formal social and health services provided by state, voluntary and commercial sectors. The pressure on 'family' to care for the elderly in the community is the major trope for neo-liberal and conservative politics but this moral imperative, articulated through common sense, media and professional advice, swiftly translates into care by daughters to look after their parents, or more taxing and problematic still, elderly people related by kinship (e.g. aunts and uncles) or by marriage (in-laws). Tensions inevitably arise within family relations over the material and emotional burdens of dealing with and managing elderly parents and relatives who can no longer live independently. Recent media attention has at last focused upon the possibility that carers may suffer from depression, often not recognized, diagnosed or treated appropriately by those with the responsibility of part- or full-time care of parents and the elderly. Such tensions are exacerbated by more complicated family networks as people divorce and remarry. Market researchers now talk about 'beanpole families' as, with divorce and remarriage, individuals shed or find it hard to sustain previous wider extended family relationships. There is much academic and media speculation that the extended family is in inexorable decline whilst beanpole families look to friendship networks rather than kinship, particularly those from obsolete and estranged marriages, for identity, support and leisure companions.

Although the elderly may prefer to live in their own home, if they are wealthy enough to possess one, sooner or later, because of physical and/or mental deterioration, probate decisions must be taken to provide long-term full-time care. Many women leave work to take care of elderly relatives; many take them into their own homes or arrange 'granny flat' accommodation. In 2013 more than 2.3 million people left their jobs to care for relatives, according to an online poll for the charity Carers UK (2013). When women and families can no longer cope with part- or full-time care, for whatever reasons (needless to say these are inexorably complex and compelling), the choice and location of residential care must be tackled. Professions in residential care have suggested that the process of choosing and deciding upon the right nursing or residential care home for the elderly or infirm parent/parents is frequently more traumatic for family members than for the elderly themselves. Then, for main carers, the rota and routines of visiting, holidays and 'days out' are embedded in, and often displace, pre-existing leisure lifestyles. Their lives and leisure lives are on hold.

Although respite care, when organized and available, may offer temporary release and a welcome option for some carers, the long-term commitment to care changes and transforms the lives and lifestyles of both elderly and carers. Some argue (Sheikh, 2012) that personal care budgets should be devolved more directly to individuals and families; this may result in a more creative use of budgets by the elderly, particularly in terms of leisure – for example, access to sport, theatre and community-based activities.

The same commitment to care and changed leisure routines reappear when the baby-boomer generation take on the role of 'grand parenting'. Although politicians such as Ed Miliband can talked of the 'squeezed middle' of the electorate, the baby-boomer generation find themselves squeezed into a caring and supportive role when they have to divide their time, energy and resources between very elderly grandparents and their own growing grandchildren. Many grandmothers feel anxious and become committed to caring routinely for their grandchildren as their own children feel compelled to pursue dual careers, with mothers often returning promptly to full- or part-time work once maternity leave runs out. The traditional gender division of labour forged two or three generations ago – men in the public sphere as breadwinners and women in the private sphere at home as carers – has long since dissolved. Although many mothers may want to choose to look after their own pre-school children rather than pay nannies, pre-school nurseries or call on granny's help and goodwill, heavy mortgages and consuming life-styles exert a compelling priority.

ACTIVE LEISURE LIFESTYLES OF THE ELDERLY

The sustained compression of morbidity or increasing the healthy lifespan has opened up both the physical and mental horizons of the 'young old' (60–80 years of age) and indeed the 'old old' (80 plus years of age). The taste for liminality, for pushing against cultural boundaries, which so animated the baby-boomer generational culture in their teenage years in the 1960s asserts a seductive, and for some, corrosive power in a variety of ways sixty years on. Whereas sexism and racism may have been seen as giants to tackle in the 1970s, ageism is seen as the new goliath at the turn of the millennium. In the 1940s and 1950s, retirement and old age were captured by the phrase 'a well-earned rest', often essential for health reasons, as the majority of the male population were employed in physically damaging skilled and unskilled manual occupations. Back then, the life stage of men on reaching retirement at 65 years of age or often earlier, was celebrated by management and work mates with the traditional leaving present of a pocket watch or a mantelpiece clock, both symbolizing release from the tyranny of work time, from the disciplines of clocking in and clocking off; an escape from the relentless pres-sure of piecework rates when 'every second counts'. Those leaving work nowadays view retirement as an opportunity for active leisure, for satiating their leisure imaginations in order to catch up with what was impossible in working lives and careers.

It is precisely this thirst for active leisure, a self-induced and self-referential quest for pleasure and leisure, that make any demands for long-term caring commitments so hard to bear. Whether that care is demanded or expected by family members (i.e. from dependent parents or growing grandchildren), many amongst the elderly cohort find such obligations easy to resist and so politely or not so politely decline. Driven on by the watchword 'it's my turn now' or the advertising slogan 'because you are worth it', the young old feel mandated to treat themselves to conspicuous consumption often in the form of longed for motorbikes, cars and mobile homes which facilitate day trips, tourist visits to favoured locations and foreign holidays. Rather than being flummoxed by the tastes and technological trends of postmodernity – namely digitalization, commodification and commercialization the majority of the young old are more or less comfortable with going 'online', Internet dating, texting on their iPhones, catching up with friends on Facebook and taking pictures with their iPads.

Because the majority of the young old are no longer constrained by work and work obligations, leisure time expands and retirees can spend and fill their time being 'busy doing nothing'. Everyday domestic routines of preparing and eating meals, cleaning the house or car, gardening, shopping and even putting the bins out may be transmogrified into leisure enthusiasms rather than chores. They provide important topics of conversation and opportunities to gossip with friends and neighbours, noted by feminist research as one important dimension to women's home-based leisure (Green, 1998; Green et al., 1990). In leisure the elderly can challenge and resist negative stereotypes of old age by participating in competitive endurance sports and some take pleasure in beating the performances and times of much younger participants, whether the form chosen is road or fell running, rowing, sportive cycling, mountain marathons or triathlons. Wisdom in old age often means sticking to sports that one has established competence in rather than embarking on careers in new sporting challenges. As one would expect, each sport organizes its own age-based masters or vets category races and competitions; all of which have been and remain fiercely contested at local, regional, national and international levels.

For those elderly people not interested in physical fitness or competitive sports, they have the time to and do volunteer, often in new areas of interest or those developed out of previous enthusiasms. The bulk of volunteering in the UK and elsewhere is diverse, often leisure based, and inevitably and reliably sustained by the middle aged, retirees and the old:

> Volunteering takes place across the spectrum of leisure settings including museums and heritage attractions, visitor information centres, parks, recreation and conservation; volunteer tourism and volunteering at sporting and other types of events, ensuring that, subject to the volunteer's needs, all forms of engagement, sustained and episodic, are on offer. In addition, the act of volunteering has also been considered as a form of leisure regardless of the organisation or setting. (Lockstone-Binney et al., 2010: 437)

At first blush the strength of volunteering in sports, arts and cultural organizations witnessed amongst the present generation of middle- and old-aged people may seem paradoxical as it flies in the face of previous arguments about the lack of local solidarity and altruism in protecting the welfare state and growing individualism under the pressures of consumer culture. But these are neo-liberal times as the state hollows out traditional functions, passing on more and more responsibilities to the voluntary sector. Even traditionally core state functions such as law and order and the management of collective transport infrastructure are in the UK parcelled out to charitable organizations and volunteers. This has been the case in managing the waterways and canal network, and will be so under recent proposals to prioritize the voluntary sector via financial incentives to take on the release and after care of offenders, which has been historically the sole province of the state, monitored through the Probation Service.

Leisure researchers suggest that the psychological benefits of volunteering focus upon self-interest rather than altruism. Older people volunteer because they are mainly following their personal interests, pursuing and sustaining leisure careers. Volunteers can benefit from free entry and access to resources as well as nourishing social networks with like-minded enthusiasts. Not everyone values the help that volunteers may offer. For example, Alan Bennett complains of the over-intrusive and patronizing nature of National Trust volunteers in their dealings with the public as they visit NT properties. Indeed, this unease provided the inspiration for his play in 2012 , *People* (Higgins, 2012). Needless to say, the very same National Trust policies, strategies, staff values and behaviour have been fiercely defended by its Chair, Simon Jenkins as he refutes Bennett's view (Jenkins, 2012).

9.2 Leisure in old age

Consider the following list. What would you put into the A–Z guide for leisure in old age?

A – Allotments; Art Galleries; Alcohol
B – Bowls; Bingo; Bridge
C – Cruises; Cinema; Caravanning; Coach Trips
D – Dancing: Tea, Ballroom, Latin American
E – Eating out
F – Fishing
G – Golf
H – Heritage sites; History Groups
L – Libraries; Listening to the Radio; 'Leisure' Shopping
M – Museums; Music Concerts
N – National Trust; Newspaper Reading
O – Opera
R – Rambling; Rail Travel
P – Pet Ownership (Cats and Dogs)
S – Shopping in Town
T – Tennis; Theatre
U – U3A
V – Volunteering; Visiting
W – Watching Sport; Watching Television

Why are the above leisure pursuits attractive or suitable for elderly people?

STRICTLY GONE BALLROOM DANCING?

For some older people, ballroom dancing and the dance floor provide a significant social and cultural space for leisure. This section provides a case study of one leisure activity associated with old age. One can focus on dance as an emancipatory practice for older people as it enables them both to belong to and enjoy social networks and also to exhibit cultural competence in performance. Dances and dance music constitute specific cultural capital that each generation develops and deploys to celebrate and to display its own distinctive historical cultural identity, but these tastes are also shared with other generations. Tastes are acquired and developed and dancing classes and dance venues are crucial sites for creating, inhibiting or realizing, physicality, gender identity and body competence.

So, historical and generational analysis provides a crucial backdrop to mapping the place of dance and dancing within leisure. Policies around the production and consumption of dance, the physicality of dancing and broader leisure trajectories underpinning getting ready and 'going out' to dances, to raves, and nights out 'clubbing', require detailed historical and ethnographic study. Such analyses immediately sensitize readers to the shifting hybridity of dance forms, fads and fashions. Processes of globalization are hard to ignore here as an essentially transatlantic trade in both song and dance has continually shaped youth and youth cultures in the post-war period.

Table 9.1 provides a rough broad-brush historical sweep over the past few decades of emergent styles. In any decade there are dominant mainstream dances as well as oppositional and emergent dancing styles. But it is important to acknowledge that trends in social dancing constantly change because 'roots can be found in generations past and its offspring discovered in dances to come' (see Driver, 2000: 13).

Table 9.1 Historical cohorts and dancing tastes: 'fads' and 'fashions'

1930s	Traditional 'English' codified ballroom dances: waltz, foxtrot, tango, QuickTime foxtrot and Charleston (quick step)
1940s	American 'swing'– jitterbug, lindy hop, samba, rumba, tango
1950s	Jazz and the beat generation: jive, rock 'n' roll, bossa nova, cha cha cha, mambo
1960s	The swinging 'expressive' revolution: twist, jazz dance, single-sex bopping and more informal dancing styles
1970s	Youth subcultures and spectacular styles: disco dancing, heavy metal and head banging, moshing, punk and pogo-ing, gay scene and the hustle
1980s	Madchester, Haçienda and Northern 'Soul', the 'rave' scene, break dancing, hip hop, popping
1990s	'Clubbing' , moonwalking and street dance; American line dancing
2000s	Salsa dancing, Strictly Come Dancing

It is beyond the scope of this case study of elderly dance tastes to offer any precise periodization of dance, it simply suggests that at any one historical moment, particular dance forms are fashionable to particular sorts of people in particular locations. So it comes as no surprise that older people like old-time ballroom dancing and dances. However, this lesson seems to have been forgotten by health experts, keen to increase physical activity levels amongst the elderly (Douglas and Carless, 2005). The suggestion that older people should embark on strenuous machine-driven exercise regimes offers no attraction to older women, some of whom value dancing because of the sheer pleasure of simply touching others, of 'messing about', of enjoying the music, having fun, as well as belonging to long-standing friendship networks. Dancing offers the possibility of reconnecting with one's youth and rekindling past (hopefully pleasant) embodied experiences, locked deep inside one's own biography. So prescriptions for gym-based exercise and the promise of future health benefits carry more appeal for a younger cohort of 55–65-year-olds who represent the fastest growing sector of the fitness industry. The perceived reluctance of the present generation of school children to engage with physical activity provides the backdrop to the current moral panic about eating habits and childhood obesity. Health strategists and health professionals are just as worried about the long-term health of young adults, of 20–30 years, given their propensity for unhealthy lifestyles around sexual relations, smoking, drug and alcohol consumption and eating patterns.

One central argument of this book is a pressing need to develop a sociological imagination and more specifically to take a generational perspective on social and cultural processes and contexts. Indeed, the structure of the book traces the post-war generation as a cohort through the decades. To use Rojek's terms (2005), one must acknowledge that every generation is emplaced quintessentially in cultural space and time. Each generation develops its own habitus, its unique predilections and tastes for all things, including leisure, yet each age cohort does so by growing up in the shadow of its parent generation. Consequently, each generation is keen to make its own space and establish its own identity, and this is forged in the light of economic, political, social and cultural circumstance. Perhaps shadow is a not too helpful metaphor as each age cohort also fragments along recalcitrant lines of class, gender and race. So, the material and cultural heritage that the next generation inherits, is in one important sense both unequal and uneven. The plethora of opportunities and constraints for the next generation depend significantly on the precise legacy and generosity of the preceding parental generation. Youth's compulsory and determined diet of opportunity and constraint is both shaped by one's whereabouts in traditional hierarchies of class, race and gender, as well as by the collective historical life course and experiences of one's own generation. At a micro level, the individual's position in the family and the family size, not least bearing in mind the complexity of modern family and household arrangements, is crucial too in determining access to parental resources over the life course.

If we turn to historical and generational perspectives towards dance, these generic arguments become clearer. During adolescence, young people are exposed to or identify with distinctive dance fads and fashions and, importantly, those forms become crystallized by peer and media pressures in the taste of that particular demographic cohort. Dancing forms are embodied and embedded within specific historical generations, and so distinctive ways of dancing and characteristic forms of music and music locations are both valued and carried on into later life. Each generation has in the tired cliché 'been there and bought the tee shirt'; each has its own experience with its own unique message. All these experiences are central in identity formation and generational solidarity, as each age cohort collectively shares its time in history, bounded by specific economic, political, social and cultural circumstances.

One could argue that there are particular moments, special episodes and key sites that crystallize, privilege and in turn symbolize both the music and dance *zeitgeists* of each historical cohort. Nevertheless, there remain iconic venues which function or functioned as dance factories, such as Blackpool's Tower ballroom, Liverpool's Cavern and Cream, Manchester's Haçienda and London's Ministry of Sound, and so on.

Just as John Bale (1993) has suggested that football grounds serve as hallowed sites for football supporters, similar emotions are generated in the hearts of dancing enthusiasts. Every urban centre of any large student city is full of distinctive discotheques and dancing clubs which offer diverse 'authentic' evenings out (Lowe and Atkin, 1997). These hallowed halls are visited and revisited during the three years of undergraduate life, particularly in times of ritual and celebration. Many students seek to live and dance on, after graduation, in their chosen university towns, as if halcyon student days and most importantly nights, will live on.

At a national level, 'special' concerts such as Woodstock, The Who at Leeds University, George Harrison's concert for Bangladesh, Bob Dylan's Isle of Wight performance and Bob Geldof's Live Aid and Life 8 have provided effervescent displays of generational identity and community. These have been crucial signifiers of taste and may be renewed by yearly events such as the Glastonbury or Reading festivals. Musical *zeitgeist* may also be symbolized and captured in television programmes, like *The Old Grey Whistle Test*, *Top of the Pops*, *The Tube* or personified in radio celebrities like John Peel. These are like tips of the iceberg, firmly embedded in the generation's unconscious as well as articulated consciousness. As we argued in Chapter 5, Sarah Thornton (1995) has suggested that there is in fact a mainstream/subculture divide, with subcultures searching out their own 'authentic' music and dance experience, unavailable in the mainstream. Hebdige's (1979) work on punk subcultural style is most helpful here, as is also Willis' (1990) study of bikers. Hebdige (1988) went on to explore the fragmentation of youth according to racial divisions while stressing the generic paradoxical desire of young people to be 'hiding in the light'. Teenagers want to be noticed but certainly not to be recognized nor supervised by their parental generation. So each generation develops its own historical taste for dance and dance music as mass media both construct, reflect and brand distinctive styles such as jive, reggae, punk, new wave, beat, acid jazz, garage, indie, house, and so on. There are always those dormant opportunities to rediscover old tunes or recycle past dances but even retrospective tunes often have a different mix so as to mark them out from the original sound tracks and ageing artists.

DANCE, IDENTITY AND INDIVIDUALIZATION

Conventional wisdom when discussing dance is one that emphasizes growing individualization. Whereas pre- and post-second world war dances were organized around heterosexual couples dancing as partners, the 1960s witnessed and legitimated dancing separately, sometimes in single-sex groups and sometimes just dancing alone. Commentators have suggested that the 1960s baby boomers' expressive revolution displaced ballroom and the more choreographed dance patterns favoured by their grandparents and parents. In winning space from the tastes of the parent generation, 1960s youth rejected the discipline and conventions of formalized dance education and training. Driven by different music genres, spectacular youth subcultures developed their more individualized dance moves, dancing styles and taste in their own prescribed, and at times proscribed, dancing locations.

While the 1960s youth generation challenged traditional values and hierarchies, it was youth growing up in the 1970s and 1980s that embraced and developed the politics of identity. Although dismissed by marketeers as Generation X or Thatcher's children, they were the new kids on the block. The gay 'scene' and black music and dance in particular challenged and subverted mainstream white culture and taste. This next youth generation, the offspring of the 1960s 'baby boomers', discovered new 'techno' music and took different recreational drugs inside new club and rave scenes. They turned towards US black urban culture for their taste in rap, clothes, trainers and dance. They also occupied key sites and sounds in particular cities and caught the attention of a newly formed Institute of Popular Culture in Manchester (see O'Connor and Wynne, 1996; Redhead, 1993, 1997). For instance, there was much interest in Manchester's 'gay village' as a new contested urban site for different sexualities and youth culture. Their parents were left behind, uncomfortably out of place, to grow old, to upgrade their favourite vinyl records into CD compilations and to attend rock concerts of their favourite groups, now themselves old-age pensioners reunited in one last tour. Worse still, those aged parents may choose to take in one of the many 1960s tribute bands playing at some small-town community-centre venue, in the spirit of re-affirmative nostalgia.

With a visible presence of gay and black youth culture, discourses about the body and dancing take on new directions. In racialized discourses around black identities, skin colour and the physicality of the body overwrite alternative discourses organized around mind, intellect and culture. Ben Carrington (2000) has emphasized cultural tensions around black hyper-masculinities and their mediatization. The black body is seen as pre-literate, primitive and naturally disposed to physical competencies in sport and dance. Paul Gilroy has tackled this question and is keen to stress cultural hybridity, rather than any racial biological essentialism, as a starting point for analysis. The fact that ethnic minorities too subscribe to racial ideologies, that they consider they are better dancers because of their natural rhythm, need not detain us here. However, it is interesting to note that in Heike Wieschiolek's (2003) study of the 'salsa scene' in Hamburg it was divided into two subcultures. One part was made up of ethnic minority dancers (Latinos/Latinas) who felt no need to go to salsa workshops or attend classes as they considered that they could 'naturally' do the complicated salsa moves and kicks (even though salsa dancing was not part of their own national cultural background). In contrast, the second subculture was made up of German dancers who would dance up to five times a week and were keen to attend classes and develop dance competencies.

DANCING CLASSES: WHO OR WHAT MAKES A GOOD DANCER?

In generational analysis particular attention must be paid to the function of the dance class in developing taste and bodily competence. What formal and instructional institutional arrangements are made to sustain traditional dance forms and pass them on to the next generation? In particular, what educational arrangements are made by the parental generation to transmit and impose their own favoured dances and traditions onto their children and the next generation? As has been suggested, 1960s teenage culture rejected established ballroom dance forms of their parents' generation and subsequently developed a plethora of rapidly changing dance styles which were less grounded in heterosexual coupledom and unconstrained by patriarchal culture. In the 1970s and 1980s the politics of identity, particularly surrounding sexualities, were further explored in youth culture in dress, music and dance. Social theory began to study the neglected body and acknowledge that human agency was grounded in embodied individuals negotiating identities within more open and liquid cultural spaces.

It is usually in primary schools where children are first introduced to dance and dancing. In this context of physical education, children learn to develop skills and competencies in bodily movement and also to understand where dance sits in the measure of things, particularly in gender relations. There is substantial research that suggests that physical education teachers have (and had) little time for dance both in in the present (and in the past). It is a problematic part of the national curriculum both in the UK and elsewhere (Gard, 2003b, 2005). Many writers have suggested that teaching dance is a challenge, particularly so when teaching boys. If boys are happy, or at the very least committed, to put their bodies on the line for sport (see Gard and Meyenn, 2000) they are less comfortable with dancing. Boys do not dance because it is seen by teachers, parents and children alike as 'a girlie' thing; dancing is simply something that girls do (see Gard, 2001). For boys, interest in dance and dancing undermines any strong claim to a dominant heterosexual masculinity. So, within the context of physical education, the equation between dance and male homosexuality is quickly drawn and calculated. This tension between playing sport and dancing is a lived experience and Keyworth (2001) provided a reflexive commentary on how male PE teachers may experience and deploy dance to subvert traditional notions of masculinity. Indeed, Keyworth (2001)

explored the feminized territory of dance inside PE and suggested that by dancing, men developed an 'oppositional consciousness' to the 'gender game'.
Ramsay Burt (1995) has argued that the history of theatre dance has ignored
gender discourses centred on dance and masculinity, while his book suggested
that dance subverted and challenged patriarchal relations. Some notion of
liminality, of transgressing boundaries, is central to Gard's (2003a) view of anti-
oppressive teaching in PE. Dance can offer boys and girls the possibility of
'being someone else', of breaking out of the rituals and routines of normal body
discipline in everyday life.

STEPPING INTO GENDER ROLES

If dance is seen as somehow abnormal for primary school boys when located
in the classroom, do older mature adult males fare any better when attending
dancing classes later on in life? Are grown-up men more confident in ignoring
traditional hegemonic masculinities and common-sense 'wisdom' which stigmatizes good dance performers as 'poofs', 'gays' or homosexuals? The dance
tutors and media celebrities have important roles to play here and *Strictly
Come Dancing*, with the 85-year-old Bruce Forsyth as compere (inevitably
'assisted' by the glamorous and much younger female companion in Tess Daly),
offers an interesting role model for older men. But dance classes, especially
amongst the elderly, provide important lessons in gender relations; it is quite
all right for women to dance with women (although it can be a constant source
of jokes during dance classes) but it is unthinkable for men to dance with men.
Whereas women seem quite prepared to learn the man's steps in any dance,
men are not prepared to take on the role of women partners. For celebrities, it
is impossible, as when the TV chef, Gordon Ramsay, demanded Darren Gough
teach him dancing and there was immediate argument about who should be
the man and lead.

So ballroom dancing and dance floors provide one important space or site
where older people can not only gain physical exercise and enjoyment, but also
demonstrate competence. Rather than being invisible, they are centre stage and
many are serious enthusiasts, conforming to the ideal type first outlined in
Stebbins' work (see Stebbins, 1992). So, go to afternoon tea dances during the
weekdays or any ballroom on Saturday nights at commercial venues and it is
the over 60s who are the ones displaying bodily competence and skill. Their
bodies are comfortable and at home dancing. Some couples dress up and some
definitely 'show off' when performing particular (presumably favourite)
dances. Many couples just sit, socialize and dance occasionally. It is all spectacle and display and the few younger middle-aged couples in attendance can
only gaze in wonder and admiration. So, ballroom dancing and specific dances
belong to the 'ants' generation. This habitus, this taste, this body competence
was developed as teenagers in the 1940s and 1950s and played out on
Saturday nights in local *palais de dance* such as the ubiquitous Mecca

Locarnos, in locations faintly redolent of Hollywood dance film musicals and celebrity dancing pairs. It is this leisure skill that some of this older generational cohort have nurtured and embodied. It survives in their attendance at afternoon tea dances in leisure venues which remain comfortably within the cost budgets of retired people, some relying solely on state pensions and income support. The death of the tea dance will coincide with the morbidity and demise of its aged practitioners.

So, a generational analysis of ballroom dancing suggests that this dance form, acquired in adolescence, provides a perfect physical activity for older people to display bodily competencies and skills to themselves and to younger generations. Unlike in a sporting contest, living inside a decaying body is no great inhibitor to successful participation and performance. Clearly some forms of physical activity are unattractive to younger generations as uncool if they symbolize the tastes of old people. But mediatization of ballroom dancing has transmogrified this traditional form of dancing, making it more attractive to a young generation as well as replenishing the tastes of the parent and, in this case, grandparent generation.

The BBC has been surprised at the massive success of *Strictly Come Dancing*, which has turned into a long-running popular series. In it the staid 1950s format of competitive ballroom dancing was recycled and upgraded, stimulated by the film *Strictly Ballroom*, released in 1992. The new postmodern format had celebrities, paired with professional dancers, having to dance competitively before judges who made up half the votes for that week's dancing performance, with the remaining votes dependent upon audience voting. It is a reality TV show like *Big Brother* or *Pop Idol*, as couples are filmed backstage struggling to learn new dances and performers have to listen to very critical commentaries from four 'expert' judges, who seldom agree with each other. This was much to the TV audience's displeasure, as fulsome praise had to be ladled out to all and this was orchestrated by the host, the ageing male Bruce Forsyth, 'you're my favourite', and the 'lovely' and much younger hostess, Tess Daly. Starting with 12 couples, the series eliminates the couple with the lowest votes until the judges eventually arrive with one celebrity winner. There was also the additional spin-off programme of *It Takes Two*, which during the week profiles the dancing couples still inside the competition and speculates on the developing relationship between the celebrity and the dancer. As is commonplace with media, there have been subsequent dance spin-off programmes.

There is little need to provide a detailed cultural analysis of *Strictly Come Dancing*, as its message is both traditional and uncompromisingly patriarchal. There is throughout a clear gender message of hyper-masculinity and hyper-femininity. The dance styles, the clothes and the expert comments are essentially heterosexual even if the judges are not. Going ballroom dancing is like stepping back in time, when men were gentlemen and women were ladies. For the elderly, who grew up with ballroom, the gender order is unproblematic: men lead and women follow. So the paradox remains as to why young postmodern men, struggling with the 'crisis of masculinity', are reluctant to put on dancing shoes and step into the less ambiguous world of ballroom dancing. But stepping backwards, into the past, is no easy move to make as it underplays the importance of historical process, demographics and the exigencies of cohort socialization. One should never underestimate the difficulty of transgressing generational boundaries and the inevitability of habitus change. A study (Wieschiolek, 2003) of the 'salsa scene' in Hamburg has suggested that modern German women, who had grown up in a culture of gender equality, were uncomfortable with the patriarchal assumptions of the dance, continually reminded as they were by the dance teacher's exhortation, 'Ladies, just follow his lead!'.

Traditional gender relationships with their prescriptive body discourse and the discipline of ballroom dancing sit easily on the shoulders of the older generation. *Strictly Come Dancing* may be linked to a generational rediscovery of past music and dance styles for re-commodification and re-exploitation but times have changed and so have the dancers. This is not the staid 1950s white 'English' world of competitive ballroom dance as filmed by the BBC, backed by the music of Victor Sylvester's orchestra, but rather a mediatized postmodern version with celebrities and cultural hybridity, epitomized by the salsa. Social dancing must be located within generational cohorts and contextualized within their collective historical experience. Ballroom dancing is not the life blood of the generation of postmodern 'butterflies' but still it is central, reinforcing and transformative for the 'ants' generation. Dancing still provides a crucial site for leisure for each generation but its significance and function differ, as each age cohort is different.

CONCLUSION

There is a pressing need for us to develop a historical and sociological imagination to understand leisure; more specifically to take a generational perspective on social and cultural processes and contexts. Indeed, the structure of the book traces the post-war generation as a cohort through the decades and now this generation inevitably must face up to the exigencies of ageing and old age. However, despite their diverse and divided biographies, it is unlikely that this generation will grow old gracefully. Many have the economic, social, cultural and political resources to participate fully in postmodern culture and are disposed to do so.

10

LEISURE AND THE FUTURE

THIS CHAPTER

- Introduces students to key debates in social analysis about the 'end of history' and post-industrialism
- Outlines the distinctive contributions of the philosopher Bertrand Russell in the 1930s, of countercultural polemists, such as Leary and Neville in 1960s, and Ivan Illich in the 1970s about the nature of leisure and future society
- Explains the significant contribution of Marxist theorists in the 1980s such as André Gorz, as well as examining the historical changes in work patterns and leisure lifestyles in the 1990s
- Concludes with some reliable predictions about the future of leisure.

This chapter considers the future of leisure – the terms in which it has been discussed by important thinkers and the predictions they have made for it. We concentrate on questions of how much leisure has been envisaged for future societies and why, and on how leisure time might be spent.

LEISURE: PAST FUTURES

The Berlin Wall, constructed in 1961 to mark the division in that city between the eastern sector controlled by the communist government of the German Democratic Republic and the part that lay within the Western 'free world', was pulled down in 1989. Later that year Francis Fukuyama, an academic and strategist for the US State Department, published an article entitled 'The end of history' in *The National Interest*, a conservative journal. The article, developed into a book in 1992, argued that the Cold War – a war, in effect, of words and diplomatic manoeuvre between the United States and the Soviet Union that had lasted since the late 1940s – had now been resolved in favour of the USA. This meant that history – in the sense of an ongoing struggle between different political systems and ideologies – was now over: Western-style governance, based on parliamentary democracies and capitalist economies, would now, it was argued, be the norm. While this proposition has attracted a good deal of (largely justified) criticism, it's a good starting point for discussing the future of leisure. After all, while a number of other political and social systems could still be found around the world in the second decade of the twenty-first century (communism in Cuba and North Korea, autocratic monarchy in Saudi Arabia, Muslim theocracy in Iran ...), the so-called 'Arab Spring' of 2011 saw the overthrow of dictatorship in Egypt and popular insurgencies against undemocratic governance in Libya, Syria, Tunisia, Yemen and Bahrain. So, if, for the sake of argument, Fukuyama's liberal democracy is the face of an inescapable future, what kind of life – and, specifically, leisure life – does that democracy promise for its citizens?

BACK TO THE FUTURE OF LEISURE

A future for humankind organized largely around the prospect of increased leisure has been the subject of growing speculation among Western social theorists, politicians and commentators – at least since the 1960s and early 1970s. One of the most thoroughgoing analyses in this regard was Daniel Bell's *The Coming of Post-Industrial Society*, first published in the United States in 1973 (Bell, 1999). In the book Bell described a process through which Western societies were moving from an economy based primarily on the production of goods to one that was predominantly concerned with the providing of services. By the time that Bell's book was published, however, writers had already begun to speculate about an imagined future for humankind – at least in the 'developed world' – in which scarcity would be a thing of the past and the necessity for work greatly diminished, workers having been replaced by automated machinery of various kinds (including, of course, computers). Some writers anticipated that the void left in human lives by the automation of work would be filled by the pursuit of pleasure. This pleasure was to take various forms.

In 1932 the philosopher Bertrand Russell published a provocative essay called 'In praise of idleness', in which he scorned the notion of the ennobling nature of 'honest toil' and prescribed a four-hour working day for each member of a modern society. Russell took his inspiration from the (centralized) organization of production in Britain (and societies like Britain) during the First World War:

> The war showed conclusively that, by the scientific organization of production, it is possible to keep modern populations in fair comfort on a small part of the working capacity of the modern world. If, at the end

of the war, the scientific organization, which had been created in order to liberate men for fighting and munition work, had been preserved, and the hours of the week had been cut down to four, all would have been well. Instead of that the old chaos was restored, those whose work was demanded were made to work long hours, and the rest were left to starve as unemployed. (Russell, 1932)

Russell, who sympathised sympathized with communism and the aims of the Russian Revolution, attacked the principle that leisure should be the pre-rogative of a small and privileged social class. Income and working hours, he argued, should be made equal. The result, he thought, would be a society seething with intellectual curiosity:

In a world where no one is compelled to work more than four hours a day, every person possessed of scientific curiosity will be able to indulge it, and every painter will be able to paint without starving, however excel-lent his pictures may be. Young writers will not be obliged to draw atten-tion to themselves by sensational pot-boilers, with a view to acquiring the economic independence needed for monumental works, for which, when the time at last comes, they will have lost the taste and capacity. Men who, in their professional work, have become interested in some phase of economics or government, will be able to develop their ideas without the academic detachment that makes the work of university economists often seem lacking in reality. Medical men will have the time to learn about the progress of medicine, teachers will not be exasperatedly struggling to teach by routine methods things which they learnt in their youth, which may, in the interval, have been proved to be untrue. Above all, there will be happiness and joy of life, instead of frayed nerves, weariness, and dys-pepsia. The work exacted will be enough to make leisure delightful, but not enough to produce exhaustion. (Russell, 1932)

Timothy Leary, an American psychologist and writer, who had worked for the American military and lectured at Harvard University, propounded a comparable vision in the 1960s and 70s. Leary suggested that for people in Western societies to embrace and explore a more creative, leisured future, they needed to change their consciousness. His critique of the middle class of post-war America was akin to Herbert Marcuse's (see Chapter 7). In his view, they had *become*, rather than been replaced by, automatons. His own life in the 1950s, he once described as that of: 'an anonymous institutional employee who drove to work each morn-ing in a long line of commuter cars and drove home each night and drank mar-tinis ... like several million middle-class, liberal, intellectual robots' (Torgoff, 2004: 72). To escape this life of unthinking conformity, Leary advocated the use of the drug Lysergic Acid Diethylamide (popularly known as LSD), which caused hallucinations – experiences which Leary styled as 'psychedelic'. Leary's vision of the future was expounded in his book *The Politics of Ecstasy* (1970) and in an interview with *Playboy* magazine – a leading advocate of a hedonistic future – in 1966. Radically-minded, curious, young people, having, via LSD, acquired their heightened consciousness, would 'drop out' of conventional society.

Leary was closely associated with a social movement known variously as 'the underground' or 'the counterculture' which flourished in North America and Europe, especially during the 1960s. Another such writer was the Australian futurist and social commentator Richard Neville, whose book *Playpower*, first published in 1970, was more specific in anticipating (and advocating) a future in which work and leisure were merged. In calling for a society in which the individual had more freedom (of sexual expression, of access to drugs and, gen-erally, to *play*) Neville drew political contours that had been less distinct in the work of Leary or, for that matter, Russell. Although a radical, Neville had little political sympathy with the organized and conventional Left. This was because he, and the people for whom he spoke, attacked the very notion of *work* – something on which virtually all left-wing politicking was predicated. 'How can hippies [Neville's constituency] be attracted to the idea of "radicalizing the trade unions" when the implicit goal – higher wages – seems obsolete to them? ... Grubby Marxist leaflets and hand-me-down rhetoric won't put an end to toil', wrote Neville. 'It will be an irresistible, fun-possessed, play-powered counter-culture' (Neville, 1971: 208–209). 'The Underground has abolished work', he continued. 'There are no Positions Vacant columns in the Underground press' (1971: 212). Instead, echoing Russell and Leary to some degree, Neville conceived of a future in which:

> 'Work is done only for fun; as a pastime, obsession, hobby or art-form and thus is not work in the accepted sense. Underground people launch poster, printing, publishing, record and distribution companies; bookshops, newspapers, information bureaux, video and film groups, restaurants ... anything that they enjoy doing. First advantage: every Monday morning is a Saturday night. (Neville, 1971: 213)

Two things are important to note about Neville's argument and this last pas-sage in particular. First, the sort of pleasurable pursuits cited by Neville are plainly a glimpse of the sort of society now prevailing in 'the West' – that is, a postmodern society based heavily on the service sector and on media-based industries in particular. Second, Neville (and, for that matter, Leary) organized their arguments around personal freedoms and did not concern themselves unduly with the organization of a wider society that might underwrite these freedoms. Unlike Russell, they were hostile to communism and Neville acknowledged the incompatibility between his ideas and the standard con-cerns of organized labour. The political logic of the 'hippie' position was there-fore that the future of leisure and pleasure that it envisioned would happen only in the ways, and to the extent, that the prevailing capitalist system permit-ted. Broadly speaking, those with the time and the financial means to explore new horizons in leisure and pleasure might do so. Moreover, questions of personal liberty were more likely to be taken up by right-wing politicians, with their characteristic hostility to state intervention, than those of the left. In 1988, for example, Timothy Leary staged a benefit for Ron Paul, then standing for the US presidency as candidate of the Libertarian Party. (Paul sought the Republican nomination for the presidency for 2008 and again for 2012. He is seen as the intellectual godfather of the far right Tea Party Movement, and an American political scientist has suggested that Paul, a member of the US Congress since 1979, has the most conservative voting record of any congress-man since 1937.)[1]

10.1 Alternative futures

Is it possible to create a society based on the ideals of idleness, fun and self-exploration envisioned by Russell, Leary and Neville?

If so how?

If not, why not?

There were, of course, other futurists throwing their hat into the ring of debate during the 1970s and 80s. Some, not unexpectedly, placed technology at the heart of their predictions; it has, after all, been the majority of theorists who have counselled that, with machines to do the work, humankind would have greater leisure time to fill. Others have been sceptical not only of the value of technology, and of the usefulness of the professionals who administered it, but of the notion that the capitalist system, to which Fukuyama saw no alterna-tive, could actually make a leisured future possible. Let's review some of these arguments.

Academic and popular discussion of the future during the 1970s and 80s was often dominated by the work of Alvin Toffler and, in particular, by his book *Future Shock*, published in 1970. Toffler was at the time working for *Fortune* magazine in the United States and subsequently became a management consult-ant; he wrote from a business perspective. Toffler's book deals essentially in the same currency as Bell and other writers who have perceived the onset of a 'post-industrial society' and a 'knowledge economy'. In his view, the future, as mapped out by Fukuyama twenty years later, would certainly be capitalist: consumer capitalism would flourish and it would be based on niche marketing, as much as on mass marketing. Technology – and computer and satellite tech-nology in particular – would be central to the generation of profits, and people would increasingly define themselves through consumption. Toffler argued:

Anti-materialists tend to deride the importance of 'things'. Yet things are highly significant, not merely because of their functional utility, but also because of their psychological impact. We develop relationships

with things. Things affect our sense of continuity or discontinuity. …
Moreover, our attitudes towards things reflect basic value judgements.
Nothing could be more dramatic than the difference between the
new breed of little girls who cheerfully turn in their Barbies for the new
improved model and those who, like mothers and grandmothers before
them, clutch lingeringly and lovingly to the same doll until it disintegrates
from sheer age. In this difference lies the contrast between past and future,
between societies based on permanence and the new, fast-forming society
based on transience. (1970: 55)

Ultimately, Toffler's vision of the future is akin to those we have previously
discussed. The stress is on the growing possibilities for human self-exploration
and self-development. People will move geographically from place to place,
from culture to culture, from organization to organization, from partner to
partner and from one sense of self to another:

The hippie becomes the straight-arrow executive, the executive becomes
the skydiver without noting the exact steps of transition. In the process
he discards not only the externals of his style, but many of his underlying
attitudes as well. … For they are no longer dealing in 'self' but in what
might be called 'serial selves'. (Toffler, 1970: 290)

Scorning what he called the 'anti-technological rhetoric' of writers such as
Marcuse, it was, said Toffler, 'the super-industrial society, the most advanced
technological society ever, that extends the range of freedom' (1970: 291).
Expectably, like Leary, Toffler found favour with the political right, being
endorsed during the 1990s by Newt Gingrich, another leading figure in
Republican Party politics in the United States (Farrell, 2001).

We can now identify two critiques of the sorts of future propounded by
Leary, Toffler and Fukuyama, one that questions the benefits of the system
through which greater leisure is said to be procured and one which questions
whether the Western system, now declared inevitable by writers such as
Fukuyama, actually *has* generated (or indeed *can* generate) the enhanced leisure opportunities widely spoken of by futurists.

The leading critic of conventional futurism during the 1970s was the
Austrian-born intellectual Ivan Illich. Illich was a Catholic priest, but his social
analysis was rooted, paradoxically, in the anarchist tradition. His radical ideas
influenced the work of the Mexican language training centre he ran for
Catholic missionaries going to South America; this brought complaints from
the American CIA and censure from the Vatican. Illich questioned the usefulness of the very economic growth upon which Western culture was predicated.
This was the economic model which 'the West' (i.e. the United States and the
societies of Northern Europe) prescribed for the rest of the world, but, in Illich's
view, conventional economic development was both inappropriate and unvia-
ble for the still largely agricultural societies of Africa, Latin America and Asia.

Illich seems to have been one of the first writers to argue that the basic premises upon which all previous speculations about the future had rested were themselves undesirable. This argument was essentially twofold. First, Illich questioned the conventional notion of development. Western societies were characterized by a series of key institutions (education systems, health care systems, etc.) and their accompanying bodies of highly trained professionals (teachers, doctors, surgeons, etc.). Not only were these institutions and the services provided by their personnel always assumed to be for the public good, but the *lack* of these institutions and trained professionals was an index of poverty. Thus, an African society which offered only, say, three years compulsory schooling, was seen as deprived and, it was thought, should be assisted towards greater provision. For Illich this simply modernized the concept of poverty. These societies should not aspire towards a cadre of highly and expensively trained professionals. Schools seldom provided people with genuinely useful knowledge in any event: most people had skills and they should educate, and impart these skills to, each other (Illich, 1970). Similarly, Western doctors created as many health difficulties as they cured; society would be better served by paramedics, with basic medical skills – like the 'barefoot doctors' of the People's Republic of China (Illich, 1975a). Second, Illich challenged the desirability of economic growth – a given in Western political discourse. All Western governments sought to promote economic growth so that, via tax revenue, they could fund their state bureaucracies (including the salaries of the many professionals, whose usefulness Illich now questioned). Illich suggested that societies should no longer aspire to growth in this sense – because to do so unduly taxed the earth's physical resources. After several Arab oil-producing countries raised oil prices in 1973, it became common in Western political circles to speak of an 'energy crisis'. This referred, clearly, to availability, but Illich used the term to describe the way Western countries *conceived* of energy in any event:

> It has recently become fashionable to insist on an impending energy crisis. This euphemistic term conceals a contradiction and consecrates an illusion. It masks the contradiction implicit in the joint pursuit of equity and industrial growth. It safeguards the illusion that machine power can indefinitely take the place of manpower. To face this contradiction and betray this illusion, it is urgent to clarify the reality that the language of crisis obscures: high quanta of energy degrade social relations just as inevitably as they destroy the physical milieu. (Illich, 1974: 15)

The implication for mainstream futurist arguments such as Toffler's, predicated as they were on the notion that humans would toil less as automation took over, was clear. People should turn their backs on an ever more mechanized future, in the interests of saving the earth. This way, Illich argued, they would re-discover the 'tools for conviviality': 'People need not only to obtain things, they need above all the freedom to make things among which they can live, to give shape to them according to their own tastes, and to put them to use in caring for and about others' (Illich, 1975b).

There is another argument – one to which many Marxists can subscribe – that says, in effect, 'Leisure? What leisure?' There are two important strands to this argument. One is that, in many societies, people seem to be working more, not less. A widely cited work here is *The Overworked American: The Unexpected Decline of Leisure* by the American sociologist Judith Schor (1991).[2] Schor revisits the issue of productivity addressed by Bertrand Russell in the 1930s: when productivity rises (as it had done steadily in the United States between 1948 and 1990) workers may either produce more in the same amount of time or produce the same amount and have time off. Whether they willed it or not, American workers, instead of taking sabbaticals or working fewer hours, had actually begun to work longer: leisure, to borrow Schor's phrase, had become 'a conspicuous casualty of prosperity' (http://users.ipfw.edu/ruflethe/american.html). Why was this?

> In part, the answer lies in the difference between the markets for consumer products and free time. Consider the former, the legendary American market. It is a veritable consumer's paradise, offering a dazzling array of products varying in style, design, quality, price, and country of origin. The consumer is treated to GM versus Toyota, Kenmore versus GE, Sony, or Magnavox, the Apple versus the IBM. We've got Calvin Klein, Anne Klein, Liz Claiborne, and Levi-Strauss; McDonald's, Burger King, and Colonel Sanders. Marketing experts and advertisers spend vast sums of money to make these choices appealing, even irresistible. And they have been successful. In cross-country comparisons, Americans have been found to spend more time shopping than anyone else. They also spend a higher fraction of the money they earn. And with the explosion of consumer debt, many are now spending what they haven't earned. (http://users.ipfw.edu/ruflethe/american.html)

In other words, it was the logic of consumer capitalism (the basis both of Toffler's things-related optimism and the cultural pessimism of the Frankfurt School of philosophers) which worked to diminish leisure – a great irony in view of the fact that consumer capitalism was supposed to *enhance* leisure. As things had turned out in the USA, according to Schor:

> consumers crowd increasingly expensive leisure spending into smaller periods of time. Contrary to the views of some researchers, the rise of work is not confined to a few, selective groups, but has affected the great majority of working Americans. Hours have risen for men as well as women, for those in the working class as well as professionals. They have grown for all marital statuses and income groups. The increase also spans a wide range of industries. Indeed, the shrinkage of leisure experienced by nearly all types of Americans has created a profound structural crisis

of time. (http://web.archive.org/web/20021128203808/users.ipfw.edu/ruflethe/american.html)

Tiredness, lack of sleep and stress-related illness were all on the rise and parents had less time either for their children or for each other.

It seemed clear, then, at least in the United States, that machines had not set people free. Schor had argued:

> After four decades of this shopping spree, the American standard of living embodies a level of material comfort unprecedented in human history. The American home is more spacious and luxurious than the dwellings of any other nation. Food is cheap and abundant. The typical family owns a fantastic array of household and consumer appliances: we have machines to wash our clothes and dishes, mow our lawns, and blow away our snow. (http://web.archive.org/web/20021128203808/users.ipfw.edu/ruflethe/american.html)

But Americans had appreciably less leisure or apparent peace of mind.

So-called labour-saving devices, then, do not necessarily save or lessen labour. But, and here we can introduce another important dimension to this debate, their clear purpose is often not to save labour, but to save capital. To take some familiar examples of mechanization and/or automation, in the late twentieth and early twenty-first centuries we saw goods increasingly loaded onto ships in containers, obviating the need for dockers; we saw the rise of automatic cash machines and Internet banking, reducing the requirement for counter staff; we saw robots deployed to construct automobiles, so that fewer car workers were now called upon. This was self-evidently not done in order to enhance the leisure experiences of dock workers, bank clerks or car assembly personnel. It was done to reduce costs – of transport, administration and production – and, thus, boost profitability. It may be that the economies wherein machinery is increasingly deployed to perform tasks previously done by humans will generate other employment possibilities for those humans. But, equally, it may not and the ones for whom it does not will likely be designated as *unemployed*, not as being *at leisure*.

These various concerns, raised by writers such as Russell, Illich and Schor, are together grasped in the work of the French Marxist theorist André Gorz, in his book *Farewell to the Working Class: An Essay in Post-Industrial Socialism* (1982). Gorz, who was particularly sympathetic to the work of Illich, wrote of the inherent balefulness of the word 'work' in the late twentieth century:

> A market gardener 'works'; a miner growing leeks in his back garden carries out a freely chosen activity. 'Work' nowadays refers almost exclusively to activities carried out for a wage. The terms 'work' and 'job' have become interchangeable: work is no longer something one *does* but something one *has*. One 'looks for work' and 'finds work' just as one 'looks for' or 'finds' a job. Work is an imposition, ... a nondescript

sale of time. ... For both wage earners and employers, work is only a means of earning money and not an end in itself. Therefore work is not freedom. (Gorz, 1982: 1–2)

(This fundamental notion has, of course, defined leisure – leisure being the time, and the parts of the self, not invested in this alienated activity.) Gorz's book called for the abolition of work, as thus conceived. However, Gorz pointed out, this would not mean 'abolition of the need for effort, the desire for activity, the pleasure of creation, the need to cooperate with others and be of some use to the community' (Gorz, 1982: 2). But how was such fulfilling, freely chosen endeavour to be promoted? Millions of jobs lost to automation would, in all likelihood, not be replaced. Keynesianism – the doctrine that the state should intervene to restore full employment – was dying; Western governments, notably those of Margaret Thatcher and Ronald Reagan in the 1980s would pursue policies of denationalization and the reduction of state social spending. The result would be (and, many would say, has been) a society based on mass unemployment. 'The outlines of a society based on the free use of time', wrote Gorz, 'are only beginning to appear in the interstices of, and in opposition to, the present social order' (Gorz, 1982: 3). Those who thus sought to develop Illich's tools for conviviality would have to break with the Marxist tradition and abandon the notion of the nobility of waged labour; indeed, they would cease to be 'the working class'. They would instead become 'a non-class of non-workers', the new vital agents of social change (Gorz, 1982: 6–7).

The citing of Keynesianism (and its apparent demise) in the debate over the future of leisure is telling and not without irony or ambiguity. As we have observed, the economist John Maynard Keynes is seen as the godfather of state intervention to combat unemployment and protect populations from financial turmoil; his doctrine, for example, strongly influenced President Franklin D. Roosevelt's New Deal policies in the United States in the 1930s and early 40s. But he is also often invoked as the prophet of the age of leisure. Daniel Bell, for example, quotes at length from an essay Keynes published in 1930 on 'The Economic Possibilities for our Grandchildren'. In it, Keynes looked to science as much as to economics as the basis for a leisured future and called for fundamental changes of attitude:

I think with dread of the readjustment of the habits and instincts of the ordinary man, bred into him for countless generations which he may be asked to discard within a few decades ... for the first time since his creation man will be faced with his real, his permanent problem – how to use his freedom from pressing economic cares, how to occupy his leisure, which science and compound interest will have won for him, to live wisely, agreeably and well. (Keynes, 1963, quoted in Bell, 1973: 462–463)

The Australian writer and politician Barry Jones also draws on this essay, reproducing a long passage from it in *Sleepers, Wake! Technology and the Future of*

Work, his book of 1982 (pp. 7–8). Like Bell, Jones, who was Australia's Minister for Science and Technology between 1983 and 1990, endorsed Keynes' vision of a leisurely future but hesitated to say that it would happen for sure: 'We face an extraordinarily ambiguous future. Technology can be used to promote greater economic equity, more freedom of choice and participatory democracy. Conversely, it can be used to intensify the worst aspects of a competitive society, to widen the gap between rich and poor ...' (Jones, 1982: 254). He did note, however, that, crucially, in his country (as elsewhere), the outcome might not lie in the hands of politicians: 'Australia is moving towards a "corporate state" in which major areas of society are run autonomously e.g. industrial relations are left to the employers, unions and the Conciliation and Arbitration Commission, and decisions about hours of work would not be made by parliament' (Jones, 1982: 255). In a television interview 20 years later Jones seemed to concede, the portentous title of his book notwithstanding, that technology had not reduced either the number of jobs or the amount of time employed people devoted to work:

> Well, we can't be sure about that. I think in fact the probability is that there will be more jobs, but they won't be the jobs that we recognise now. I've often thought that the best guide, the best rough cut to where employment services are being created ... where employment's being created, are the Yellow Pages. If you look at the Yellow Pages, and you can see that there's about 4,000 pages in Melbourne, a similar number in Sydney, and you look down the list of jobs that are there, you'll see that a tremendous number of those jobs didn't exist 10 or 15 years ago. Many of them are the sort of things that are, for example, the provision of substitute services for people who are in two-income families. In other words, if you've got a two-income family and people are working pretty hard, they need somebody perhaps to pick up the kids or mow the lawn, or to take the dog for a walk, and so on. (http://www.abc.net.au/dimensions/dimensions_future/Transcripts/s616084.htm (accessed 20 September 2011))

It is of course an open question as to whether many or any of these jobs in the Sydney Yellow Pages met the criteria of Illich's 'tools for conviviality' or Gorz's work 'freely chosen'.

In 2006 Judith Schor confirmed that the trend she had identified in the early 1990s had been maintained. The twenty-first century 'crisis of leisure' foretold by experts had not materialized: '... instead of boredom, time poverty and high levels of daily life stress appear to be widespread' (Schor, 2006: 203). She added:

> The experience of the United States, where both predictions and explanations of the 'growth of leisure time' were pervasive, is an even more cautionary tale for the teleological, modernist perspective. According to internationally comparative sources, working hours rose 3 per cent in the period 1980–2000, and a whopping 16 per cent per working-age person. (2006: 203)

The balance of evidence, then, suggests that of the leisure futures predicted by an array of thinkers scattered across the political spectrum, there is so far little sign. Whether they were predicated on economic growth, the need to reject economic growth, the primacy of play, the redefinition of work or the recourse to consciousness-changing drugs, these futures have so far failed to materialize in a range of resilient capitalist societies. That should not stop us, however, from speculating further about the future of leisure as we advance into the twenty-first century.

POSSIBLE FUTURES: LEISURE PROSPECTS FOR OUR GRANDCHILDREN

Here we will consider two areas of expectation: the degree of access to leisure and the nature of leisure time activity that future generations may enjoy. On the first question, the political winds are not unduly difficult to read. During the first decade of the twenty-first century, largely due to failures in the banking system, several major economies in the Western world – those of the United States, the United Kingdom, Greece, Italy, Spain, Portugal and the Republic of Ireland among them – went into crisis. As we observed earlier, Keynesian measures such as Roosevelt's New Deal were no longer considered appropriate and the governments concerned, pressed by the International Monetary Fund (IMF), introduced what in Britain were termed 'austerity measures'. This had two clear implications for the debates we have been considering. First, in the USA and a range of European societies, public spending was subject to often severe reductions, with a huge number of public sector jobs lost. With forecasts of low, or no, growth in these countries, the prospect of the now redundant public employees finding jobs in the private sector seemed bleak. In the summer of 2010, for example, it was reported that:

> An overwhelming 83% of senior financial and legal professionals believe private sector growth over the next 2 years will not be enough to support the influx into the labour market caused by public sector spending cuts, according to a recent survey by FRP Advisory LLP, the restructuring, recovery and insolvency specialist.[3]

Huge swathes of the previously employed population of the Western world were therefore now faced with enforced leisure and the task, perhaps, of developing their own tools for conviviality.

The second, equally important, consequence of the economic crisis was the formal postponement of access to leisure in the form of the raising of the retirement age. Plans for this had already been announced by the Labour government in Britain in 2006: as a consequence of greater life expectancy, the state retirement age would rise from 65 to 66 in 2024, then a further year each decade until it reached 68 in 2044 (Grice, 2006). In 2010 the French government stated that the French retirement age of 60 for both men and women was no longer affordable, the German government said its retirement age would be raised and the Italian government imposed a six-month delay on those Italian workers retiring in 2011; the Spanish government was being urged by the IMF to take similar measures (Lichfield and Roussel, 2010). In a number of countries, then, the long-term more-work/less-leisure trend identified by Judith Schor was now receiving state affirmation and a virtual guarantee that it would continue for much of the twenty-first century.

Turning now to the typical leisure experiences that may characterize this coming century, we can certainly set down the likely social parameters of these experiences. The sociologist most influential in defining these parameters has been the Polish émigré Zygmunt Bauman, although the terms that he and others have used in doing so have varied: ours has been described as the period of postmodernity (by Bauman (1992) and others), high modernity (a term chiefly associated with the sociologist Anthony Giddens (1990)) and 'liquid modernity' (a phrase coined subsequently by Bauman (2000)). This period, whichever name we might choose for it, is generally agreed to be one in which the following have a pre-eminence: the service-, media- and information-related industries; diversity of cultures and lifestyles; individuality; consumption; and the decline of class politics and the rise of 'identity politics' based on social difference (gender, sexuality, disability) or specific issues (the environment, the arms trade, etc.). Life in contemporary (and foreseeable) societies is agreed to centre, among other things, on the search for identity. This quest is endless because identity itself is elusive. Bauman writes: 'Whenever we speak of identity, there is at the back of our minds a faint image of harmony, logic, consistency: all those things which the flow of our experience seems – to our perpetual despair – so grossly and abominably to lack' (2000: 82). Moreover, according to Bauman, our despair is deepened by the fact that experts – what he calls 'interpreters' – are no longer relevant to matters of culture: in other words there are now no persons privileged to tell us who and what we should be (Bauman, 1992: 1–25). Instead we seek ourselves primarily through consumption – via the media, shopping, popular entertainment and elsewhere. With all this in mind, and drawing on what can be observed from current leisure trends, we can now make some reasonably reliable statements about the future of leisure:

- The seeking and affirmation of personal identity will become more and more important to people in their leisure lives, largely because their work lives – particularly in the service sector – are, arguably, more and more circumscribed: people who work in a variety of occupations are required to wear the uniform and insignia of the company employing them; call centre personnel are given a prescribed list of things to say; the behaviour of a range of employees is closely regulated by supervisors administering regimes of performance indication; and so on.

- One crucial context for identity seeking will be the 'neo-tribe' – the term popularized by Bauman and the French sociologist Michel Maffesoli for a large, imagined community. A religion could certainly fit his description and Islam (wrongly styled by its opponents as anti-modernist) springs to mind, but secular neo-tribes, for instance in the world of sport, now command huge support: in 2007 it was estimated that the football club Manchester United might have 333 million supporters worldwide (Cass, 2007).

- Similarly, celebrities, already ubiquitous in Western popular culture, will be central to leisure lives. The evidence is that people, paradoxically perhaps, have begun to form increasingly intimate attachments to people that they don't know: witness the outpouring of public grief at the death of famous people, such as Diana, Princess of Wales in 1997 and singer Amy Winehouse in 2011. Celebrities have recently reciprocated, regularly publishing their previously private thoughts on Twitter. In a world, to use Bauman's words, 'tightly packed with means, yet notoriously unclear about ends' (2000: 68), celebrities (what they say, what they do, what they recommend) will continue to suggest a way forward to many: huge numbers of people, for example, now follow their favourite celebrity's every utterance on Twitter.

- The historic debate over good leisure, while now muted, is unlikely ever to be concluded. As we've seen, in the nineteenth century, an age when experts still presided over matters of culture, policy makers and social commentators promoted 'rational recreation' – a use of leisure which was intended to improve people morally. In the 1930s the Frankfurt School of Marxist philosophers fretted over the harmful effects of passive or mass entertainment. Today it's an axiom of postmodern culture that such moral judgements are not made and that people make their own discriminations via the market. For much of the latter part of the twentieth century there were widely expressed fears over the degrading of culture through the market: commercial broadcasting, for instance, was thought to bring 'dumbing down' or a reduction of programming to 'the lowest common denominator'. Bauman suggests instead that it 'is arguable whether market domination of culture does indeed promote cultural uniformity, middle-, low- or any other brow. There is plenty of evidence that the opposite is the case. The market seems to thrive on cultural diversity ...' (Bauman, 1992: 18). Cultural judgements, of course, are still – and will continue to be – made, but they will not, as was the case until the 1960s, be made by a self-confident cultural elite. There will be those, for example, who deride others as 'chavs' – a synonym, as one writer argued recently, for working class people who are perceived to make bad choices in consumption and taste (Jones, 2011). Others, of course, are not so sure. Critics of the popular 'X Factor' television format, for instance, claim that it deals in unduly narrow definitions of popular music and occasionally internet campaigns have been mounted to prevent X Factor winners from topping the charts (see Lashua, 2011).

- This brings us to the question of politics. It is arguable that voting in TV talent contests is the nearest that many people come to participating in any kind of democracy – an indication of the postmodern condition, wherein individuals are defined more as consumers than as subjects of the state. Some of the Frankfurt School were pessimistic about the possibilities of politics in advanced industrial societies – Marcuse, for example, wrote of politics in the late twentieth century as a closed and Orwellian discourse (1972: 81) – and politicians have continued to decline in popularity and legitimacy in a range of countries. This is expressed in the fall in the number of people voting, the growing popularity of political satire and recurrent poll findings that the public hold politicians in low regard. In November of 2010, Rory Bremner, impressionist and Britain's leading exponent of political satire, announced that he was taking a break 'because there are simply no politicians in the new government that anybody recognises. That does make life a bit trickier for me' (Walker, 2010). Similarly in September 2011, Ed Miliband, leader of the British Labour Party (a party that had been in government for 13 of the previous 14 years) was publically advised by party sympathizers on what he needed to do to 'get noticed' (Sherwin, 2011). This does not of course mean that politics will cease to preoccupy people in their leisure time. Far from it. They will have meetings, march for causes, stage demonstrations and distribute leaflets, just as they have done for centuries, and they will debate via the Internet. Indeed the Internet itself will continue to be a conduit for political intervention, as already witnessed by the rise of 'hacktivism', the issuing of 'dot.communist manifestos' and so on (see Jordan and Taylor, 2004). Nor should X Factor-style media phenomena be thought to be without political import: in 2011, when the government of the People's Republic of China banned the TV talent contest *Super Girl*, sections of the Western press claimed that it was because the programme entailed 'too much democracy'(*Daily Mail*, 2011). Similarly, the fall of the autocratic governments of Tunisia and Egypt in the 'Arab Spring' of 2011 was widely attributed to the Internet social networking facility Facebook.[4]

- It is an open question as to whether tourism will flourish as a leisure time activity in the coming century. Governments have in the recent past been committed to the expansion of air travel, but powerful factors seem now to militate against this. For example, the British government confirmed plans for a third runway at London's Heathrow airport in 2009, but dropped them in 2010, almost certainly on grounds of expense. There is growing opposition to air travel, however, principally on ecological grounds: considerations of climate change have seen the founding of such pressure groups as Plane Stupid (in 2005) and brought the term 'carbon footprint' into popular usage. Popular opposition to air travel now ranges across a number of organizations and societies. (For details of those in the UK go to the *airportwatch* website: http://www.airportwatch.org.uk/.) Besides this, the costs or air travel are unlikely to diminish and will be beyond the purse of the majority of the world's population.

- Conversely, for that section of the world population that has grown in prosperity, *leisure counselling* will increasingly be available. Edwards and Bloland write: 'Today the executives whose success enables them to slow down, the housewives whose children have grown, the young people who wish to develop their potential, the retired workaholics all are potential candidates for this emerging helping service'(1980: 435). Although the notion of leisure counselling may seem novel, these words were actually written over thirty years ago and are clearly predicated on the conventional notions of the coming of a leisure society that we have discussed in this chapter.

- One key area for specific leisure counselling and the expression of self-identity will continue to be the body. Sociologists such as Chris Shilling (see, e.g., Shilling, 1993) some time ago recognized the body as an important site for the expression of self-identity. The best example here is health and fitness: this preoccupation seemed to develop in the 1980s – Jane Fonda's famous *Workout Book* and video, for instance, had sold 4 million copies by 1986[5] – but witness also the more recent proliferation of gymnasia and fitness trainers and workout instruction. Other examples are cosmetic surgery – evoking the stress placed in postmodern culture on 'image' and the visual and, like gym membership, a leisure pursuit of the more affluent – and body art. Tattoos are probably the best example of the latter. Historically having a tattoo may have been a predominantly male and working-class proclivity and, in Britain, tattoo parlours still seem most likely to be found in working-class districts. But this is clearly beginning to change. In 2003 a survey found that 15% of the US adult population had at least one tattoo; that number rises to over a quarter for adults under 25; moreover women are as likely to have tattoos as men (Kang and Jones, 2003).

- One final, but reliable, prognostication is that censorship of visual material will be relaxed, the spirit of the postmodern age being one of consumer sovereignty, deeming individuals (as viewers and as the parents of viewers) to be the best judges of what they and/or their children should see. Action to assert the offensive nature of media material is more likely to come from private than from state, or state-sanctioned, bodies. A good example here would be the protests mounted by the religious pressure group Christian Voice against the broadcasting by the BBC of *Jerry Springer: The Opera* in 2005. This protest was staged by a private body and directed against a broadcast institution established by royal charter as a public service.

10.2 Forward thinking

Consider your own thoughts on the future.

What are 'tools of conviviality? Will it be possible to use them and what influence will they have on the future of humankind?

Is the future one of more work or more leisure? Give reasons for your answer.

Now that economic growth is being called into question by some people, what are the alternatives?

NOTES

1. See http://voteview.com/Is_John_Kerry_A_Liberal.htm (accessed 12 September 2011).
2. For a summary of Schor's argument, go to http://users.ipfw.edu/ruflethe/american.html (accessed 19 September 2011).
3. 'Private sector growth not strong enough to absorb public sector cuts', posted 11 August 2010: http://www.mynewsdesk.com/uk/view/news/survey-by-frp-advisory-shows-private-sector-growth-not-strong-enough-to-absorb-public-sector-cuts-9118.
4. Witness, for example, the television documentary *How Facebook Changed the World: The Arab Spring*, BBC2, 5 September 2011.
5. See http://eightiesclub.tripod.com/id314.htm (accessed 25 September 2011).

BIBLIOGRAPHY

Abrams, P. (1982) *Historical Sociology*. Shepton Mallet: Open Books.

Adams, J. (1999) *The Social Implications of Hypermobility*. OECD Env. Directorate, pp. 95–134.

Aitchison, C. (2000) 'Poststructural feminist theories for representing others: A response to the crisis in the leisure studies' discourse'. *Leisure Studies* 19(3): 127–144.

Allison, L. (2001) *Amateurism in Sport: An Analysis and a Defence*. London: Frank Cass.

Anderson, B. (1991) *Imagined Communities: Reflections on the Origins and Spread of Nationalism* (revised edition). London and New York: Verso.

Appadurai, A. (1990) 'Disjuncture and difference in the global cultural economy', in M. Featherstone (ed.) *Global Culture: Nationalism, Globalization and Modernity*. London: Sage, pp. 295–310.

Appignanesi, R. and Zarate, O. (1992) *Freud for Beginners*. Cambridge: Icon Books.

Argyle, M. (1993) *The Social Psychology of Leisure*. Harmondsworth: Penguin.

Argyle, M. (2001) *The Psychology of Happiness*. London and New York: Routledge. (First edition published 1987.)

Armistead, N. (ed.) (1974) *Reconstructing Social Psychology*. Harmondsworth: Penguin Books.

Arnold, M. (1960) *Culture and Anarchy*. Cambridge: Cambridge University Press. (First published 1869.)

Bach, L. (1993) 'Sports without facilities: The use of urban space by informal sports'. *International Review for the Sociology of Sport* (28(2 and 3): 281–295.

Bailey, P. (1978) *Leisure and Class in Victorian England: Rational Recreation and the Contest for Control, 1830–1885*. London: Routledge and Kegan Paul.

Bale, J. (1993) *Sport, Space and the City*. London: Routledge.

Bandura, A. (1971a) *Principles of Behavior Modification*. New York: Holt, Rinehart and Winston.

Bandura, A. (1971b) *Social Learning Theory*. New York: General Learning Press.

Bandura, A. (1986) *Social Foundations of Thought and Action: A Social Cognitive Theory*. Englewood Cliffs, NJ: Prentice-Hall.

Banton, M. (1967) *Race Relations*. London: Tavistock Publications.

Barker, C. (2000) *Cultural Studies: Theory and Practice*. London: Sage.

Bataille, G. (1988) *The Accursed Share* (Vols 1–3). New York: Zone Books.

Batty, D. (2005) 'Charity urges human rights protection for older people'. *Guardian*, 2 August.

Bauman, Z. (1987) *Legislators and Interpreters: On Modernity, Post-modernity and Intellectuals*. Cambridge: Polity Press.

Bauman, Z. (1988) 'Is there a postmodern sociology?' *Theory, Culture and Society* 5(2): 217–237.

Bauman, Z. (1992) *Intimations of Postmodernity*. London: Routledge.

Bauman, Z. (1996) 'From pilgrim to tourism or a short history of identity', in S. Hall and P. du Gay (eds) *Questions of Cultural Identity*. London: Sage, pp. 16–34.

Bauman, Z. (1999) *Globalisation*. Cambridge: Polity Press.

Bauman, Z. (2000) *Liquid Modernity*. Cambridge: Polity Press.

Bauman, Z. (2002) *Society Under Siege*. Cambridge: Polity Press.

Bauman, Z. (2005) *Liquid Life*. Cambridge: Polity.

Bauman, Z. (2006) *Liquid Fear*. Cambridge: Polity.

Bauman, Z. (2007) *Liquid Times: Living in an Age of Uncertainty*. Cambridge: Polity.

Beck, U. (1992) *Risk Society: Towards a New Modernity*. London: Sage.

Beck, U. and Beck-Gernsheim, E. (2002) *Individualization: Institutionalized Individualism and its Social and Political Consequences*. London: Sage.

Bell, D. (1973) *The Coming of Post-industrial Society*. Harmondsworth: Penguin.

Bell, D. (1999) *The Coming of Post-industrial Society*. New York: Basic Books. (first published 1973.)

Bennett, A. (1994) *Writing Home*. London: Faber and Faber.

Berger, P. and Luckmann, T. (1968) *The Social Construction of Reality*. Harmondsworth: Penguin.

Berman, M. (1983) *All That is Solid Melts into Air: The Experience of Modernity*. London: Verso.

Berne, E. (1967) *Games People Play: The Psychology of Human Relationships*. New York: Grove Press.

Berry, Chuck (1956) 'Roll over Beethoven'. Chicago: Chess Records.

Birch, S. (2013) 'Leisure trusts help councils save money'. *Guardian*, 21 March.

Bishop, J. and Hoggett, P. (1986) *Organizing Around Enthusiasms: Mutual Aid in Leisure*. London: Comedia.

Blackshaw, T. (2003) *Leisure Life: Myth, Masculinity and Modernity*. London: Routledge.

Blackshaw, T. (2005) *Zygmunt Bauman*. London and New York: Routledge.

Blackshaw, T. (2010) *Leisure*. London and New York: Routledge.

Blackshaw, T. (2012) 'The man from leisure: An interview with Chris Rojek'. *Cultural Studies* 26(1): 1–17.

Boorstin, D.J. (1963) *The Image or What Happened to the American Dream*. Harmondsworth: Penguin.

Boseley, S. (2013) 'Fifth of hospitals failing to treat older patients with dignity, says review'. *Guardian*, 19 March.

Bourdieu, P. (1984) *Distinction: A Social Critique of Taste*. London: Routledge.

Brake, M. (1980) *The Sociology of Youth Culture and Youth Subcultures: Sex and Drugs and Rock 'n' Roll?* London: Routledge and Kegan Paul.

Bramham, P. (2003) 'Boys, masculinity and PE'. *Sport, Education and Society* 8(1): 57–71.

Bramham, P. (2006) 'Leisure studies and "useless" knowledge'. *Leisure Studies Association Newsletter* 75: 29–30.

Bramham, P. and Spink, J. (2009) 'Leeds – becoming the postmodern city', in P. Bramham and S. Wagg (eds) *Sport, Leisure and Culture in the Postmodern City*. Farnham: Ashgate Publishing, pp. 9–32.

Braudel, F. (1949) *La Mediaterranée* (Paris) translated as *The Mediterranean in the Age of Philip II* (2 vols, London).

Brewer, J. and Styles, J. (eds) (1980) *An Ungovernable People: The English and their Law in the Seventeenth and Eighteenth Centuries*. London: Hutchinson.

Brown, N. (1968) *Life after Death: The Psychoanalytical Meaning of History*. London: Sphere. (First published 1959.)

Bryson, B. (2004) *A Short History of Nearly Everything*. London: Black Swan.

Burke, P. (1980) *Sociology and History*. London: George Allen & Unwin.

Burt, R. (1995) *The Male Dancer: Bodies, Spectacle and Sexualities*. London and New York: Routledge.

Burton, R. (1991) 'Cricket, carnival and street culture in the Caribbean', in G. Jarvie (ed.) *Sport, Racism and Ethnicity*. London: Falmer Press.

Butler, J. (1990) *Gender Trouble*. London: Routledge.

Butler, J. (2006) *Gender Trouble: Feminism and the Subversion of Identity*. New York and London: Routledge.

Callinicos, A. (1989) *Making History: Agency, Structure and Change in Social Theory*. Cambridge: Polity Press.

Campbell, D. (2011) 'Drink deaths: Failure to act will cost an extra 250,000 lives by 2031, say doctors'. *Guardian*, 21 February.

Carers UK (2013) *The State of Caring 2013* http://www.carersuk.org/professionals/resources/research-library/item/3090-the-state-of-caring-2013 (accessed 15 February 2014).

Carrington, B. (2000) 'Double consciousness and the Black British athlete', in K. Owusu (ed.) *Black British Culture and Society: A Text Reader*. London and New York: Routledge, pp. 133–156.

Carrington, B. (2011) 'Leeds and the topographies of race: In six scenes', in P. Bramham and S. Wagg (eds) *Sport, Leisure and Culture in the Postmodern City*. Farnham: Ashgate, pp. 99–128.

Cass, B. (2007) 'United moving down south as fan base reached 333 million', *Daily Mail*, 15 December. Available at: http://www.dailymail.co.uk/sport/football/article-502 574/United-moving-south-fanbase-reaches-333-million.html (accessed 23 September 2011).

Centre for Contemporary Cultural Studies (CCCS) (1982) *The Empire Strikes Back: Race and Racism in 70s Britain*. London: Routledge.

Chibnall, S. (1977) *Law and Order News: An Analysis of Crime Reporting in the British Press*. London: Tavistock.

Children's Play Council (2004) Children's Play Council Policy Positions: *The Objectives of Good Play Provision*. Available at: http://www.ncb.org.uk/cpc/dcms.htm#object (accessed 9 September 2004).

Chisholm, K. (2002) 'A tonic for the nation' [review of *Gin: The Much Lamented Death of Madam Geneva* by Patrick Dillon]. *The Telegraph*, 9 June. Available at: http://www.telegraph.co.uk/culture/4727944/A-tonic-for-the-nation.html (accessed 6 November 2013).

Choonara, E. (2011) 'Is there a precariat?' *Socialist Review* October. Available at: http://www.socialistreview.org.uk/article.php?articlenumber=11781 (accessed 15 October 2013).

Clarke, J. and Critcher, C. (1985) *The Devil Makes Work: Leisure in Capitalist Britain*. Basingstoke: Macmillan Press.

Coffey, T.M. (2013) *The Long Thirst: Prohibition in America, 1920–1933*. New York: W.W. Norton & Co.

Cohen, A. (1985) *The Symbolic Construction of Community*. London and New York: Tavistock Publications.

Cohen, P. (1975) 'Subcultural conflict and working-class community', in E. Butterworth and D. Weir (eds) *The Sociology of Modern Britain*. Glasgow: Fontana/Collins, pp. 92–102.

Cohen, S. and Young, J. (1981) *Manufacture of News: Social Problems, Deviance and the Mass Media* (revised edn). London: Constable.

Cole, L. (2008) *Dusty Springfield: In the Middle of Nowhere*. London: Middlesex University Press.

Colley, L. (1992) *Britons: Forging the Nation 1707–1837*. London: Pimlico.

Collinson, P. (2011) 'Over 55s struggle as savings and income levels plunge'. *Guardian*, 7 December. Available at: http://www.theguardian.com/money/2011/dec/07/over-55s-savings-income-plunge.

Connell, R.W. (1995) *Masculinities*. Cambridge: Polity Press.

Cowper, W. (1980) *The Poems of William Cowper, Volume 1, 1748–1782* (edited by John D. Baird and Charles Ryskamp). Oxford: Clarendon Press.

Critcher, C. (2003) *Moral Panics*. London and New York: Routledge.

Critcher, C. (2011) 'Double measures: The moral regulation of alcohol consumption, past and present', in P. Bramham and S. Wagg (eds) *The New Politics of Leisure and Pleasure*. Basingstoke: Palgrave Macmillan, pp. 32–44.

Csikszentmihalyi, M. (1975) *Beyond Boredom and Anxiety*. San Francisco: Jossey-Bass.

Csikszentmihalyi, M. (1990) *The Psychology of Optimal Experience*. New York: Harper & Row.

Csikszentmihalyi, M. (1992) *Flow: The Psychology of Happiness*. London: Ryder.

Cunningham, H. (1980) *Leisure in the Industrial Revolution, c.1780–c.1880*. London: Croom Helm.

Daily Mail (2011) 'Chinese X Factor is banned from TV after viewer voting started to look a little bit like democracy', *Daily Mail*, 19 September. Available at: http://www.dailymail.co.uk/news/article-2039135/Chinese-X-Factor-banned-TV-westernised-dress-sense-offends-older-viewers.html (accessed 25 September 2011).

Dawkins, R. (1976) *The Selfish Gene*. Oxford: Oxford University Press.

de Castella, T. (2011) 'Why is "chav" still controversial?' *BBC News Magazine*, 3 June. Available at: http://www.bbc.co.uk/news/magazine-13626046 (accessed 12 November 2013).

Deci, E.L. and Ryan, R.M. (1985) *Intrinsic Motivation and Self-determination in Human Behavior*. New York: Plenum.

Deci, E.L. and Ryan, R.M. (2002) *Handbook of Self-determination Research*. Rochester, NY: University of Rochester Press.

Deem, R. (1986) *All Work and No Play? The Sociology of Women and Leisure*. Milton Keynes: Open University Press.

Delingpole, J. (2006) 'A conspiracy against chavs? Count me in'. *The Times*, 13 April, p. 25.

Delves, A. (1991) 'Popular recreation and social conflict in Derby, 1800–1850', in E. Yeo and S. Yeo (eds) *Popular Culture and Class Conflict 1590–1914*. Hassocks: Harvester Press.

Dennis, N., Henriques, F. and Slaughter, C. (1969) *Coal is Our Life: An Analysis of a Yorkshire Mining Community* (2nd edition). London: Tavistock Publications. (Previous edition published by Eyre & Spottiswoode, 1956.)

Department for Culture, Media and Sport (2004) *Getting Serious about Play: A Review of Children's Play*. Available at: http://www.culture.gov.uk.

Dilley, R. and Scraton, S. (2010) 'Women, climbing and serious leisure'. *Leisure Studies* 29(2): 125–141.

Dorling, D. (forthcoming) '"What have the Romans ever done for us?" Child poverty and the legacy of "New" Labour', in S. Wagg and J. Pilcher (eds) *Thatcher's Grandchildren? Politics and Childhood in the Twenty First Century*. Basingstoke: Palgrave Macmillan.

Douglas, K. and Carless, D. (2005) *Physical Activity in Older Women in Cornwall* (A qualitative research study commissioned by the Women's Sport Foundation). Bristol: University of Bristol, Department of Exercise and Health Sciences.

Douglas, M. (1970) *Natural Symbols: Explorations in Cosmology*. London: Barrie & Rockliff, Cresset Press.

Doyle, J. (2009) 'When Harry met Petula, April 1968'. PopHistoryDig.com, 7 February. Available at: http://www.pophistorydig.com/?p=850 (accessed 7 November 2013).

Driver, I. (2000) *A Century of Dance*. London: Hamlyn.

Dubin, R. (1956) 'Industrial workers' worlds: A study of the "central life interests" of industrial workers'. *Social Problems* 3(3): 131–142.

Dunning, E., Murphy, P. and Williams, J. (1986) 'Spectator violence at football matches: Towards a sociological explanation'. *British Journal of Sociology* 37(2): 221–244.

Durkheim, E. (1982) *The Rules of Sociological Methods*. New York and London: Free Press. Edited by Steven Lukes. Translated by W.D. Halls.

Edwards, P.B. and Bloland, P.A. (1980) 'Leisure counselling and consultation', *The Personal and Guidance Journal*, February: 435–444. Availindiana.edu/~leisure/module2/unit5_LA2/readings/Leisure%20Counseling-Edwards.pdf (accessed 25 September 2011).

Eldridge, J. (1980) *Recent British Sociology*. London and Basingstoke: Macmillan Press.

Elliott, A. (2002) *Psychoanalytic Theory: An Introduction*. Basingstoke: Palgrave.

Ellis, M. (1973) *Why People Play*. New York: Prentice Hall.

Farrell, S. (2001) 'Gingrich, Toffler and Gore: A peculiar trio'. Available at: http://www.enterstageright.com/archive/articles/0701thirdwayp3.htm (accessed 15 September 2011).

Featherstone, M. (ed.) (1988) *Postmodernism: Theory, Culture and Society*. London: Sage.

Featherstone, M. (1990) *Postmodernism and Consumer Culture*. London: Sage.

Featherstone, M. (1995) *Undoing Culture*. London: Sage Publications.

Foster, J. (1974) *Class Struggle and the Industrial Revolution: Early Capitalism in Three English Towns*. London: Weidenfeld and Nicolson.

Foucault, M. (1975) *Discipline and Punish*. New York: Random House.

Foucault, M. (1990) *The History of Sexuality (Volume 1)*. London: Penguin.

Foucault, M. (1992) *The History of Sexuality (Volume 2)*. London: Penguin.

Foucault, M. (1998) *The History of Sexuality (Volume 3)*. London: Penguin.

Foucault, M. (2003) *Society Must Be Defended* (translated by D. Macey; edited by M. Bertani and A. Fontana). New York: Picador.

Foucault, M. (2006) *Madness and Civilisation*. London: Routledge. (First published 1961.)

Freud, S. (1920) 'Beyond the pleasure principle', in *The Standard Edition of the Complete Psychological Works of Sigmund Freud*, Vol. 18 (translated by J. Strachey). London: Hogarth Press.

Friese, H. and Wagner, P. (1999) 'Not all that is solid melts into air: Modernity and contingency', in M. Featherstone and S. Lash (eds) *Spaces of Culture: City, Nation, World*. London: Sage, pp. 101–115.

Fukuyama, F. (1989) 'The end of history', *The National Interest*, Summer. Available at: http://www.wesjones.com/eoh.htm.

Fukuyama, F. (1992) *The End of History and the Last Man*. New York: Free Press.

Flusty, S. (2000) 'Thrashing Downtown: Play as resistance to the spatial and representation regulation of Los Angeles', *Cities*, 17(2): 149–158.

Gammon, V. (1981) '"Babylonian performances": The rise and suppression of popular church music in England, 1660–1870', in E. Yeo and S. Yeo (eds) *Popular Culture and Class Conflict 1590–1914*. Hassocks: Harvester Press.

Gard, M. (2001) 'Dancing around the "problem" of boys and dance'. *Discourse: Studies in the Cultural Politics of Education* 22(2): 213–225.

Gard, M. (2003a) 'Being someone else: Using dance in anti-oppressive teaching'. *Educational Review* 55(2): 211–223.

Gard, M. (2003b) 'Moving and belonging: Dance, sport and sexuality'. *Sex Education* 3(2): 105–118.

Gard, M. (2005) 'What does "relevant" physical education mean?' *Journal of Physical Education New Zealand* 38(1): 30–40.

Gard, M. and Meyenn, R. (2000) 'Boys, bodies, pleasure and pain: Interrogating contact sports in schools'. *Sport, Education and Society* 5(1): 19–34.

Garfield, S. (2008) You calling us old? We never felt so young'. *The Observer*, 29 June.

Genoe, R. (2010) 'Leisure as resistance in the context of dementia'. *Leisure Studies* 29(3): 303–320.

Gershunny, J. (2000) *Changing Times: Work and Leisure in Postindustrial Society*. Oxford: Oxford University Press.

Giddens, A. (1979a) *Studies in Social and Political Theory*. London: Hutchinson.

Giddens, A. (1979b) *Central Problems in Social Theory: Action, Structure and Contradiction in Social Analysis*. London: Macmillan.

Giddens, A. (1990) *The Consequences of Modernity*. Cambridge: Polity Press.

Giddens, A. (1991) *Modernity and Self-identity*. Cambridge: Polity Press.

Giddens, A. (1994) 'Living in a post-traditional society', in *Reflexive Modernisation: Politics, Tradition and Aesthetics in the Modern Social Order*. Cambridge: Polity Press.

Giddens, A. (1999) 'Runaway world', Reith Lectures, BBC, UK.

Gilroy, P. (1987) *'There Ain't No Black in the Union Jack': The Cultural Politics of Race and Nation*. London: Routledge.

Gilroy, P. (2000) 'The Black Atlantic as a counter culture of modernity', in K. Owusus (ed.) *British Black Culture and Society. A Text Reader*. London and New York: Routledge, pp. 439–452.

Glyptis, S. (1989) *Leisure and Unemployment*. Milton Keynes: Open University Press.

Glyptis, S., McInnes, H. and Patmore, J. (1987) *Leisure and the Home*. London: Sports Council/Economic Research Council Joint Panel on Leisure and Recreation Research.

Goffman, E. (1961a) *Encounters: Two Studies in the Sociology of Interaction*. Indianapolis: Bobbs-Merrill.

Goffman, E. (1961b) *Asylums: Essays on the Social Situation of Mental Patients and Other Inmates*. Garden City, NY: Doubleday.

Goffman, E. (1971a) *The Presentation of Self in Everyday Life*. Harmondsworth: Penguin. (First published in the USA: New York, Doubleday, Anchor Books, 1959. First published in the UK: London, Allen Lane the Penguin Press, 1969.)

Goffman, E. (1971b) *Relations in Public: Microstudies of the Public Order*. London: Allen Lane.

Goffman, E. (1974) *Frame Analysis: An Essay on the Organization of Experience*. London: Harper & Row.

Goffman, E. (1981) *Forms of Talk*. Oxford: Basil Blackwell.

Goldthorpe, J. and Lockwood, D. (1969) *The Affluent Worker in the Class Structure*. Cambridge: Cambridge University Press.

Gorz, A. (1982) *Farewell to the Working Class: An Essay in Post-Industrial Socialism*. London: Pluto Press.

Gough, J. and Macnair, M. (1985) *Gay Liberation in the Eighties*. London: Pluto Press.

Gray, R.Q. (1974) 'The labour aristocracy in the Victorian class structure', in F. Parkin (ed.) *The Social Analysis of Class Structure*. London: Tavistock Publications, pp. 19–38.

Grayling, A.C. (2000) 'The last word on leisure'. *Guardian*, 10 September.

Green, E. (1998) 'Women doing friendship: An analysis of women's leisure as a site of identity construction, empowerment and resistance'. *Leisure Studies* 17(3): 171–185.

Green, E., Hebron, S. and Woodward, D. (1990) *Women's Leisure, What Leisure?* Basingstoke: Macmillan.

Gregory, D. and Urry, J. (eds) (1985) *Social Relations and Spatial Structures*. London: Macmillan.

Grice, A. (2006) 'Government to raise the retirement age ahead of schedule'. *The Independent*, 25 May. Available at: http://www.independent.co.uk/news/uk/politics/government-to-raise-the-retirement-age-ahead-of-schedule-479633.html (accessed 21 September 2011).

Griffiths, J. (1999a) *Pip Pip: A Sideways Look at Time*. London: Flamingo.

Griffiths, J. (1999b) 'Time bandits'. *Guardian*, 3 November.

Guardian (2013) 'More than two million people give up work to care for relatives'. *The Guardian*, 7 March.

Guralnick, P. (1995) *Last Train to Memphis: The Rise of Elvis Presley*. London: Abacus.

Hall, S. (1980) 'Cultural studies and the Centre: Some problematics and problems'. Working papers in cultural studies, 1972–79, in S. Hall, D. Hobson, A. Lowe and P. Willis (eds) *Culture, Media, Language*. London: Hutchinson, pp. 15–47.

Hall, S. (1990) 'Cultural identity and diaspora', in J. Rutherford (ed.) *Identity: Community, Culture, Difference*. London: Lawrence and Wishart, pp. 222–237

Hall, S. (1992) 'The west and the rest: Discourse and power', in S. Hall and B. Gieben (eds) *Formations of Modernity*. Cambridge: Polity Press, pp. 275–335.

Hall, S. and Gieben, B. (eds) (1992). *Formations of Modernity*. Cambridge: Polity Press.

Hall, S. and Jacques, M. (1983) *The Politics of Thatcherism*. Lawrence Wishart in association with Marxism Today.

Hall, S. and Jefferson, T. (eds) (1976) *Resistance Through Rituals: Youth Subcultures in Post-War Britain*. London: Hutchinson

Hall, S., Critcher, C., Jefferson, T., Clarke, J. and Roberts, B. (1978) *Policing the Crisis: Mugging, the State and Law and Order*. London: Macmillan.

Harré, R. and Secord, P. (1976) *The Explanation of Social Behaviour*. Oxford: Blackwell.

Harris, D. (2004) *Key Concepts in Leisure Studies*. London, Thousand Oaks, New Delhi: Sage Publications.

Harvey, D. (1989) *The Condition of Postmodernity: An Enquiry into the Conditions of Cultural Change*. Oxford: Blackwell.

Hayward, K. and Hobbs, D. (2007) 'Beyond the binge in "booze Britain": Market-led liminalization and the spectacle of binge drinking'. *British Journal of Sociology* 58(3): 437–456.

Haywood, L., Kew, F., Bramham, P., Spink, J., Capenerhurst, J. and Henry, I. (1995) *Understanding Leisure* (2nd edn). Cheltenham: Stanley Thornes.

Hebdige, D. (1979) *Subculture: The Meaning of Style*. London: Routledge.

Hebdige, D. (1988) *Hiding in the Light*. London: Comedia.

Higgins, C. (2012) 'Alan Bennett takes a swipe at the National Trust in new play'. *Guardian*, 30 October.

Highmore, B. (ed.) (2002) *The Everyday Life Reader*. London: Routledge.

Hill, J. (2002) *Sport, Leisure and Culture in Twentieth-century Britain*. Houndmills: Palgrave.

Hines, B. (1968) *A Kestrel for a Knave*. Harmondsworth: Penguin.

Hobsbawm, E. and Ranger, T. (eds) (1983) *The Invention of Tradition*. Cambridge: Cambridge University Press.

Hockey, J. and James, A. (2003) *Social Identities Across the Life Course*. Houndmills: Palgrave Macmillan.

Hoggart, R. (1957) *The Uses of Literacy: Aspects of Working Class Life*. London: Chatto and Windus.

Holt, R. (1992) *Sport and the British: A Modern History*. Oxford: Clarendon Press.

Hoskyns, B. (2012) 'Southern rock's passion and romance is marred by racism and bigotry'. *Guardian*, 5 April. Available at: http://www.theguardian.com/music/musicblog/2012/apr/05/southern-rock-passion-marred-racism (accessed 7 November 2013).

Huddle, R. (2004) 'Rock against racism – 1970s'. *Socialist Review*, June. Available at: http://www.socialistreview.org.uk/article.php?articlenumber=8931 (accessed 7 November 2013).

Hutton, W. (1995) *The State We Are In*. London: Jonathon Cape.

Illich, I. (1970) *Deschooling Society*. Harmondsworth: Penguin.

Illich, I. (1974) *Energy and Equity*. London: Calder and Boyars.

Illich, I. (1975a) *Medical Nemesis: The Expropriation of Health*. London: Calder and Boyars.

Illich, I. (1975b) *Tools for Conviviality*. London: Fontana Collins. Available at: http://opencollector.org/history/homebrew/tools.html#nid03 (accessed 16 September 2011).

Ingham, R. (1986) 'Contributions to the psychological study of leisure – Part one'. *Leisure Studies* 5(4): 255–279.

Ingham, R. (1987) 'Contributions to the psychological study of leisure – Part two'. *Leisure Studies* 6(1): 1–14.

Ingham, R. (1990) 'Leisure, health and well-being', in J. Long (ed.) *Leisure, Health and Wellbeing*. Eastbourne: LSA Publications, No 44.

Innes, S. (1995) *Creating the Commonwealth: The Economic Culture of Puritan New England*. New York: W.W. Norton and Co.

Jarvie, G. and Maguire, J. (1994) *Sport and Leisure in Social Thought*. London: Routledge.

Jenkins, S. (2012) 'Why Alan Bennett is wrong about the National Trust'. *Guardian*, 21 November.

Jones, B. (1982) *Sleepers, Wake! Technology and the Future of Work*. Brighton: Wheatsheaf Books.

Jones, O. (2011) *Chavs: The Demonization of the Working Class*. London: Verso.

Jordan, T. and Taylor, P.A. (2004) *Hacktivism and Cyberwars: Rebels With a Cause?* London: Routledge.

Kang, M. and Jones, K. (2003) 'Why do people get tattoos?' *Contexts* 6(1): 42–47.

Kaplan, M. (1975) *Leisure: Theory and Policy*. New York: Wiley.

Kay, N. (2008) 'Chelsy the chav: Prince Harry's girlfriend pictured wearing a baseball cap, tracksuit and tasteless jewellery'. *Daily Mail*, 6 September. Available at: http://www.dailymail.co.uk/femail/article-1053175/Chelsy-chav-Prince-Harrys-girlfriend-pictured-wearing-baseball-cap-tracksuit-tasteless-jewellery.html (accessed 12 November 2013).

Kelly, J. (1980) 'Leisure adaptation to family diversity', in Z. Strelitz (ed.) *Leisure and Family Diversity*. Eastbourne: Leisure Studies Association.

Kelly, J. (1983) *Leisure Identities and Interactions*. London: George Allen and Unwin.

Kettle, M. (2003) 'My name is Britain and I have a drink problem'. *Guardian*, 31 May.

Keynes, J.M. (1963) 'The economic possibilities for our grandchildren', in *Essays in Persuasion*. New York: W.W. Norton & Co 1963. (First published 1930.) Available at: http://www.econ.yale.edu/smith/econ116a/keynes1.pdf.

Keyworth, S. (2001) 'Critical autobiography: "Straightening" out dance education'. *Research in Dance Education* 2(2): 117–137.

Kirkwood, T. (2001) 'The end of age', Reith Lectures, BBC.

Kumar, K. (1978) *Prophecy and Progress: The Sociology of Industrial and Post-industtrial Society.* Harmondsworth: Penguin.

Kynaston, D. (2007) *Austerity Britain 1945–51.* London: Bloomsbury.

Kynaston, D. (2009) *Family Britain 1951–57.* London: Bloomsbury.

Lash, S. (2002) *Critique of Information.* London: Sage.

Lash, S. and Urry, J. (1994) *Economies of Signs and Space.* London: Sage.

Lashua, B. (2011) 'Between the devil and the deep blue sea: Music and leisure in an era of X Factor and digital pirates', in P. Bramham and S. Wagg (eds.) *The New Politcs of Leisure and Pleasure.* Basingstoke: Palgrave Macmillan, pp. 225–244.

Leary, T. (1970) *The Politics of Ecstasy.* London: Paladin Books.

Leavis, F.R. (1948) *The Great Tradition.* London: Chatto and Windus.

Lichfield, J. and Roussel, C. (2010) 'Sarkozy follows Europe in raising retirement age'. *The Independent*, 27 May. Available at: http://www.independent.co.uk/news/world/europe/sarkozy-follows-europe-in-raising-retirement-age-1983938.html (accessed 21 September 2011).

Lockstone-Binney, L., Holmes, K., Smith, K. and Baum, T. (2010) 'Volunteers and volunteering: Social science perspectives'. *Leisure Studies* 29(4): 435–455.

Lowe, M. and Atkin, I. (1997) *Dance Clubs and Disco(rd)s: The Search for Authentic Experience.* Roehampton Institute.

Lowerson, J. and Myerscough, J. (1977) *Time to Spare in Victorian England.* Hassocks: The Harvester Press.

Luft, O. (2009) 'Jade Goody effect boosts red top sales'. *Guardian*, 9 April. Available at: http://www.theguardian.com/media/2009/apr/09/abcs-jade-goody-red-top-sales (accessed 12 November 2013).

Mac an Ghaill, M. (1996) '"What about the boys?": schooling, class and crisis masculinity'. *The Sociological Review.* 44(3): 381–397.

Macpherson, C. (1962) *The Political Theory of Possessive Individualism: Hobbes to Locke.* Oxford: Oxford University Press.

Macpherson, C. (1977) *The Life and Times of Liberal Democracy.* Oxford: Oxford University Press.

Magee, G. (2011) 'Zeitgeist', *The Hegel Dictionary.* London: Bloomsbury Publishing.

Malcolmson, R. (1973) *Popular Recreations in English Society, 1700–1850.* Cambridge: Cambridge University Press.

Mannheim, K. (1952) 'The problem of generations', in K. Mannheim (ed.) *Essays on the Sociology of Knowledge.* London: Routledge and Kegan Paul, pp. 276–320.

Marcuse, H. (1972) *One Dimensional Man.* London: Abacus.

Margolick, D. (2000) *Strange Fruit: Billie Holiday, Café Society and an Early Cry for Civil Rights.* London: Running Press.

Marqusee, M. (2005) *Redemption Song: Muhammad Ali and the Spirit of the Sixties.* London: Verso.

Martin, B. (1981) *A Sociology of Contemporary Cultural Change.* Oxford: Basil Blackwell.

McGuigan, J. (1999) *Modernity and Postmodern Culture.* Buckingham: Open University Press.

McGuigan, J. (2002) *Cultural Populism.* London: Routledge.

McLeish, K. (ed.) (1993) *Bloomsbury Guide to Human Thought.* London: Bloomsbury Publishing.

Mennell, S. (1979) 'Theoretical considerations on the study of cultural "needs"'. *Sociology* 13(2): 235–257.

Miles, R. and Phizacklea, A. (1979) *Racism and Political Action in Britain*. London: Routledge and Kegan Paul.

Mills, C.W. (1951) *White Collar: The American Middle Classes*. Oxford: Oxford University Press.

Mills, C.W. (1970) *The Sociological Imagination*. Harmondsworth: Penguin.

Mommaas, H., van der Poel, H., Bramham, P. and Henry, I. (eds) (1996) *Leisure Research in Europe: Methods and Traditions*. Wallingford: CAB International.

Morris, R.J. (1979) *Class and Class Consciousness in the Industrial Revolution 1780–1850*. London: Macmillan.

Mumford, L. (1967) *The Myth of the Machine*. London: Secker and Warburg.

Mumford, L. (1970) *The Pentagon of Power*. New York: Harcourt, Brace and Jovanovich.

Murdock, G. (1978) 'Class stratification and cultural consumption: some motifs in the work of Pierre Bourdieu', in M. Smith, (ed.) *Leisure and Urban Society*. Eastbourne: LSA Publications, No. 6.

Neville, R. (1971) *Playpower*. St Albans: Paladin.

Nichols, G. (ed.) (2003) *Volunteers in Sport* (Vol. 80). Eastbourne: Leisure Studies Association.

O'Connor, J. and Wynne, D. (1996) *From the Margins to the Centre: Cultural Production and Consumption in the Post Industrial City*. Aldershot: Arena.

O'Neill, B. (2011) 'The culture war on toffs and chavs'. *Spiked*, 2 June. Available at: http://www.spiked-online.com/newsite/article/10568#.UoJzoOI_a1t (accessed 12 November 2013).

Orwell, George (1986–87) *The Complete Works of George Orwell. Volume Five: The Road to Wigan Pier* (edited by Peter Davison). London: Secker and Warburg.

Parekh, B. (2000) *Rethinking Multiculturalism: Cultural Diversity and Political Theory*. London: Macmillan Press.

Paxman, J. (1998) *The English: a Portrait of a People*. London: Michael Joseph.

Pearson, G. (1983) *Hooligan: A History of Respectable Fears*. London: Macmillan.

Platt, J. (1976) *Realities of Social Research: An Empirical Study of British Sociologists*. London: Chatto and Windus for Sussex University Press.

Playboy magazine (1966) 'Playboy interview: Timothy Leary', September. Available at: http://ia700307.us.archive.org/6/items/playboylearyinte00playrich/playboyleary-inte00playrich.pdf (accessed 8 September 2011).

Plummer, K. (ed.) (1981) *The Making of the Modern Homosexual*. London: Hutchinson.

Poulantzas, N. (1973) *Political Power and Social Classes*. London: Sheed and Ward/New Left Books.

Powers, R. (2007) *Mark Twain: A Life*. London: Pocket Books.

Rapoport, R. and Rapoport, R. (1975) *Leisure and the Family Life Cycle*. London: Routledge.

Ravenscroft, N. and Gilchrist, P. (2011) 'Outdoor recreation and the environment', in P. Bramham and S. Wagg (eds) *The New Politics of Leisure and Pleasure*, Basingstoke: Palgrave Macmillan, pp. 45–62.

Redhead, S. (1993) *Rave Off: Politics and Deviance in Contemporary Youth Culture*. Aldershot: Avebury.

Redhead, S. with D. Wynne and J. O'Connor (1997) *The Clubcultures Reader: Readings in Popular Cultural Studies*. Oxford and Cambridge, MA: Blackwell.

Reid, D. (1976) 'The decline of St. Monday, 1766–1876'. *Past & Present* 71: 76–101.

Reid, D. (1982) 'Interpreting the festival calendar: Wakes and fairs as festivals', in R.D. Storch (ed.) *Popular Culture and Custom in Nineteenth-century England*. London: Croom Helm.

Rex, J. (1970) *Race Relations in Sociological Theory*. London: Weidenfeld & Nicolson.

Rex, J. (1973) *Race, Colonialism and the City*. London: Routledge and Kegan Paul.

Ritzer, G. (1994) *The McDonaldization Society: An Investigation into the Changing Character of Contemporary Social Life*. Thousand Oaks, CA: Pine Forge Press.

Roberts, J. and Sutton-Smith, B. (1971) 'Child training and game involvement', in J. Loy and G. Kenynon (eds) *Sport, Culture and Society*. London: Macmillan.

Roberts, K. (1970) *Leisure*. London: George, Allen & Unwin.

Roberts, K. (1978) *Contemporary Society and the Growth of Leisure*. London: Longman.

Roberts, K. (1999) *Leisure in Contemporary Society* (1st edn). Wallingford: CABS International.

Roberts, K. (2004) *The Leisure Industries* (1st edn). London: Palgrave Macmillan.

Rojek, C. (1985) *Capitalism and Leisure Theory*. London and New York: Tavistock Publications.

Rojek, C. (1993) *Ways of Escape*. London: Macmillan.

Rojek, C. (1995) *Decentring Leisure*. London: Sage Publications.

Rojek, C. (2000) *Leisure and Culture*. Basingstoke: Palgrave.

Rojek, C. (2001) *Celebrity*. London: Reaktion.

Rojek, C. (2005) *Leisure Theory: Principles and Practice* (1st edn). Basingstoke: Palgrave Macmillan.

Rojek, C. (2010a) 'The labour of leisure: The culture of free time'. Available at: http://ezproxy.leedsmet.ac.uk/login?url=http://www.dawsonera.com/depp/reader/protected/external/AbstractView/S9781849204392.

Rojek, C. (2010b) 'Leisure and emotional intelligence'. *World Leisure Journal*, 52(4): 240–252.

Rose, S. and Rose, H. (eds) (1982a) *Against Biological Determinism*. London: Allison and Busby.

Rose, S. and Rose, H. (eds) (1982b) *Towards a Liberatory Biology*. London: Allison and Busby.

Russell, B. (1932) 'In praise of idleness'. Available at: http://www.zpub.com/notes/idle.html (accessed 8 September 2011).

Russell, B. (2002) *In Praise of Idleness*. London and New York: Routledge Classics.

Ryan, A. (1970) *The Philosophy of the Social Sciences*. London: Macmillan.

Ryan, R.M. (2012) *The Oxford Handbook of Human Motivation*. New York and Oxford: Oxford University Press.

Savage, M. et al. (2013) 'A new model of social class? Findings from the BBC's Great British Class Survey experiment'. *Sociology* 47(2): 219–250.

Schor, J. (1991) *The Overworked American: The Unexpected Decline of Leisure*. New York: Basic Books.

Schor, J.B. (2006) 'Overturning the modernist predictions: Recent trends in work and leisure in the OECD', in Chris Rojeusan, M. Sand and A.J. Veal (eds) *A Handbook of Leisure Studies*. Basingstoke: Palgrave.

Schur, E. (1973) *Radical Non-intervention: Re-thinking the Delinquency Problem*. Englewoods-Cliffs: Prentice Hall.

Select Committee on Public Service and Demographic Change (2013) *Ready for Ageing?* London: House of Lords.

Shaw, S.M. (2001) 'Conceptualizing resistance: Women's leisure as political practice'. *Journal of Leisure Research*, 33(2): 186–201.

Sheikh, S. (2012) 'Study into personal budgets finds encouraging results'. *Guardian*, 23 October.

Sherwin, A. (2011) 'What the Labour leader must do to get noticed – the experts' advice', *The Independent*, 24 September, p. 7.

Shields, R. (1992) *Lifestyle Shopping: The Subject of Consumption*. London: Routledge.

Shilling, C. (1993) *The Body and Social Theory*. London: Sage Publications.

Sillitoe, A. (1960) *Saturday Night and Sunday Morning*. London: Pan Books.

Simpson, B. (2005) 'Cities as active playgrounds: Active Leisure for Children as a Human Right', in P. Bramham and J. Caudwell, (eds) *Sport, Active Leisure and Youth Cultures*. Eastbourne: Leisure Studies Publications No. 86.

Sivanandan, A. (1990) *Communities of Resistance*. London: Verso.

Skeggs, B. (2004) *Class, Self, Culture*. London: Routledge.

Smith, A. (1776) *Inquiry into the Nature and Causes of the Wealth of Nations*. Chicago: University of Chicago Press.

Sontag, S. (1978) 'The double standard of ageing', in V. Carver and P. Liddiard (eds) *An Ageing Population*. Milton Keynes: Open University Press.

Spink, J. (1994) 'Leisure and retailing', in F. Kew (ed.) *Leisure: Into the 1990s* (Vol. 4). Bradford: Bradford and Ilkley College, pp. 1–10.

Spink, J. and Bramham, P. (1999) 'The myth of the 24-hour city', in P. Bramham and W. Murphy (eds) *Policy and Politics: Leisure, Culture and Commerce*. Eastbourne: Leisure Studies Association, pp. 139–152.

Spink, J. and Bramham, P. (2000) 'Leeds: Re-imaging the 24 hour European city', in M. Collins (ed.) *Leisure Planning in Transitory Societies*. Brighton: Leisure Studies Association, pp. 1–10.

Spivak, G. (2006) *In Other Worlds: Essays in Cultural Politics*. Abingdon and New York: Routledge. (First edition published 1987.)

Spracklen, K. (2011) *Constructing Leisure: Historical and Philosophical Debates*. Basingstoke: Palgrave Macmillan.

Standing, G. (2011a) *The Precariat: The New Dangerous Class*. London: Bloomsbury.

Standing, G. (2011b) 'Who will be a voice for the emerging precariat?' *Guardian*, 1 June. Available at: http://www.theguardian.com/commentisfree/2011/jun/01/voice-for-emerging-precariat (accessed 15 October 2013).

Steadman Jones, G. (1983) *Languages of Class: Studies in English Working Class history, 1832–1982*. Cambridge: Cambridge University Press.

Stebbins, R. (1992) *Amateurs, Professionals and Serious Leisure*. Montreal and Kingston: McGill/Queen's University Press.

Stedman Jones, D. (2012) *Masters of the Universe: Hayek, Friedman, and the Birth of Neoliberal Politics*. Princeton: Princeton University Press.

Stedman Jones, G. (1983) *Languages of Class: Studies in English Working Class History 1832–1982*. Cambridge: Cambridge University Press.

Storch, R.D. (1975) 'The plague of blue locusts: Police Reform and popular resistance in northern England, 1840–57'. *International Review of Social History* XX: 61–90.

Storch, R.D. (1976) 'The policeman as domestic missionary: Urban discipline and popular culture in northern England, 1850–1880'. *Journal of Social History* IX: 481–509.

Storch, R.D. (1977) 'The problem of working-class leisure: Some roots of middle-class moral reform in the industrial north, 1825–50', in A. Donajgrodzki (ed.) *Social Control in Nineteenth Century Britain*. London: Croom Helm, pp. 138–162.

Storch, R.D. (1982) '"Please to remember the fifth of November": Conflict, solidarity and public order in southern England, 1815–1900', in R.D. Storch (ed.) *Popular Culture and Custom in Nineteenth Century England*. London: Croom Helm.

Strinati, D. (1992) 'Postmodernism and popular culture'. *Sociology Review* 1(4): 2–9.

Sylvester, C. (1999) 'The Western idea of work and leisure: Traditions, transformations and the future', in E. Jackson and T. Burton (eds) *Leisure Studies: Prospects for the*

Twenty-first Century. Pennsylvania: Venture Publishing, Inc. State College, Pennsylvania, pp. 17–34.

Taylor, L., Evans, K. and Fraser, P. (1996) *A Tale of Two Cities: Global Change, Local Feeling and Everyday Life in the North of England – A Study in Manchester and Sheffield*. London: Routledge.

Taylor, M., Burn-Murdoch, J. and Butler, P. (2013) 'Council cuts will bring local government "to its knees"'. *Guardian*, 26 March.

The Women's Studies Group (1978) *Women Take Issue: Aspects of Women's Subordination*. London: Hutchinson.

Thomas, K. (1997) 'The defensive self: A psychodynamic approach', in R. Stevens (ed.) *Understanding the Self*. London: Sage.

Thompson, E.P. (1967) 'Time, work-discipline and industrial capitalism'. *Past and Present* 38(1): 56–97.

Thompson, E. P. (1968) *The Making of the English Working Class*. Harmondsworth: Penguin.

Thompson, E.P. (1977) *Whigs and Hunters*. Harmondsworth: Peregrine Books.

Thornton, S. (1995) *Club Cultures: Music, Media and Subcultural Capital*. Cambridge: Polity Press.

Tilly, C. (1981) *As Sociology Meets History*. New York: Academic Press.

Toffler, A. (1970) *Future Shock*. New York: Random House.

Tomlinson, A. (1989) 'What side are they on? Leisure studies and cultural studies in Britain'. *Leisure Studies* 8: 97–106.

Topham, G. (2012) 'National Express rues loss of coach concessions'. *Guardian*, 24 October.

Torgoff, M. (2004) *Can't Find My Way Home: America in the Great Stoned Age*. New York: Simon and Schuster.

Toynbee, P. (2011) 'Chav: the vile word at the heart of fractured Britain'. *The Guardian*, 31 May. Available at http://the guardian.com/commentisfree/2011/may31/chav-vile-word-fractured-britain (accessed 11 November 2013).

Tucker, R.C. (1972) *The Marx-Engels Reader*. New York: Norton

Tyler, I. (2008) '"Chav mum, chav scum": Class disgust in contemporary Britain' *Feminist Media Studies* 8(1): 17–34. Available at: http://mafaldastasi.files.wordpress.com/2012/03/tyler-2008-chav-mum.pdf (accessed 12 November 2013).

Urry, J. (1990) *The Tourist Gaze*. London: Sage.

Veblen, T. (1994) *The Theory of the Leisure Class*. New York: Penguin. (First published 1899.)

Vincent, J.A. (2000) 'Age and old age', in G. Payne (ed.) *Social Divisions*. Basingstoke: Palgrave, pp. 133–151.

Walker, P. (2013) 'Government using increasingly loaded language in the welfare debate'. *Guardian*, 5 April.

Walker, T. (2010) 'Rory Bremner is left with a bad impression of Nick Clegg', *The Telegraph*, 25 November. Available at: http://www.telegraph.co.uk/news/celebritynews/8158004/Rory-Bremner-is-left-with-a-bad-impression-of-Nick-Clegg.html (accessed 25 September 2011).

Wallace, M. and Spanner, C. (2004) *Chav! A User's Guide to Britain's New Ruling Class*. London: Bantam Books.

Walton, J. and Poole, R. (1982) 'The Lancashire wakes in the nineteenth century', in R.D. Storch (ed.) *Popular Culture and Custom in Nineteenth Century England*. London: Croom Helm.

Walvin, J. (1978) *Leisure and Society 1830–1950*. London: Longman.

Wearing, B. (1995) 'Leisure and resistance in an ageing society'. *Leisure Studies*, 14: 263–279.

Wearing, B. (1998) *Leisure and Feminist Theory*. London: Sage.

Weeks, J. (1981) *Sex, Politics and Society*. London: Longman.

West, E. (2011) 'There's nothing wrong with having a go at chavs'. *The Telegraph*, 1 June. Available at: http://blogs.telegraph.co.uk/news/edwest/100090254/theres-nothing-wrong-with-having-a-go-at-chavs/ (accessed 12 November 2013).

Wheaton, B. (ed.) (2004) *Understanding Lifestyle Sports: Consumption, Identity and Difference*. London and New York: Routledge.

Whelehan, I. (2000) *Overloaded: Popular Culture and the Future of Feminism*. London: The Women's Press.

White, M. (2011) 'The class war: Why everyone feels insecure', *U TV*, 30 May. Available at: http://www.u.tv/articles/article.aspx?cat=news&guid=916a786c-edfd-44b9-9e6e-cab04c55837c (accessed 12 November 2013).

Wieschiolek, H. (2003) 'Ladies, just follow his lead!: Salsa, gender and identity', in N. Dyck and E. Archetti (eds) *Sport, Dance and Embodied Identities*. Oxford and New York: Berg, pp.115–138.

Wilensky, H. (1960) 'Work, careers and social integration'. *International Social Science Journal* 4(4): 543–560.

Williams, R. (1977) *Marxism and Literature*. Oxford: Oxford University Press.

Willis, P. (1977) *Learning to Labour: How Working Class Kids Get Working Class Jobs*. Farnborough: Saxon House.

Willis, P. (1978) *Profane Culture: Symbolic Work at Play in the Everyday Cultures of the Young*. London: Routledge and Kegan Paul.

Willis, P. (1988) *The Youth Review: Social Conditions of Young People in Wolverhampton*. Aldershot: Avebury.

Willis, P. (1990) *Common Culture: Symbolic Work at Play in the Everyday Cultures of the Young*. Milton Keynes: Open University Press.

Winship, J. (1987) *Inside Women's Magazines*. London: Pandora Press.

Wittgenstein, Ludwig (1963) Philosophical Investigations. Translated by G.E.M. Anscombe. Oxford: Blackwell. Available at: http://www.homodiscens.com/home/embodied/ludens_sake/lang_games/indexhtm (accessed 7 February 2014).

Wynne, D. (1998) *Leisure, Lifestyle, and the New Middle Class: A Case Study*. London: Routledge.

Young, J. (1974) 'Mass media, drugs and deviance', in M. McIntosh and P. Rock (eds) *Deviance and Social Control*. London: Tavistock, pp. 229–260.

Young, M.D. and Willmott, P. (1957) *Family and Kinship in East London*. London: Routledge & Kegan Paul,

Young, M.D. and Willmott, P. (1973) *The Symmetrical Family: A Study of Work and Leisure in the London Region*. London: Routledge and Kegan Paul.

Zukin, S. (1991) *Landscapes of Power*. Los Angeles: University of California Press.

INDEX